Images in an Antique Book

Dante in Shakespeare

Vivienne Robertson was born in Castlemaine, Victoria. She completed a B.A. at the University of Melbourne, an M.Litt. at the University of New England and a Ph.D. at the University of New South Wales. She has taught English at all levels in Victoria, New South Wales and Queensland, and also in Italy and England. Her Italian experience led her to Dante, where she found several passages strongly reminiscent of Shakespeare. Further research produced her doctoral thesis which then became this book. Dr Robertson, now retired, lives with her husband in Castlemaine.

Images in an Antique Book

Dante in Shakespeare

VIVIENNE ROBERTSON

AUSTRALIAN SCHOLARLY

for John
with whom I have shared the warm and colourful
Autumn of our lives.

First published 2019 by
Australian Scholarly Publishing Pty Ltd
7 Lt Lothian St Nth, North Melbourne, Vic 3051

Tel: 03 9329 6963 / Fax: 03 9329 5452
enquiry@scholarly.info / www.scholarly.info

ISBN 978-1-925801-78-1

Cover: Portrait of Dante Alighieri by Luca Signorelli (c.1445–1523), fresco. Chapel of the Madonna di San Brizio, Orvieto Cathedral, Orvieto, Umbria, Italy

Cover design: Wayne Saunders

Contents

Prologue

We are on the Indian Pacific, the transcontinental, hurtling westwards from Sydney to Perth. The train, almost a kilometre long, left Central Station on time. Ponderously, it rolled through Redfern out of the city, then slowly glided smoothly through the endless Western Suburbs. When eventually the houses were not so close together and the trees became taller and more prevalent we realised that we were climbing the eastern slopes of the Blue Mountains. As the sun set, the views of orange coloured cliffs, deep gorges and endless navy blue forest gradually faded. The dark closed in around us as we began to pick up speed, racing along towards Broken Hill—our first stop.

It's the first night on board and we are tired but excited. When John pushes open the door into the Lounge, the noise rushes up to greet us and I see people smiling widely, talking animatedly and laughing loudly. Waiters are moving round with platters of delicious looking canapés and trays of empty glasses. The long, narrow room is full. There is still half an hour to go before dinner. There's only one vacant seat in sight on the end of a sofa near us where two people are talking quietly.

"You sit here," says John into my ear. "I'll go and get something to drink."

He's gone and I move to the vacant seat next to a pleasant looking man who smiles up at me as if he knows me.

Actually, no one knows anyone. It's the first night of the journey. People are ready to meet fellow travellers, to chat, to share opinions. I see immediately that we are in the right place. Everyone looks, in a way, like us—retired, in their sixties or seventies and delighted to be on this adventure.

"Let me introduce myself," says the smiling man. "I'm Don. We are from Sydney and we're only going to Adelaide. What about you?" I introduce myself and tell him we are from Victoria and that we're going the full distance. His wife has begun to talk to someone on the other side.

Don wants to talk. He is a chemical engineer and worked at Sydney University. But, he tells me, his smile growing wider, his great interest is Shakespeare. I am amazed, as he expects me to be. I tell him briefly of my own experience with Shakespeare—my doctoral thesis completed in 2002. I don't elaborate too much. I have learned not to expect much interest. But he *is* interested. He is listening to me. He says, "I suppose you have read *The Truth Will Out*?" I haven't. For the last 13 years I have been living in a country town. I have left academia behind me. I am relatively newly married. I have been busy trying to run a house, re-learn to drive, meet new people, join various groups, take a few classes at U3A.

He is telling me about the book. I am listening. I can hardly believe what he says—and yet this was what I had vaguely considered in the course of my research. I begin to feel quite strange.

Don has stopped talking. He is looking at me, concern on his face.

"Are you all right? Would you like a glass of water?" He looks round anxiously, no doubt hoping to see my husband.

And I am not all right. My heart is pounding. My mind is going back almost 20 years to when I was so busy researching and writing. And now, all the problems I had then seem to be disappearing. I am seeing in my mind the few missing pieces from the enormous jigsaw puzzle that was my doctoral thesis. As I listen they are suddenly falling into place.

On the edge of the Great Australian Desert, the black night rushes past outside. I am thousands of miles and hundreds of years away from the worlds of Shakespeare and Dante, far from the University libraries where I had pored over multitudinous books, argued with professors and tutors, wiped dust off ancient tomes and wondered why I was doing all this.

Suddenly I see that all my questions can be answered.

The Saints of Poetry

*Shakspeare and Dante are the Saints of Poetry; really, if we
think of it, Canonised, so that it is impiety to meddle with them.*
Lectures on Heroes,[1] Thomas Carlyle

The decent knight retired with sober rage,
"What! no respect", he cry'd, for Shakespear's Page!"
The Dunciad,[2] Alexander Pope

It is not my intention to "meddle with" either Dante or Shakespeare, but
rather to link them in a new way, and in so doing, to draw attention to yet
another facet of Shakespeare's learning and genius. I do not see these poets
as surrounded by a kind of religious aura, as did Carlyle and many literary
lions of his time, and I believe that adding to currently accepted knowledge
of the great English playwright can only increase our understanding and
appreciation of his work. T. S. Eliot often thought of Dante and Shakespeare
together, as did A. C. Bradley and Ezra Pound. They saw similarities in
themes, in atmosphere, in images. They did not however, venture to suggest
that Shakespeare may have known the work of Dante and been influenced
by it.

It is my intention to do exactly that. There are a number of close
parallels in the works of the two great writers and if they cannot be found
to be a result of both writers working from the same source, or sheer
coincidence, then it must be that Shakespeare was aware of Dante's work
(directly or indirectly) and used ideas from it in his own writing.

The books written about Shakespeare's sources are legion. Holinshed's histories provided information for many of the history plays. Selma Guttman[3] in her listing of Shakespeare's foreign sources found many Italian authors from whose work various writers believe Shakespeare borrowed material. Not all of these were translated into English. This would suggest that Shakespeare had some considerable knowledge of the Italian language or knew well someone who did.

My goal has been to establish this claim but before I continue I need to introduce the two main characters, Dante and Shakespeare. There is considerable information on the life of Dante and I have given some of it below. Those of us who have studied Shakespeare have been given very scarce information on the life of the man from Stratford. There is his birth in 1564, education at Stratford Grammar School (for which there is no evidence), marriage in 1582, birth of his three children and the death of one, time on the stage in London, dealings in real estate in Stratford and London and then death in 1616. There is little here to account for the amazing achievements of this man Shakespeare, and for many years there have been all kinds of candidates who many believe to be more likely as the author of the poetry and plays than the man from Stratford.

Dante Alighieri was born in Florence in 1265. His mother died when Dante was very young and the father married again. At the age of nine Dante saw Beatrice Portinari (aged eight) for the first time, and his devotion to her lasted for the rest of his life. Apart from a brief greeting when he was eighteen, there was no personal relationship between them. Dante's father died in 1283 and in the same year Dante married Gemma Donati. Marriages were made for many reasons, the least of which was the preference of the two young people involved. Beatrice had married very young and died in 1290.

Dante was well educated and clearly talented in literary and other fields. He read widely from the *Aeneid* (which he claimed to know by heart), the Latin Bible, Aristotle, Cicero, the Christian scholars and theologians, Livy, Pliny, Virgil and many, many others. Traces of these works remain in the *Divina Commedia*.

He entered politics in 1295—a violent and dangerous world in mediaeval Florence where the two conflicting parties, the Whites (of which Dante was a member) led by the Cerchi family and the Blacks, led by the Donati family, fought for power. In 1300 Dante was appointed one of the seven priors (supreme magistrates) for a two month period. In 1301 he was sent on an embassy to Pope Boniface VIII, but while he was still on this mission, he was accused of graft and corruption, found guilty and sentenced to exile. Soon after, he was permanently banished from Florence, with the penalty of being burnt alive should he return. In 1315 Florence offered to repeal the sentence of exile on the condition that Dante acknowledge his guilt, but he refused. In 1315 he was living in exile in Verona with the Scala family and in 1319 he had moved to live as a guest of Guido Novella da Polanta at Ravenna. Here, in 1321 he completed the *Divina Commedia*. He died in that same year.

The *Divina Commedia* is meticulously planned and carefully structured. It is in three parts, the *Inferno*, the *Purgatorio* and the *Paradiso*. Each part, or *cantica*, contains 33 cantos but the first book, *Inferno*, actually has 34 cantos, the first of which is an introduction. There are 100 cantos. All of this is written in the *terza rima*, a rhyme scheme which Dante invented for this work, where the first and third line of a three line verse, rhyme (a b a). The next *tiercet* uses the second line rhyme in the first and third lines of the next (b c b). This makes it difficult to translate if one tries to replicate this rhyme scheme. If one does not, the poem may be more accurately translated but loses the rhythmic sound which makes it so appealing to the ear.

The structure of the *Divina Commedia* is based on the "mystic" number three, which was a symbol of the Trinity. These numbers had a special religious significance for Dante and they also contribute to making his book a work of art in its precision, its music and its beauty. Dante wrote his *Divina Commedia* not in Latin, as was the custom for a work of some significance at that time, but in Tuscan, the vernacular spoken in Florence and from which modern Italian has evolved.

Dante's Inferno is a cone shaped segment beneath the surface of the Earth where unrepentant sinners at the time of their death, come to receive their deserts. At the base of the cone, which is at the centre of the Earth, are the greatest sinners of all—the traitors. The worst of these are in the mouth of Satan himself and they are Judas, who betrayed Christ, the founder of the Church, and Brutus and Cassius who betrayed Julius Caesar, the founder of the Empire. The worst of all is Lucifer, or Satan, who was cast out of Heaven for the sin of pride.

Dante has carefully evaluated the relative gravity of each transgression, and while the souls in the first circle are relatively blameless, those who were born before the coming of Christ for example, or unbaptised babies, those in the lowest circle are the traitors. In between these extremes are all the other sinful souls—the sluggish, the lustful, the gluttonous, the avaricious, the wrathful, the heretical, the violent, the fraudulent. These souls come from real life, from ancient stories, from mythology or the Bible. Dante has designed a *contrapasso* for them all. Some are given what they always sought while others are given the exact opposite. The ethic is basically biblical: "Wherewith a man sinneth, by the same also shall he be punished" (Wisdom 6:16).

The Italian dictionary gives the definition of *contrapasso* (now spelt *contrappasso*) as an ancient punishment which involved inflicting on the guilty person the same suffering that he has inflicted on others. In *Inferno*, the punishment is always related to the crime. For example, those who were Fortune Tellers and have, by forbidden arts, attempted to look into the future, have their heads turned round so that they can look only at the past. Because they attempted to look forward in time, they are condemned to look backwards for all eternity.

In Purgatory are those who died repentant within the Church. Here, the soul can be cleansed and presumably it may then progress to Paradise. Purgatory is a mountain at the top of which is the Garden of Eden, which all strive to reach. All these souls are saved but they must labour to purge themselves of the sins of which they were guilty. Progress is possible only when the sun (Divine Wisdom) shines.

Paradiso is an eternity of absolute happiness where the human soul comes to an understanding of its Maker. It is more difficult to understand than the other two *cantiche* both in language and in concepts. It is a series of spheres with the Earth at the centre. Paradiso is the Kingdom to Come.

These are extremely limited summaries of the *Divina Commedia*, but they will be sufficient for my purpose at this stage. To those who wish to know more I can only suggest, as did Chaucer in *The Monk's Tale*,

> Whoso will hear it in longer wise.
> Reade the great poet of Itale,
> That Dante hight, for he can devise
> From point to point, not a word will he fail.
>
> *The Monk's Tale*[4]

The plot of the *Divina Commedia* is the journey of Dante (the Pilgrim) through these other worlds. John Ciardi's translation[5] creates the atmosphere in the first six lines of *Inferno:*

> Midway in life's journey, I went astray
> from the straight road and woke to find myself
> alone in a dark wood. How shall I say
>
> what wood that was! I never saw so drear,
> so rank, so arduous a wilderness!
> Its very memory gives a shape to fear.
>
> *Inferno* I.1–6

It is Easter in 1300. Dante (the Pilgrim) is 35 years old. He sets off but soon finds the way difficult and then is joined by Virgil (symbolising Reason) and continues through the appalling chaos on the different levels of suffering souls. Finally, he emerges to see the Mountain of Purgatory before him.

Here, the feeling is quite different. The souls waiting to free themselves of their sins, strive to move up the mountain. Dante continues upward with Virgil and at the top, just as Virgil leaves him, Beatrice appears. She reprimands him for not making proper use of his gifts and then leads him to drink from the river Lethe for his final purification. She goes with him to Paradise.

Paradise is "a visualised allegory rather than an interpretation of concrete reality".[6] There are the various spheres and planets where the souls whose goodness has had some earthly stain find themselves. But all are content in the knowledge that they are doing God's Will. At the end of *Paradiso,* Dante is granted the Vision of God.

As we read the *Divina Commedia* we are aware that there are two voices of Dante. One is the man making the journey (Dante the Pilgrim) and the other is the man who recounts the story after the journey is complete (Dante the Poet).

My own involvement with the idea that Shakespeare may have been familiar with Dante's work happened quite by chance. I am not an academic but I am deeply interested in Shakespeare and his work. It had occurred to me quite often that for a man with little formal education, no travel experience and virtually no biography, it was astonishing that he should have such a broad knowledge of the world and of the many aspects of human nature that are revealed in his writing.

In the early 1990s I was teaching in a small Catholic School in the Eastern suburbs of Sydney. My subject was mainly senior English but I also had a class of girls at a lower level studying Italian. Having spent several years living and working in Italy in the 1960s, I felt confident about teaching Italian at this level, but then it became necessary to have a tertiary qualification for any subject taught at higher levels and consequently I needed a tertiary qualification in Italian.

The University of New England offered a distance education course at this time and so I enrolled, since it was possible to take the course without too much disruption. There would be several brief sessions at

UNE Armidale during the year and the rest of the course involved reading, writing essays, doing language exercises at home, and then posting them off for assessment.

In the third year of the course, the subject of Dante was introduced. Up to then my knowledge of this great writer had been limited to the occasional epigraph by Dante in the poetry of T.S. Eliot, whose work was studied in senior English classes. It was easy enough to translate these verses, but of course with no understanding of the context, it was often difficult to grasp their significance in the Eliot poem. I was also familiar with the charming painting done by Henry Holiday in 1883, where we see Dante on the Trinita Bridge, the Ponte Vecchio in the background. He stands, hand on his heart as the elegant and proud Beatrice walks by attended by her servants and apparently unaware of his passionate love and devotion.

Early in the year I noticed a striking parallel between a passage in Shakespeare's *Macbeth* and one in *Inferno*. I made some enquiries, discussed it with my lecturer and wrote an essay[7] on this. Thus began a new direction in my life. I was close to retirement and soon I would have time to study full time. I began with this Diploma, went on to an M.Litt. in 1999 and then to a Ph.D. in 2002. This book is the result of research done at that time—but that is not the end of the story.

CHAPTER 1

The Question:
Had Shakespeare Read Dante?

*If Shakespere had known Dante, he would have used him, and
so often, as to leave no doubt on that point.*

F.J. Furnivall

The Reverend H. F. Cary, translator of the second complete English version[1]
of the *Divina Commedia* in 1814, commented in his footnotes on passages
which he found remarkably similar to ideas or phrases in Shakespeare. He
did not, however, attempt to account for this similarity and we can only
conclude that he was somehow assuming the coincidence of great minds.
He also noted in his footnotes parallels between Dante's work and that of
Chaucer and Milton, both of whom were known to have been familiar with
Dante's work.

Another early writer to notice a very striking coincidence of idea in
Shakespeare and Dante was James Russell Lowell,[2] writing in 1868. He
noted and discussed the parallel, but did not suggest that Shakespeare
may have read Dante. Four years later in 1872, Wilhelm König, writing
in German, claimed that Shakespeare was certainly familiar with Dante's
work and had used material from it in his plays. König's paper, forty-three
pages long, concentrated on the similarity of ideas he found in the works of
the two poets. In his conclusion he claimed:

> we are convinced that he [Shakespeare] did know Dante's
> work. We are led by the fact that the great Florentine was

highly acknowledged in Shakespeare's time, even though the main ideas in his poems were misunderstood. England was quite familiar with his works, much like the European continent in general. When it comes to Shakespeare himself being familiar with Dante's work, we can assume that the very literate British poet had access to a masterpiece like the *Divina Commedia*. I would even say that the opposite— namely Shakespeare being totally ignorant of such an acclaimed poet—seems impossible.[3]

These claims, here presented by König without supporting evidence, are considered in more detail in Chapter 2.

Several English writers in this decade, mostly amateurs of Dante, noted similarities, only to find an almost universal rejection of their ideas by English literary experts, expressed sometimes in a rather scathing and dismissive tone, even on occasions with a humorous flight of fancy to show just how absurd the notion was. The acknowledgement of the fact that some writers had noted certain parallels in the works of the two poets was usually followed by a refusal to accept that these similarities could be attributed to anything other than chance or coincidence. After this, there was sometimes even a personal attack on whoever had dared to suggest the possibility of a "borrowing".

In 1878 Dr F. J. Furnivall wrote a brief note in *Notes and Queries* in response to two other writers who had noticed some striking parallels between the works of the two poets. They sought some expert guidance on whether Shakespeare could have been familiar with Dante. Touching on a few of the now well-known parallels, one of them, Erato Hills, had concluded "[t]hese coincidences seem scarcely accidental. Was there a translation of Dante in Shakespeare's time?"[4]

Furnivall's response is interesting not so much for its scholarly authority on the subject, as for its note of firm certainty in spite of an admitted ignorance:

I do not know enough to give a real opinion, but I feel *sure* that Shakespere had no such knowledge of Dante as Chaucer had; bits from Dante don't come out in Shakespere as they do in *The Second Nun's Tale*, the last stanzas etc. of *Troilus*, the *Parlement of Foules*, *The House of Fame;* and that the highest Judge should be called by Shakespere "the top of judgment" seems to me so likely and natural as to need no suggestion from Dante ... My belief is, that if Shakespere had known Dante he'd have used him, and so often, as to leave no doubt on the point.[5]

Lorenzo Mascetta-Caracci's paper, written in Italian and published in 1897,[6] began by claiming that there could be no doubt that Shakespeare had some knowledge of the Italian language and literature. He gave passages from Shakespeare's plays in which he said the playwright was clearly using ideas from Ariosto, Petrarch, and Tasso. He then went on to comment that Shakespeare had borrowed less from Dante than from other Italian writers, but he gave a number of parallels—about ten—in the work of the two great poets. He was rather tentative about some of them. Unfortunately Mascetta-Caracci did not go beyond selecting verbal similarities or Dantean ideas which he claimed Shakespeare had translated for his own purposes. He commented, however, that the two geniuses:

had in common great width and depth of intellect, breadth of imagination, profound knowledge of human nature and great vigour and power of style. That would have conformed to English literary tradition, because, not to speak of others, Chaucer before Shakespeare and Milton after, are packed full with Dantean references.[7]

This opinion was not shared by Lewis Einstein, whose fascinating study *The Italian Renaissance in England*[8] was published in 1902. In it he traced the Italian influences in many areas of English life during this period, and the work is remarkable for its detailed information on the many Italians whose lives and ideas served to change England from a medieval society to a new and vibrant Renaissance civilization. Einstein's discussion of the Italian effect on English literature began, of course, with Chaucer, who, he claimed, was "the first to express the influence of Italy".[9]

But while Petrarch and Boccaccio were named, Dante was not, unless we are to assume his presence in the phrase "the Tuscan poets". There was some discussion of Spenser and his knowledge of Italy and Italian, but again, the possible influence of Dante was not mentioned. Considerable information was also given on John Florio and the range and effect of his writing and teaching, but no mention was made of the fact that he had used Dante's work in the compilation of his dictionary *Queene Anna's New World of Words*. On Shakespeare, Einstein claimed that "the sources of fourteen of his dramas are found in Italian fiction",[10] but Dante's name did not appear in the discussion, even as a non-influence or as a *grande assente*. Dante was simply ignored as one of the specific Italian influences on English literature, though there was a general reference to "the schools of Dante, Ariosto and Petrarch".[11]

Although in a footnote Einstein mentions the fact that "two English bishops, Hallam and Bubwith, meeting John of Serravalle at the Council of Constance (1414–18), induced him to write a commentary on Dante's *Commedia*,"[12] he does not follow the line of thinking which this would seem to suggest. There must have been at that time some considerable interest in Dante's work in England, since the request for the provision of a Latin commentary (no small task) was clearly a request for accessibility. Someone must have read this work, and it must have had some influence. In fact, Toynbee tells us that a copy of this work (and a Latin translation of the *Divina Commedia* in prose, also by John of Serravalle) was noted in the libraries of Oxford and Wells by Leland in his capacity as "King's antiquary" when he toured England in the years 1536–42. The work was recorded as:

Oxoniae in bibliotheca publica

Commentarii Joannes de Seravala, episcopi Firmani, ordinis
Minorum, Latine scripti, super opera Dantis Aligerii, ad
Nicolaum Bubwice, Bathon, et Wellensem episcopum, et
Robertum Halam, episcopum Sarisbur: commentarii editi
sunt tempore Constantiensis consilii.[13]

Bishop Nicholas Bubwith founded and endowed the library at Wells
and "no doubt presented to it a copy of Serravalle's work, perhaps the
copy[14] seen by Leland when he visited Wells".[15] Toynbee believed that the
copy seen by Leland "was probably identical with the *Commentaria Dantes*
presented to the University by Humphrey, Duke of Gloucester in 1443."[16]

Einstein discussed the contribution of Duke Humphrey to the English
Renaissance in some detail and mentioned his donation of between three
and four hundred Italian books to Oxford, noting that among these were
"the text and commentaries of Dante".[17] But he did not consider the effect
that reading these must have had on English minds either in the time of
Duke Humphrey in the fifteenth century, or later in the late sixteenth
and early seventeenth centuries. And yet William Thomas had written his
Dictionarie for the Better Understanding of Boccace, Petrarche and Dante
in 1550 and Thomas Sackville had written his *Induction* to *A Mirror for
Magistrates* in 1559 with a similar structure to Dante's *Inferno*. Florio, too,
had remarked in the dedication of his *Worlde of Wordes* in 1598 that "Dante
is hardest, but commented. Some doubt if all aright" and had used the
Divina Commedia as a source for his dictionary of 1611. But to the writers
of the early twentieth century it was as though Dante's work had made no
impact—though there was much discussion on the influence of Petrarch
and Boccaccio (along with so many other Italian writers) on the great
Elizabethan writers, of whom Shakespeare is the greatest.

One reason for the absence of any mention of Dante in this context
could have been the practices adopted by some editors and printers up to
about 1550. Editors of Petrarch, Boccaccio and Ariosto, particularly Bembo
in Venice, produced editions of the works of these writers with glossaries

and grammar notes for less able readers, including women and young people. But Bembo felt that Dante took excessive liberties with language and so in the first half of the sixteenth century there were no editions of Dante with this kind of assistance for the reader.

Another reason for the lesser popularity of Dante may have been its philosophical and theological content. But from the 1540s to the 1570s there was new interest in the poem, due, according to Brian Richardson,[18] to a new and different moral and intellectual climate. He points out that there was always more interest in the *Divina Commedia* in times of political and religious crisis. If there were fewer editions of Dante's work available and accessible to the general public than of the work of the other great Italian writers of the period, it would seem logical that his work would have less influence. But the fact remains that a number of Elizabethan and Jacobean writers *had* read it.

In 1909, Paget Toynbee, in his meticulously researched tome *Dante in English Literature* (Vol. 1), listed some sixty-two English writers from the time of Chaucer to that of Milton who were familiar with, or made some mention of, the work of Dante. Shakespeare was not among them. Included in the list were such names as Chaucer, Greene, Whetstone, Spenser, Harington, Florio, Drayton, Meres, Donne and Jonson. Shakespeare would have been familiar with the work of most of these and would have known some of them personally. Given his penchant for using foreign sources, particularly Italian, it seems scarcely credible that Shakespeare would *not* have known something of Dante's work and revealed this knowledge somewhere in his own writing—as had the sixty-two writers on Toynbee's list.

Toynbee however, in his Introduction, would not entertain the idea. In highly coloured language which left no doubt as to his feelings about such a claim, he wrote,

> The question as to whether Shakespeare had any knowledge
> of Dante has been discussed of late years at great length, and,
> it must be confessed, with a certain lack of sobriety, by sundry

Italian and Shakespearean scholars. Shakespeare's works have been ransacked for traces of Dante's influence, and considerable ingenuity has been expended in attempting to prove his indebtedness. Many parallel passages and so called imitations have been adduced, as in the case of Spenser, but the result is far from convincing. Some of the parallels are fairly close and one or two are striking [examples omitted][19] but the majority are wholly illusive.[20]

The examples given by Toynbee, most of which were taken from the article by Lorenzo Mascetta-Caracci published in 1897, were dismissed, but with no discussion, except for the comment that Shakespeare could have written them himself, without having to go to Dante. His conclusion to the paragraph (and the discussion) was as follows:

Few who have examined the evidence, such as it is, will have any hesitation in endorsing the conclusion of the well-known Shakespearean scholar, who expressed his belief that "if Shakespeare had known Dante, he would have used him, and so often, as to leave no doubt on that point".

The "well-known Shakespearean scholar" was, of course, F. J. Furnivall.

Toynbee's line of argument was still being followed sixteen years later, in 1925, when Michele Renzulli, an Italian writer, considered the subject. Equally dismissive of the idea that Shakespeare might have read Dante, he conceded Shakespeare's excellent knowledge of Italian topography, especially in the Veneto, but concluded that there was nothing in the plays to remind him of Dante:

[I]n all his marvellous and fruitful poetic works, we do not find a single line which reminds us even distantly of Dante. We must conclude that Shakespeare either knew the *Commedia* only by name or, having a vague idea of it, never made it an object of his attention, otherwise, given his nature, Shakespeare would have derived such, and so much material from the work of Dante as to leave no doubt at all concerning his debt to the Divine Poet.[21]

This very clear and total dismissal of any connection between the two writers, and the repetition of the idea that Shakespeare would have used a great deal of Dante's work if he had known it, was made in spite of the fact that Renzulli cited, in a footnote, the parallel first noted by Lowell, and mentioned above, between an idea in *Inferno* II and a strikingly similar one in *Hamlet*. Renzulli made no comment on whether he found this parallel close, but given his conclusion, presumably he did not.

Apart, then, from König in 1872, the two writers in *Notes and Queries* in 1878, and Mascetta-Caracci in 1897, up to the 1920s there was no voice, English, Italian or German, to argue that Shakespeare may have read Dante. While Cary and Lowell had also noted similarities, and Toynbee had used material by some of the above writers for his survey, only König and Mascetta-Caracci were prepared to suggest Shakespeare's possible knowledge of Dante. König expanded on his theme, giving a large number of parallels. Mascetta-Caracci gave only the examples.

But in 1921 Clara Longworth, Comtesse de Chambrun,[22] writing in French, claimed:

> Numerous allusions spread throughout the work of Shakespeare show us that the poet was familiar with the works of Petrarch, Dante and Machiavelli.[23]

She directed our attention to the dream of Clarence in *Richard III* and the vision of Claudio in *Measure for Measure* as evidence of Shakespeare's knowledge of *Inferno* V, but did not pursue the argument further, which was hardly surprising, since this was not the subject of her book.

Writing in 1949, and also considering the possibility that Shakespeare may have known Dante's work, was Ernesto Grillo, Head of the Department of Italian Language and Literature at Glasgow University from 1910 to 1940. He commented that "students of Dante had noted parallels in Shakespeare to thoughts or images in the *Divina Commedia,* but these were too few and too slight in themselves to have much weight as evidence".[24] He was convinced, however, that Shakespeare had a good knowledge of the Italian language and had probably visited Italy.

Some twenty years later several papers appeared in which the authors were (sometimes reluctantly) prepared to allow that Shakespeare may have known Dante, or at least some small parts of his work. Reginald Saner, writing in 1968, found a strong parallel between a passage in *Purgatorio* XXIII and another in *King Lear,* but ridiculed those who suggested that Shakespeare had read Dante and claimed, quite rightly, that "the single parallel offered in this note is not proof that he did".[25] He was, however, prepared to concede rather grudgingly that "the greatest English poet" might have known "at least some passages or episodes from Italy's greatest poet".[26]

Saner, like Furnivall and Toynbee, even took a rather patronisingly satirical tone on the absurdity of such a notion and entertained us with the following little piece of whimsy:

> Almost annually we read assertions that Shakespeare must have known Italian, assertions based on a familiar hypothetical formula. It usually begins with the Earl of Southampton's circle, stresses the fact that learning Italian was widespread and fashionable, introduces (optionally) one or more sea-captains from Venice or Genoa, assembles these elements with Shakespeare at a quiet room in the Mermaid, and finally adds a touch of Florio in the night.[27]

In 1971, an American writer, Joseph Satin, published a paper entitled "Macbeth and the Inferno of Dante". His subject was the similarities between *Macbeth* and *Inferno* and, in particular, the strange parallel between the classification of various types of betrayal in the final cantos of

Inferno and the speech "He's here in double trust …" (*Macbeth,* I.7.12–20).
In a footnote, Satin commented:

> Whether Shakespeare read Dante, and if so in what language,
> or whether Shakespeare merely had the *Divine Comedy*
> outlined to him at some time is a topic as haunting as it is
> inexplicable. To date, the reader of both Shakespeare and
> Dante must content himself with knowing that the English
> genius borrowed from the Italian one in several of his plays.[28]

In the 1976 *Enciclopedia Dantesca,* under the heading "Shakespeare,
William" a number of parallels in thought and similarities in words or
phrases were given, then the writer went on to conclude that direct influence
could not be proven:

> In the vast field of poetry and drama of the greatest English
> poet … it is not surprising that parallels of thought and verbal
> similarities should be seen in the ideas and lines of Dante's
> works, but in the end one must admit the impossibility of
> identifying direct influences.[29]

The material used to compile the entry is largely the same as that mentioned
by Toynbee and some of the other writers mentioned above. After listing
these parallels between the texts of the two writers, the *Enciclopedia*
concluded without a great deal of conviction that in Shakespeare's plays,
there did seem to be some knowledge of Dante's work:

> At most he had some knowledge of *Inferno,* perhaps in the
> period in which he was writing *Measure for Measure.*

Francis Fergusson wrote in 1977 that "There is no reason to
think that Shakespeare ever read Dante,"[30] but he went on to discuss
the kinship between them and attributed this largely to the fact that

"they were both brought up on Aristotelian ethics, metaphysics and psychology which was the standard philosophy from Dante's Aquinas to Shakespeare's Hooker".[31] He found parallels between *Romeo and Juliet* and Dante's tale of Paolo and Francesca, between *Macbeth* and the tale of Ugolino and so on, but did not ever suggest that Shakespeare had seen Dante's work. Robin Kirkpatrick believed in 1995 that "Shakespeare had almost certainly not read Dante",[32] but commented on the similarities in treatment of the themes of love and justice by the two poets. In 2001 Stuart Gillespie noted two writers who had observed parallels in the work of Shakespeare and Dante, but commented:

> Dante was virtually unknown in early modern England: the snippets in Florio's Italian-English dictionary, uninspiring enough in themselves, are the only plausible route suggested to Shakespeare.[33]

The subject does not seem to have attracted a great deal of interest in recent years and one senses that it is not a popular one. One of the objections to the notion that Shakespeare may have borrowed from Dante is the fact that there was not an English translation of the *Divina Commedia* in Shakespeare's time and it is therefore assumed that he could not have had access to it.

It is true that the first translation of part of the *Divina Commedia* did not appear till 1782, some 166 years after Shakespeare's death. David Wallace wrote that in that year:

> William Hayley translated three cantos of the *Inferno* ... and William Rogers published a blank verse translation of the entire *Inferno*. In 1802 the first complete English translation of the *Commedia* was published by an Irishman, Henry Boyd. It was not until 1814 however, that H. F. Cary, an Anglican clergyman, brought the English-speaking world face to face

with a powerful, accurate, and poetically moving translation of Dante.[34]

Since there was no English translation, then the possibilities are two, if we accept for the moment that parallels are the result of "borrowing". The first of these is that Shakespeare had enough knowledge of the Italian language, and access to a copy of the *Divina Commedia,* so that he could consult it and adapt ideas and images to his own use. The alternative is that his knowledge was filtered through another person or persons whose writings or conversations relayed enough of Dante's ideas and images to provide a source for Shakespeare. It may even be that both of these alternatives operated. It is hardly necessary to establish that Shakespeare was, as a writer, known to have "borrowed" ideas from the work of many other writers.

All of the points listed in the paragraph above are crucial to the establishment of the hypothesis that Shakespeare had read Dante, and after a brief consideration here, they will all be discussed in detail in Chapter 3, 4 and 5 of this book.

That Shakespeare had some knowledge of the Italian language seems highly likely and many modern writers[35] accept this. Leonard Barken, writing in 2001 on the revolutionary effect of translations from 1560 onwards on the material available to Shakespeare says:

> Though the dramatist's familiarity with passages in the original is often demonstrable, Shakespeare's plays would scarcely have been possible without: Hoby's Castiglione (1561), Adlington's Apuleius (1566), Golding's Ovid (1567), North's Plutarch (1579), Harington's Ariosto (1591), Chapman's Homer (1598, in part), Hollands' Livy (1600), Fairfax's Tasso (1600) and Florio's Montaigne (1603). To say that, of course, is to return to 'small Latin and less Greek': as a reader, Shakespeare was pretty much like most of us who have a reasonable command of a foreign language. Faced

with the bulk of something like *Orlando Furioso,* we would still prefer a reliable trot; and the chances of our experiencing the whole work and of going back to it in the original are vastly increased by the existence of a good translation.[36]

We can see from his plays that Shakespeare's interest in Italian culture began sometime before 1593 or 1594 when *Two Gentlemen of Verona* and *The Taming of the Shrew* appeared. After that, there were so many plays with Italian plots, Italian settings, Italian names and even the occasional Italian phrase that we must assume that somehow Shakespeare had access to a large library of Italian books. Some of these had been translated into English, but many had not, and in Chapter 4 a number of Shakespearean passages which seem to have come from untranslated Italian sources are considered in some detail. Several writers claimed that even when the Italian source was translated, there were cases where Shakespeare's version was closer to the original Italian than to the translation.

It also seems likely that there was in his circle someone with a good knowledge of the Italian language and culture, who discussed these with the playwright and encouraged his interest. Shakespeare had certainly read John Florio's Italian/English language manuals, evidence for which claim is presented in Chapter 4. Lowell mentions in passing that "one of the few books which Shakespeare is known to have possessed was Florio's *Montaigne*",[37] a copy of which is in the British Library, inscribed with Shakespeare's name. One would assume that Shakespeare read the language manuals in an attempt to learn the language, or perhaps because he knew Florio, who was Italian teacher to the Earl of Southampton, believed to be Shakespeare's famous patron. Certainly, Shakespeare must have known both Southampton and Florio, and since both men knew the Italian language well, it is very possible that Shakespeare may have had considerable assistance from one or both of these, in himself learning the language.

Ernesto Grillo presented an excellent case for Shakespeare's knowledge of the language, and also argued that "at least on one occasion he must have visited Italy."[38] The modern novelist, travel-writer and italophile Jonathan Keates expounded on the same theme:

> [T]here is something just a shade too coincidental in the fact that all Shakespeare's Italian plays are set in the same carefully demarcated area, stretching from Milan to Venice, bounded on the south by Mantua and on the north by Bergamo. Why no Naples, no Florence, no papal Rome?[39]

He went on to discuss how the very details which so called "experts" use to demonstrate that Shakespeare did not know Italy, seem to prove the contrary. Whatever the truth of this, there is no historical evidence that Shakespeare had visited Italy.

That there were copies of Dante's *Divina Commedia* in England in Shakespeare's time is clear from the number of other English writers who were familiar with this work, and from contemporary library catalogues. Both of these aspects will be considered in Chapter 3 and 4. It is even possible to discover where particular copies were located. Some of them were in the possession of persons in a social circle to which Shakespeare had access.

That Shakespeare was a "borrower" is indisputable. Shelves of volumes have been written on Shakespeare's sources. Only one of his plays, *Love's Labour's Lost,* seems not to have a plot taken from an identifiable written literary source[40]—the others all use plots of other writers both English and foreign. Many of Shakespeare's ideas seem to have their origins in Greek and Roman classics,[41] the Bible, emblem books, well-known proverbs, a large number of Italian tales and also various stories from the French, Spanish, German and Dutch.[42] Selma Guttman in her exhaustive study of foreign sources, found twenty-seven Italian authors from whom Shakespeare had probably taken ideas. She also provided information on whether these works were translated when Shakespeare was writing.

Dante too, used many of the sources listed above, and if there are parallels between his work and Shakespeare's, it is always possible that common sources might account for them. When this could be the case, I have not considered these parallels as "borrowings". Emblem books, some first appearing in English versions in 1586, were popular when Shakespeare was writing, and may have been one way in which he could have learned of Italian ideas, whether the book was translated or not. The emblematic representations of abstract ideas were often visual and since many of these originated from classical sources (Ovid, Livy, Plutarch, Terence, Virgil, Pliny, Horace and others), as did much of Dante's work and Shakespeare's, it would hardly be surprising if there were a number of parallels in the work of the Italian poet and the English playwright.

A 1611 Italian reprint of Cesare Ripa's *Iconologia* listed in its index of authors who had expressed views similar to those implicit in the personifications of abstract qualities, fifteen references to Dante's *Divina Commedia*. Three of these coincide with passages we have considered in this study, but by the time this book appeared and even though it was an expanded version of a 1603 edition, Shakespeare would have already written two of the plays in which the parallels appear, before he saw this edition. The other parallel is considered in Chapter 2.

The genre flourished in the seventeenth century and then went out of fashion, but these books reflect the Elizabethan and Jacobean interest in allegory and certainly influenced Shakespeare's thinking. Mario Praz[43] found the influence of emblem books in the works of Florio, Lyly, Sidney, Greene, Spenser, Daniel, Drummond of Hawthornden, Marlowe, Marston, Chapman, Jonson and, of course, Shakespeare. He gave several examples of this influence in Shakespeare's work but none of these coincides with passages considered here as parallels with Dante. Since much of Dante's work is allegorical, Shakespeare's knowledge of *emblemata* and *iconologia* could account for some of the apparent parallels between the two writers. When this could be the case, I have acknowledged the possibility.

It may be apposite to comment here on Elizabethan attitudes to "borrowing". In Shakespeare's time, authorship was often shared and so it may not always be possible to consider any one play to be the exclusive work of one playwright. At the same time, sources were usually not acknowledged and plagiarism was not a consideration. Jeffrey Masten quotes Timothy Murray,[44] who notes that "identification and glorification of sources was not a convention cherished by the players, who preferred disguised sources, collaboration, alterable texts".[45]

Jonathon Bate points out that "Renaissance thinkers believed passionately that the present could learn from the past; the belief was the starting point of education and a formative influence upon writing in the period. It was the essence of what we now call Renaissance humanism."[46] It may be that those who are so reluctant to admit the possibility of Shakespeare's borrowing from Dante are concerned about the moral implications of plagiarism, seeing the practice quite differently through modern eyes. It may also be that they attribute parallels to the use of common sources. And yet no-one disputes the fact that Shakespeare took so many of his plots from other Italian sources. It seems that the blind spot is reserved exclusively for Dante.

It could also be that those passages considered to be "borrowings" were contributed to the play by another person, who was himself familiar with Dante's work. To investigate this, one can only consider the scenes which contain such passages and try to determine the identity of the other contributing writers—if they exist. Where there is some doubt concerning the authorship of a passage from Shakespeare, and where there also seems to be a "borrowing", I acknowledge the possibility that this knowledge of Dante's work may be attributed to another writer.

Certainly, Shakespeare read widely, and it seems that much of what he read somehow became part of the fabric of his plays and poetry. Robert Miola in his *Shakespeare's Reading*[47] made some interesting observations on the *way* in which Shakespeare read, noting that, among other things, he was "alert to parallels and analogues, sensitive to moral and political meanings". Miola went on to comment that the dramatist read retentively and reminiscently, forgetting very little, able to recall appropriate material easily. He altered the text, added to it, shifted the emphasis, combined it with the ideas of someone else. Echoes of other writers abound, but sometimes an element appears which cannot be traced and a footnote often acknowledges this fact.

In some of these cases, the untraced element could have come from Dante.

Shakespeare's genius lies largely in his ability to absorb plots, characters, settings, atmospheres, and philosophies from all he has read and heard, and then to adapt and re-present them in language which is imaginative and creative and which appeals to the mind and senses. Ernesto Grillo wrote:

> Shakespeare was in reality the possessor of a vast store of learning; and in saying this we do justice not only to England but to the most illustrious of her sons. Besides his most fertile imaginative power he possessed the faculty of assimilating the characteristic details of the works which he read ... In Shakespeare's case the assimilative factor reinforced his imaginative fertility. He had made a profound study of the literature of his own time; and the fruits of his reading were immediately digested, assimilated, transformed by his powerful imagination; and when they reappeared in some concrete form they bore, with rare exceptions, the stamp of his individuality rather than the traces of their origin.[48]

It was this very ability to "digest" and "assimilate" so effectively which allowed Furnivall to make his claim that "bits from Dante don't come out in Shakespere as they do in Chaucer".[49] The "bits" are already too well "digested".

But today, it is not fashionable to talk about sources. Roland Barthes claimed that:

> The intertextual in which every text is held, it itself being the text-between of another text, is not to be confused with some origin of the text: to try to find the "sources", the "influences" of a work, is to fall in with the myth of filiation; the citations which go to make up a text are anonymous, untraceable, and yet *already read*: they are quotations without inverted commas.[50]

It is an interesting but dubious claim. The citations which go to make up a text may be anonymous, but they are not always untraceable. Anything written is the expression of the thoughts of the writer, influenced perhaps by the thoughts of others whose ideas the writer may have heard or read. The process could extend backwards indefinitely, but sometimes the similarity between the present piece of writing and one immediately preceding it can be striking.

The greatest writers have read widely, and they express ideas which are the processed product of all they have learned. To search for the origins of these ideas is simply a fascinating exercise—rather like searching the face of a child for features we recognise from some other family member or remote ancestor. And sometimes we may see in the face a quite different feature—one that we did not expect or do not recognize. Or we may recognize a feature and be astonished at its presence. The ideas of a good writer in part adapted from an earlier source become something fresh and original—much as a child's face, though perhaps recognisable in its separate features, is still its own. The new work—or the new face—is peculiar to the new owner, though the source of a particular idea or feature may be easily recognised.

But it is certainly true that ideas on what might be a "source" are changing. Stuart Gillespie in his Introduction comments:

> What Robert S. Miola calls "our recently expanded understanding of sources" involves the assumption, generally made now, that a text may derive from a source quite obliquely, when it is part of a "tradition" or "context" for a work; and the understanding, now common enough, that evidence about a source can be derived from a "scenic form, thematic figuration, rhetorical strategy, structural parallelism, ideational or imagistic concatenation" as well as more straightforward kinds of "verbal iteration".[51]

This wider scope for the investigation of sources allows new and different ways in which texts may be related and it is therefore reasonable to expect that claims of "borrowing" which once may have been rejected, can now be considered.

The other alternative mentioned earlier to explain Shakespeare's apparent knowledge of Dante is that he may have found information on or excerpts from the *Divina Commedia* in the works of past or contemporary English writers—or of foreign writers in English translation. Certainly Chaucer used quite long passages from Dante, acknowledging his source, and Shakespeare is known to have read Chaucer.[52] While it is necessary to consider this possibility, so many parallels in Shakespeare's work emerged in the course of research, some of them so verbally exact, that it became increasingly unlikely that Shakespeare could have acquired the sheer volume of knowledge he had of Dante from anything other than an actual copy of the text.

It became necessary early in the research process to develop criteria for what could be considered a genuine parallel and a probable "borrowing". Earlier writers seem to have been content to note a verbal similarity, and certainly this is always the most obvious. But when we are working in two languages, this is sometimes confusing. Some writers, working from an English translation of Dante, found what they thought was a verbal parallel. On investigation, though, it emerged that the translator, having found an idea he recognised, and being familiar with Shakespeare's work, had simply appropriated Shakespeare's phrase. What looked like an exact verbal parallel was not. On other occasions, a translator, trying desperately to find a rhyme or to keep to a certain metre, changed, condensed or even omitted an idea so that what could have been a parallel was lost in the attempt to translate Dante into English poetry.

But even a very close verbal parallel can be a matter of coincidence. In studying two prolific writers it would not be really surprising to find that sometimes their expression of a similar idea would emerge in a quite similar form—even given the language difference. Sometimes too, a verbal parallel could be explained by both writers working from another common source. Where this seems possible, I have not claimed that the similarity is a "borrowing".

In the course of this investigation it soon became apparent that when there was a verbal parallel, or a very similar idea, there was often a parallel in the context in which this passage occurred. Saner noted this phenomenon in his paper *Gemless Rings*[53] and went on to claim that he believed this parallel to be "the closest thing to a Dante borrowing yet discovered in Shakespeare".[54]

For the purposes of this book, only if there was a verbal parallel, or similarity of idea, *in conjunction with* the parallel in context, was the parallel deemed to be an actual "borrowing". The verbal parallel alone may well have been a "borrowing", but unless it was very exact, there was no way of establishing that it had, in fact, originated in Dante. One might object that even with the requirement that there be a verbal parallel associated with a parallel of context, this similarity could still have been a matter of coincidence—and if it had happened once then that was certainly a possibility. But when it happened time and time again, to use the word "coincidence" seemed to distort the meaning of the word.

There were however, several exceptions to this rule. In a parallel observed between a short passage in *The Tempest* and another in *Inferno* XIII, there was no close similarity of context. But on closer examination of Shakespeare's play, so many ideas which also appeared in *Inferno* XIII were identified that it was absurd not to concede a "borrowing". As the number of apparent parallels began to accumulate, it was necessary to allow that this very accumulation and combination of similarities was, in itself, evidence of another kind for my hypothesis. While no one of the parallel ideas taken in isolation was necessarily a "borrowing", the *collocation* of ideas was striking as evidence of a connection between the two writers. As J. M. Robertson points out in his discussion of whether one can consider this collocation between the work of Bacon and Shakespeare as evidence that Bacon was the author of Shakespeare's work:

> Noting that the collocation is exceptional ... we have two hypotheses open. Either both writers copied a previous

one—as they may very well have done—or Bacon recalled some lines he had heard at the theatre ...[55]

In the present case, the argument is identical. Either both Shakespeare and Dante were working from a common source (as they sometimes were) or Shakespeare recalled passages from Dante.

I have used the parallels noted by (in chronological order) the Reverend H. F. Cary,[56] James Lowell,[57] Wilhelm König,[58] Erato Hills,[59] Lorenzo Mascetta-Caracci,[60] Paget Toynbee,[61] Clara Longworth de Chambrun,[62] Kenneth Muir,[63] Reginald A. Saner,[64] Eric Vincent,[65] and Joseph Satin.[66] Many of these found the same parallels or were discussing the ideas of other writers and so their works overlap. The other examples of "borrowing" have been the result of my own research. I consider one of these, the passage from *Measure for Measure* describing Isabella as "enskied and sainted", in view of the verbal parallel and the many exact and detailed parallels of context, to be compelling and incontrovertible evidence that Shakespeare had read at least this part of Dante's *Paradiso*.

As a general rule I have used various Arden editions of Shakespeare's plays and of his poems, where I found the footnotes to be particularly informed and useful—and in some cases to mention Dante, though only for the plays, never for the poems. For similar reasons, I have used generally the modern editions of the *Divina Commedia* with commentary by Natalino Sapegno. Where possible, I used the old editions which were available to Shakespeare. For biblical references in relation to Shakespeare, I have used the Bishops' Bible (1584), accepting Richmond Noble's claim that "there can be no reasonable doubt that some way or another, he had access to the Bishops' Bible."[67] For the translation of passages from the *Divina Commedia* I have chosen to use the work of Charles Singleton, since he makes no attempt to translate into verse, and is therefore less likely to distort the meaning in the quest for rhyme or rhythm. There are some occasions however, where he has altered the order of phrases, and thus lost the structural parallel of a sentence. When this occurs, I have pointed it out in a footnote or used the work of another translator.

In the light of the publication of Diana Price's *Shakespeare's Unorthodox Biography*, and the fascinating ideas presented by Calvin Hoffman in *The Murder of The Man Who Was Shakespeare*, Joseph Sobran in *Alias Shakespeare* and Cecil Cragg's translation of Abel LeFranc's *Under the Mask of William Shakespeare*, it is probably even necessary to define what is meant here by the name "Shakespeare". For the purposes of my argument in this book, I use the name "Shakespeare" to describe the author of the plays and poems which we understand to be the work of this great playwright and poet—whoever he may have been. For an exhaustive list of his plays, I have used *Annals of English Drama, 975–1700*, by A. Harbage and revised by S. Schoenbaum, Methuen, London, 1964. For dates of Shakespeare's poetry I have used the list published in "The Canon and Chronology of Shakespeare's Plays" in Stanley Wells and Gary Taylor, eds., *William Shakespeare: A Textual Companion*, pp. 77ff., Oxford, 1987. When a date or a title is used in this book, it is from these sources, although I am aware that there are a number of divergent views on the actual texts and dates given in the above publications.

The purpose of this book is to argue that Shakespeare had read Dante's *Divina Commedia* in the original Italian—at least in part—and had used ideas and images from it in his own writing. The idea is indeed "haunting", as Joseph Satin claimed, but it is certainly not "inexplicable". In conjunction with this, it must be shown that the knowledge of Dante's work demonstrated by Shakespeare could not have been acquired via another person of his acquaintance, or via the work of another writer. By investigating the knowledge of Dante's work revealed in the work of other English writers, it can be established whether this is sufficient to explain the "borrowings" that I believe are to be found in Shakespeare's work.

As other writers have commented, a close parallel between several passages in the work of these two great writers is not proof of any direct connection. But a large number of such parallels is rather more convincing, particularly if the parallels are more than verbal. Given Shakespeare's voracious appetite for new material for his plays, his demonstrated interest in Italian sources and his wide reading list established by a large number of researchers in this field, it would be astonishing if Shakespeare had *not* read Dante.

Perhaps the most striking and compelling parallels appear in characterisations. Dante presents a vast kaleidoscope of characters—from life, from literature, from history and from mythology—he seems not to differentiate. They are sketched with skill, colour and economy, and allocated whichever place God (or Dante) has deemed just, according to their performance measured against Dante's complex system of moral philosophy. Like Shakespeare's characters, they are presented dramatically, telling their own story, rationalising their behaviour, performing the actions which constitute their punishment or reward. Unlike Shakespeare's characters, they cannot develop, as they have already passed beyond this life.

Shakespeare, too, has myriad characters, and sometimes in one of them, there suddenly appears a striking similarity to one of Dante's personages in the *Divina Commedia*. Initially, there may seem to be just a similar word or phrase—but then, on investigation, the similarity extends to the context in which the character appears, or the details of his life. It is as though Shakespeare, in creating his character, has been reminded of someone else—a Dantean creation—and has used (perhaps sometimes unconsciously) details he remembers from his reading. Often, the details evoke the same emotional response in the reader as they had in Dante—surely intentionally—so that we cannot imagine that Shakespeare could have chanced, quite independently, on precisely the same set of circumstances as that used by Dante. This material is the subject of Chapter 2.

The second area in which the two poets seem to coincide is on the matter of particular moral, ethical or philosophic values and ideas. This is hardly surprising in two writers from staunchly Christian societies, but sometimes the parallel is so exact in matters of detail not to be found in the Bible or the writings of the great Christian teachers and philosophers, that we are almost forced to concede the possibility of some direct connection between the two great writers.

Many writers who were familiar with the work of both Dante and Shakespeare have commented on the similarity of atmosphere or the "feeling" which is created in the work of each. For the reader of *Macbeth* and *King Lear* particularly, it is difficult not to be reminded of the torment and gloomy chaos of Dante's *Inferno*. It is the similarity of atmosphere which perhaps first suggests to a reader that Shakespeare may have read Dante and been influenced by his ideas.

The objection given in the past to the hypothesis presented in this book has always been that there is no persuasive evidence of Shakespeare's knowledge of Dante, although most writers would agree that *if* the playwright had known Dante's work, he would certainly have used it. I have therefore begun my argument by presenting all the available evidence of Shakespeare's knowledge of Dante, as revealed in the canon of his plays and poems.

The subject of Chapters 3, 4 and 5 is the means by which Shakespeare *could* have been familiar with Dante's work—despite the apparent language barrier and the matter of whether he could have had access to a copy of the *Divina Commedia*.

Most persuasive for my argument, as evidence of Shakespeare's knowledge of Dante is, I believe, the similarity of the context in which many of the parallels occur. If the hypothesis presented here is correct, then we can place one more piece in the complex jigsaw of facts which gradually create for us a more detailed, accurate and complete portrait of William Shakespeare himself. We can imagine someone rather different from the perhaps rather insular actor from Stratford and we can see him in a culture more in touch with European society and less isolated by the Reformation than we might have imagined. The dates of the plays in which he seems to be "borrowing" from Dante give us an indication of the period in which he was most influenced by these different ideas and contribute to our understanding of the expansion of his thinking and the development of his mind.

CHAPTER 2

The Evidence

I

Macbeth (1606)

> *Hell is murky.*
>
> *Macbeth*, Shakespeare

Hell is murky indeed, particularly the Hell created by Dante in *Inferno*. When Lady Macbeth makes this comment in *Macbeth* (V.1.22) she is in a Hell of her own making. "Murky" describes her situation accurately. The Concise Oxford Dictionary gives the meaning as "dark, gloomy (of darkness), thick, dirty and suspicious, obscure". She is in a darkened room, insisting that she have "a light by her continually". Demented, she re-lives the terrible night of the murder. Now, in retrospect, she is horrified at what she and her husband have done. "Murky" would also describe the murder itself—dirty (literally and metaphorically), arousing suspicions and initially obscuring the truth.

In the murky depths (the ninth and tenth circles) of Dante's Inferno were the four categories of traitors in icy concentric circles. Those who had betrayed family were on the outer circle (named Caina, after Cain) and immersed in the ice up to the neck. In the next circle (named Antenora after a Trojan who betrayed his city to the Greeks) were those who had betrayed their country or party. These were immersed in the ice up to the chin. Inside this was a circle (named Tolomea after Ptolomea, who murdered his father-in-law at a banquet). In this circle were those who had betrayed their host or guest, and only their faces emerged above the ice. And in the final circle (called Giudecca, after Judas Iscariot) were those who had betrayed their benefactors. Here is Judas, betrayer of Christ, the founder of the Church. Here are Brutus and Cassius, betrayers of Julius Caesar, the founder of the Empire.

This code of ethics is interesting as is the order in which these betrayals are graded. The least despicable treachery was betrayal of family, followed by betrayal of country, then of host or guest—and finally of benefactors. I felt that I had heard this code somewhere before, but where?

Then I remembered. It was in *Macbeth* in the scene where Macbeth argues against his earlier plan to kill Duncan.

I wondered if Shakespeare had read Dante. The generally accepted belief was, it seemed, that he had *not*. Dante's great work was not translated at that time and Shakespeare did not know Italian. And yet, so many of his plays were set in Italy and involved Italian plots and characters. What's more, there was always the feeling that Shakespeare had actually *seen* the places in which he had set his plays.

Fascinated, I read further. It seemed that most English writers from the last two centuries were convinced that Shakespeare did *not* know Dante's work—and yet so many English writers from Shakespeare's time and before, were familiar with it! I looked again at the passage in *Macbeth*. It seemed to me that the parallel was striking, and somehow, it did not seem like a Christian ethic. I had never heard it before and no one seemed to remember it from the Bible or Christian teachings.

In *Macbeth*, the witches address Macbeth correctly as Thane of Glamis, and then predict that he will become Thane of Cawdor and "King hereafter". On hearing this, and then almost immediately inheriting the title of Thane of Cawdor, Macbeth contemplates the murder of Duncan, the king. Lady Macbeth, even more ambitious than her husband, encourages him. He is persuaded, but left alone, he reconsiders, and presents his reasons in a soliloquy on why he should not follow this plan:

... He's here in double trust:
First, as I am his kinsman and his subject,
Strong both against the deed: then, as his host,
Who should against his murtherer shut the door,
Not bear the knife myself. Besides, this Duncan
Hath borne his faculties so meek, hath been
So clear in his great office, that his virtues
Will pleade like angels, trumpet tongu'd against
The deep damnation of his taking-off.

Macbeth I.7.12–20

At this point Lady Macbeth enters the scene to tell her husband that the king (who is their guest) has asked for him, and Macbeth, reverting to his own argument, decides:

We will proceed no further in this business:
He hath honoured me of late; and I have bought
Golden opinions from all sorts of people,
Which would be worn now in their newest gloss,
Not cast aside so soon.

Macbeth I.7.32–5

The parallel was remarkable. Not only are Macbeth's reasons for *not* killing Duncan identical to the types of treachery Dante lists, but they are also in the same order:

Dante, *Inferno*	Shakespeare, *Macbeth*
Traitors in the 9th circle	**Reasons not to kill Duncan**
those betraying kin	"I am his kinsman ..."
those betraying country or party	"and his subject ..."
those betraying guest or host	"as his host ..."
those betraying a benefactor	"he hath honoured me of late"

I was not able to find elsewhere any other mention of this ethic. What I did find was in another edition of *Macbeth*, a footnote by Kenneth Muir in which he writes:

> Shakespeare may not have been aware that in Dante's *Inferno* XXXII–XXXIV, those who were traitors to their kin, to their country, to their friends and guests, and to their lords and benefactors are tortured together in the Ninth or *frozen* Circle of Hell. Macbeth might be regarded as a traitor to his kinsman Duncan, to his country, Scotland, to his friend, Banquo, to his guest, lord and benefactor, Duncan.[1]

The negative construction used here—that Shakespeare *"may not have been aware"* of this, seems to imply that Muir believes that he *could have* been, and probably was aware of it. Muir had noted this parallel (and several others) years earlier and had written a brief note on them in *Notes and Queries*. He concluded "I am far from suggesting that these parallels can be regarded as proof presumptive that Shakespeare knew Dante; but they may be enough to encourage scholars to re-open the subject."[2]

I was certainly encouraged. Further research revealed that an article had been published in 1971 where the writer[3] had made the same observation as had I, and wrote:

> Duncan is his kinsman: Duncan is the leader of the party Macbeth supports: Duncan is his guest; Duncan is a fine king. Dante's *Inferno, and only in Dante's,* is a cone-shaped series of ever-narrowing circles, the lowest of which houses four kinds of traitor-murderers whom Dante encounters in the following order: murderers of kinsmen, traitors to party or country; murderers of guests; murderers of kings.
>
> The four reasons Macbeths lists for hesitating to murder Duncan are, *in order,* the same four crimes that Dante, and only Dante, lists as the punishments in the lowest level of hell.[4]

If Shakespeare had Dante's traitors in mind, then Macbeth is guilty on all four counts. The punishment for Dante's traitors in *Inferno* is submersion in a frozen lake. They have lost all warmth in their hearts for other people, and so they are tortured in the cold for all eternity. Would Shakespeare, with Dante's traitors in mind, have continued this parallel any further in the play?

That Macbeth and his wife, after the murder of Duncan, are actually in Hell (or Inferno), is made quite clear. When the idea to murder Duncan is first accepted by Lady Macbeth, she cries "Come thick night/And pall thee in the dunnest smoke of Hell" (I.5.50–1). It seems that her request is granted. In the last lines of Act II, Scene I, when Macbeth hears the bell, their signal, he says:

> Hear it not Duncan, for it is a knell
> That summons thee to Heaven or to Hell.
>
> *Macbeth* II.1.66–7

He is as yet unaware that the bell tolls indeed to summon Duncan— but probably to Heaven. The summoning to Hell is for Macbeth himself. It is he, who, in the next scene, having murdered the King, finds himself in a Hell of his own creation. In the closing scene of the play, when Macbeth refuses to give his name because "Thou't be afraid to hear it," Siward cries:

> No, though thou call'st thyself a hotter name
> Than any is in Hell.

When Macbeth identifies himself, Siward continues:

> The devil himself could not pronounce a title
> More hateful to mine ear.
>
> *Macbeth* V.7.5–9

Moments later, Macduff confronts him with "Turn, Hell-hound, turn!" Clearly these characters see Macbeth as a creature from Hell, and even the Porter (II. 3), awakened by the knocking at the door after the murder of Duncan (of which he is still unaware), imagines himself as "porter of Hell-Gate". Having pondered a little on whom he might expect to meet at such a gate, he concludes "but this place is too cold for Hell. I'll devil-porter it no further." This is more than mere whimsy. He, like many of his contemporaries, may have seen Hell as "th'everlasting bonfire", but in the play, Shakespeare, perhaps thinking of Dante, has made this Hell at Inverness as cold as the depths of Dante's Inferno.

The cold is not just physical. One by one his supporters desert him. Even when he hears the news that "The Queen, my Lord, is dead," he can only respond, "She should have died hereafter:" There is a coldness there which is a sad reminder of his affectionate "my dearest love" earlier in the play. Rapidly his supporters withdraw from him. His close friend Banquo is murdered on Macbeth's own orders. Macduff, suspicious after the discovery of Duncan's body, refuses to go to the coronation. Angus reports of Macbeth as the English army with Malcolm move towards Dunsinane:

> Those he commands move only in command,
> Nothing in love: now does feel his title
> Hang loose about him, like a giant's robe
> Upon a dwarfish thief.
>
> *Macbeth* V.2.19–22

Like Dante's traitors he is out in the cold, isolated and bereft of all support and loyalty.

But Macbeth is not just a traitor. As King, he is a tyrant. Macduff refers to him as an "untitled tyrant bloody-sceptred". Young Siward addresses him as "abhorred tyrant". Macduff talks of how they will put Macbeth's head "painted upon a pole, and underwrit, /"Here may you see the tyrant." He has killed Duncan, the two grooms, Banquo, Macduff's wife and family and then, we hear, countless others. Macduff reports to Malcolm:

... Each new morn
New widows howl, new orphans cry; new sorrows
Strike heaven in the face, that it resounds
As if it felt with Scotland, and yell'd out
Like syllable of dolour.

Macbeth IV.3.4–8

In Canto XII of *Inferno*, Dante's tyrants are immersed in a river of boiling blood, the Phlegethon. They are in the first round on the seventh circle, for the violent. Because they have wallowed in the blood of others, they are immersed in the river of blood according to the degree of their violence. Along the banks of the river the Centaurs gallop, armed with bow and arrow and ready to shoot at those who dare to rise above the designated level of their immersion.

Macbeth too, is in a river of blood. After he has killed Banquo, he comments:

… I am in blood
Stepp'd in so far, that, should I wade no more,
Returning were as tedious as go o'er.

Macbeth III.4.135–7

This is metaphorical, but from the moment of Duncan's murder, blood is everywhere and the image is very apt. We are spared the horror of Duncan's murder on stage but immediately after it, Macbeth, shocked at the sight of his own bloodstained hands, wonders:

Will all great Neptune's ocean wash this blood
Clean from my hand? No, this my hand will rather
The multitudinous seas incarnadine,
Making the green one red.

Macbeth II.2.59–62

We have seen the bloodstained hands of Macbeth and his wife, the besmirched dagger of his imagination, the blood-smeared vision of Banquo's ghost at the banquet, the gory murders of Lady Macduff and her children and the blood of the final fight to the death of Macbeth. Macbeth is, like Dante's tyrants, immersed in a river of blood. "Who would have thought the old man to have so much blood in him?" asks Lady Macbeth, talking in her sleep and recalling the night of Duncan's murder.

Alone and apart from her husband, the demented Queen, sleepwalking, cries out when she sees the imagined bloody spot on her hand. The metaphoric expression of guilt in ordinary language—blood on the hands—has become for her, a literal truth.

But her main sin might be seen as the advice she gave to her husband when he had decided to "proceed no further in this business". She taunts him for his cowardice and for the fact that he has broken his "enterprise" to her. She manages to override the reasons he had given earlier for not committing the murder and she is very successful. If she were in Dante's Inferno, she would be in the circle of the Evil Counsellors.

Dante's *contrapasso* for the Evil Counsellors in *Inferno* is ingenious and very apt. In life they have had the gift of skillful and powerful speech, but they have abused this and given advice which was harmful. The punishment therefore is that they retain their voice but the rest of their body is eternally consumed by an inner flame which resembles a tongue. When Dante, in his journey through Inferno, reaches the eighth *bolgia* of the eighth circle, he sees initially what appear to be millions of fireflies, but they are the flames of the Evil Counsellors.

He speaks with two of the souls here, Ulysses and Count Guido da Montefeltro. Ulysses had persuaded his sailors to take the ship through the Pillars of Hercules (the Straits of Gibraltar) where, according to Dante's account, the ship sank and all were lost. Guido da Montefeltro had given bad advice on the condition that the Pope Boniface VIII would absolve him in advance. His advice has been evil, though perhaps what the listener wanted to hear. "Long promise and short observance is the road that leads to the sure triumph of your throne."

We last see Lady Macbeth before her death by "self and violent hands", sleepwalking with a lighted taper in her hand. It is night and she believes she is alone. In fact she is being watched by the nurse and a doctor. She speaks apparently incoherently, until we realise that she is re-enacting the night of Duncan's murder. All is revealed—although by now everyone knows. The audience, watching the darkened stage, sees dimly in the light of her taper and hears the terrified voice. She "rubs her hands" endlessly. She had dismissed her part in the murder of Duncan with the offhand remark "A little water clears us of this deed/How easy is it then!" Now, she believes "All the perfumes of Arabia cannot sweeten this little hand."

It seems that Shakespeare has exploited the intensely dramatic possibilities of Dante's invention, and with spine-chilling effect on the stage. Her mind has gone and all that remains of her is the disembodied voice and the light beside her. Like the other souls Dante (the Pilgrim) meets in the circle of the Evil Counsellors, she insists on telling her story. The scene has no original in Holinshed or any other historical sources. As an Evil Counsellor, Shakespeare has given her precisely the fate that Dante designed for this "sin" in *Inferno*.

Also often noted by the reader or audience is the atmosphere of *Macbeth*. For those who are familiar with the Scotland of this play, to venture into the world of Dante's *Inferno* evokes the flickering sensation of *déjà vu*. It is as though one has been there before, in the half light and ever deepening gloom where no crime to too terrible and where hideous images seem oddly familiar. Gradually we realise that it is the *same* country—a metaphorical country—where the light of Good does not shine and where those who knowingly choose evil, live with this choice eternally. That both writers have chosen the same metaphor for the consideration of Evil is not really surprising, but as we read on, it seem increasingly likely that the similarities between the two works are more than coincidental.

Dante describes the evening at the beginning of Canto II:

Lo giorno se n'andava, e l'aere bruno,
Toglieva li animali, che sono in terra
Dalle fatiche loro; ed io solo uno

Inferno II.1–3

[The light was departing. The brown air drew down
All the earth's creatures, calling them to rest
From their day a-roving, and I one man alone.]

Macbeth says:

... Light thickens; and the crow
Makes wing to th'rooky wood;

Macbeth III.2.49–51

Both poets capture the moment when the air seems to almost solidify and earth's creatures instinctively feel the need to return to the safety of their shelter. Both writers create a sense of fear, Dante because he is about to begin his terrifying journey through Inferno and Macbeth because he has ordered the murder of Banquo and is anxious to know the outcome. Both poets seem to evoke the force of nature, from which, at this moment, the human stands outside in isolation.

Perhaps what strikes us most about *Macbeth* is the darkness and gloom in which almost all of the action supposedly takes place. From time to time there is the mention of "lightning", or "torches" or a "taper", but of the twenty-nine scenes, fifteen are in imagined darkness or semi darkness, either on the heath or in a dimly lit castle. Even life for Macbeth, eventually becomes a "brief candle" and clearly the darkness is a metaphor for life without the light of Good or, for a Christian, the love of God. Dante's Inferno too, is a place without the light of God's love.

In *Inferno* Dante and his guide venture ever lower in the gloom: the darkness is broken occasionally as the travellers descend into the abyss, first by the fires of the city of Dis, *il foco etterno* (the eternal fire) which causes the minarets to glow from within, then later by the burning tombs of the heretics of Cantos IX and X. In Cantos XXVI and XXVII the talking flames of Ulysses and Guido da Montefeltro briefly illuminate the gloom. Again the symbolism is clear. In the depths the two poets see only

> Come quando una grossa nebia spira
> O quando l'emispeiro nostro annotta,
>
> *Inferno* XXXIV.4–5

[as when a thick fog breathes, or when our hemisphere darkens to night]

For them, as for Lady Macbeth, "Hell is murky."

The witches, too, contribute much to the atmosphere of fear and evil that prevails in *Macbeth*. They are "so wither'd, and so wild in their attire" that Banquo cries:

> ... You should be women,
> And yet your beards forbid me to interpret
> That you are so.
>
> *Macbeth* I.3.40–7

We are reminded of Dante's:

> tre furie infernal di sangue tinte
> che membra feminine avieno e atto,
>
> *Inferno* IX.38–9

[three hellish blood-stained Furies had instantly risen up. They had the limbs and bearing of women.]

He meets these hideous creatures as he waits at the gates of the city of Dis and they threaten the two poets, calling Medusa to come and turn them to stone. Virgil explains that they are the servants of the *regina dell'etterno pianto* (queen of endless woe) (*Inferno* IX, 44), who is, according to the footnote,[5] Hecate or Proserpina, wife of Pluto. Macbeth's witches are also servants or followers of Hecate,[6] who, when questioned by them about her obvious anger, replies:

> Have I not reason, beldams as you are,
> Saucy and overbold? How did you dare
> To trade and traffic with Macbeth,
> In riddles, and affairs of death;
> And I, the mistress of your charms,
> The close contriver of all harms,
> Was never call'd to bear my part,
> Or show the glory of my art?
>
> *Macbeth* III.5.2–9

Dante's *Erine* are even more frightening than Shakespeare's witches and they are certainly also "wither'd and wild in their attire":

> ... con idre verdissime eran cinte;
> serpentelli e ceraste avean per crine,
> onde le fiere tempie erano avvinte.
>
> *Inferno* IX.40–2

[... they were girt with greenest hydras. For hair they had little serpents and cerastes bound about their savage temples.]

In both cases the dubious femaleness of these creatures, their ugliness, and even their number—three—gives them a terrifying presence and a kind of magical power which inspires in us a sense of horrified disgust and intense fear.

The close parallel between the witches and the *Erine*, however, could be the result of both poets being inspired by the same classical writers, where the Three Furies, or Erinyes, were responsible for hurrying ghosts entrusted to their care across the Phlegethon and into Hades. Dante's *Erine* attempt exactly that, but are foiled by Virgil's warning that Dante should keep his eyes shut so that he is not literally petrified by the sight of Medusa, and then by the arrival of God's Messenger. Shakespeare's witches certainly succeed in hurrying Macbeth into his own Hell.

In creating the atmosphere for *Macbeth,* Shakespeare has, in a sense, recreated the world of Dante's *Inferno* for the English theatregoer. There is the pervasive dark, the ever increasing sense of confusion and chaos, the sound of "sighs, and groans, and shrieks that rent the air", and a profusion of blood, all of which are part of the backdrop in Dante's *Inferno,* particularly in the cantos which we have discussed in this chapter. For dramatic purposes, and because of the limitations imposed by the problems of staging, Shakespeare keeps his Hell on one level and reduces the sinners to a number manageable on stage. It is nevertheless the same world—gloomy, dark, mesmerising, with a nightmare effect. Thunder growls, lightning flashes, terrifying creatures and apparitions leap from the darkness. Blood and suffering are everywhere. Both writers have created the same objective correlative for Evil.

Macbeth is about treachery. Shakespeare is clearly deeply preoccupied with the traitor, his particular treachery and the consequences of this for the victim of the betrayal, and for the perpetrator. If he were searching for some ideas on the subject, what better place to look than in the gloomy, freezing depths of Dante's Inferno?

II

King Lear (1605)

when we are sick in fortune, ... we make guilty of our disasters
the sun, the moon, and stars; as if we were villains on necessity.

King Lear, Shakespeare

If Shakespeare was using Dante's *Divina Commedia* in 1606, he may well have been reading it a year earlier, 1605, when *King Lear* appeared. In fact the storm scenes of *King Lear* immediately recall the chaos and gloom which so characterise *Macbeth* and *Inferno*. It is seldom possible to cite particular lines as parallels, but A. C. Bradley, the great Shakespearean authority of the early twentieth century, was clearly aware of this likeness in his lectures on the play, and his descriptions of the strange and fearful atmosphere evoked in it could equally be descriptions of the atmosphere of Dante's *Inferno*. Bradley mentioned the *Divina Commedia* no less that four times in his Lecture VII on *King Lear* and it is clear that memories of Dante's work were foremost in his mind as he wrote. He did not, however, suggest that Shakespeare might have been familiar with Dante's work; it was merely that he could not think of *King Lear* without recalling aspects of the afterworld of the *Divina Commedia*.

The lecture on *King Lear* began with the claim that while this was "Shakespeare's greatest work", it was also, in his opinion, the "least popular of the famous four" and the least often presented on the stage. Bradley commented:

> When I am feeling that it is greater than any other of these
> (*Hamlet, Othello, Macbeth*), and the fullest revelation of
> Shakespeare's power, I find I am not regarding it simply as a
> drama, but am grouping it in my mind with works like the
> *Prometheus Vinctus*, and *The Divine Comedy*, and even with
> the greatest symphonies of Beethoven and the statues in the
> Medici chapel.[7]

He went on to argue that *King Lear* was "too huge for the stage" and listed (among other things) to support his claim, the immense scope, the variety of experience, the vastness of the convulsion both of nature and human passion, the vagueness of the scene, and

> the strange atmosphere, cold and dark, which strikes on us as we enter this scene, enfolding these figures and magnifying their dim outlines like a winter mist: the half-realised suggestions of vast universal powers working in the world of individual fates and passions.[8]

All these elements, he believed, made the play difficult to present on stage, and, Bradley claimed, *King Lear* demanded "a purely imaginative realisation".[9] He went on to discuss some of the scenes which he felt were not always successful on stage and a number of inexplicable elements in the play, concluding that the greatness of *King Lear* consisted partly in "imaginative effects of a wider kind", for example the vagueness in the locality and the number of figures, events and movements. He believed that these elements, while perhaps hampering an effective stage production, gave

> a feeling of vastness, the feeling not of a scene or particular place, but of a world ... This world is dim to us, partly from its immensity, and partly because it is filled with gloom; and in the gloom shapes approach and recede, whose half-seen faces and motions touch us with dread, horror, or the most painful pity—sympathies and antipathies which we seem to be feeling not only for them, but for the whole race. This world, we are told, is called Britain; but we should no more look for it in an atlas than for the place called Caucasus, where Prometheus was chained by Strength and Force and comforted by the daughter of Ocean or for the place where Farinata stands erect in his glowing tomb, "Come avesse lo Inferno in gran dispetto.[10]

The description presented here of the place called Britain could just as well be of the place called Inferno; it is accurate in every detail, and Bradley was making the point that both places are, in the imagination, objective correlatives for the site of Evil. Again it is clear from his reference to Farinata that this parallel with Dante was firmly in Bradley's mind.

In the storm scenes Lear is subjected to thunder, lightning, wind and rain—and this storm, we understand, is a representation of the storm within, as he copes with the realisation of his daughters' ingratitude and the results of the actions that his anger has prompted him to take. His "sin" in Dante's terms, has been to allow his passions to override his reason, and Dante's *contrapasso* for this (although Dante is concerned with sexual passions specifically in *Inferno* V) is to be swept eternally about in tempestuous winds. But more specifically, when Lear allows his emotions to dominate his reason, he is blinded by anger and for this Dante would have sent him to the dark cornice in Purgatory (since Lear *does* repent) where, in a pall of acrid and blinding smoke, the wrathful endure the purification process. Just as anger obscures perception of the truth and of the true light of God, so the smoke here plunges all into darkness—a metaphorical blindness.

Many characters in *King Lear* are concerned with the reasons for evil and many characters are blind, literally or metaphorically. There is also the feeling that Shakespeare himself, at this time in his life, would have also liked to find an answer to this problem. It may be merely coincidence that a very similar consideration of this problem, with identical alternative theories, arises in Dante's work in the area where the wrathful, lost in a cloud of smoke as Lear seems to be lost in a storm, are subjected to the purgatorial process.

In this play, through several of the characters, Shakespeare presents various theories on why evil exists, or who can be blamed for its existence. Lear's greatest mistake is caused by his mindless anger and the consequent disastrous errors he makes because he is blinded by it. In Dante's *Purgatorio*, the wrathful wander round in a great cloud of acrid smoke, the objective correlative for the blindness men suffer when they give way to rage. When Dante (the Pilgrim) meets one of the spirits there, Marco Lombardo, he comments that *Lo mondo è ben così diserto /d'ogni virtute* (the world is ...

truly bare of every trace of good) and asks him why it is that there is so much evil on earth. Marco has a very firm view on the matter:

> Voi che vivete ogne cagion recate
> per suso al cielo, pur come se tutto
> movesse seco di necessitate.
>
> *Purgatorio* XVI.67–9

[You who are living refer every cause upward to the heavens alone, as if they of necessity moved all things with them.]

He does not accept this general belief that the heavens are responsible for our fate, and points out that we also have reason to allow us to judge right from wrong, and therefore Free Will. Dante is extremely interested in the concept of Free Will. If men do not have the possibility of choice in what they do, then there is little point in designing places for them to go after death, in terms of reward or punishment. If their actions are governed by the stars or the gods, then they cannot be held responsible for what they do, and there is no incentive to choose morally.

This is a subject very close to Shakespeare's heart in *King Lear* and he, too, allows his characters to give their various opinions on why things are as they are. To Kent, a sympathetic character, he gives the view (rejected by Marco Lombardo) that

> ... It is the stars,
> The stars above us, govern our conditions;
>
> *King Lear* IV.3.32–3

Edgar does not subscribe to this view. He believes,

> The Gods are just, and of our pleasant vices
> Make instruments to plague us.
>
> *King Lear* V.3.169–70

Gloucester's view is quite the opposite. He believes,

> As flies to wanton boys, are we to th'gods:
> They kill us for their sport.
>
> *King Lear* IV.1.36–7

It is Edmund, the villain of the piece, who introduces the notion of Free Will. When Edmund informs Gloucester that Edgar is plotting against him, the father is outraged to think that a son could do such a thing. He lists all the misfortunes of the time, "machinations, hollowness, treachery, and all ruinous disorders", concerned, as Dante is, that the world is devoid of every virtue—and attributes these evils to "[t]hese late eclipses in the sun and moon". Edmund answers:

> This is the excellent foppery of the world, that, when we are sick in fortune, often the surfeits of our own behaviour, we make guilty of our disasters the sun, the moon, and stars; as if we were villains on necessity, fools by heavenly compulsion, knaves, thieves, and treachers by spherical predominance, drunkards, liars, and adulterers by an enforc'd obedience of planetary influence.
>
> *King Lear* I.2.115.ff.

This is a very close paraphrase of Marco Lombardo's theory on the reason for so much evil. Edmund expands, gives examples, and even takes on much the same rather superior, world-weary tone evident in the speech of Marco Lombardo. There is also a close verbal and grammatical parallel between Marco's *pur come se tutto/ movesse seco di necessitate* (as if they of necessity moved all things with them) and Edmund's "as if we were villains on necessity". The translator here has changed the order of phrases. If he had left "of necessity" at the end of the clause, as Dante has done, then the parallel would appear closer, i.e. "as if they moved all things with them of necessity".

König,[11] too, noted this parallel between the views of Edmund and Marco Lombardo on the cause of evil, and also commented on a very similar view expressed by Iago, a precursor of Edmund and another "villain". Roderigo, in love with Desdemona, has learned that she has married Othello, and tells Iago, "I confess it is my shame to be so fond, but it is not in my virtue to amend it" (*Othello* I.3.317–18). Iago's response is cynical. He does not accept the notion that we have fixed characteristics: we are, he believes, able to be whatever we want to be, "tis in ourselves, that we are thus, or thus:" He goes on to present a detailed image of the body as a garden, where we plant what we wish and "the power, and the corrigible authority of this, lies in our wills" (I.3.325–6). He expands the idea:

> If the balance of our lives had not one scale of reason, to poise
> another of sensuality, the blood and baseness of our natures
> would conduct us to most preposterous conclusions. But we
> have reason to cool our raging motions, our carnal stings, our
> unbitted lusts;

> *Othello* I.3.326–32

Again, we hear an echo of Marco Lombardo:

> Lo cielo i vostri movimenti inizia;
> non dico tutti, ma, posto ch'i'l dica,
> lume v'è dato a bene e a malizia,
> e libero voler;

> *Purgatorio* XVI.73–6

[The heavens initiate your movements; I do not say all of them, but supposing I did say so, a light is given you to know good and evil, and free will.]

Dante's answer to the question is that some part of our fate is determined by the stars, but we have reason to allow us to make decisions and we need good laws, both religious and civil, to guide us. Shakespeare does not come to a conclusion, unless we must judge his personal philosophy by who is "successful"—and this is Edgar, subscriber to the "gods are just" theory. It would be possible to interpret his "and of our pleasant vices/make instruments to plague us" as a version of Dante's *contrapasso* in the sense that we make our own punishment to fit the sin of which we are guilty, and that this may be seen as a kind of Divine Justice.

The impression left is that Shakespeare has read Dante's *Purgatorio* XVI. Some of the characters in *King Lear* are considering possible explanations for the existence of evil, and in the discussion between Marco Lombardo and Dante (the Pilgrim) in this canto, some of the same theories occur. It is not possible to claim that this is a "borrowing", but there is certainly a sense that Shakespeare is writing with the knowledge of Dante's ideas on the subject. The smoke-filled setting of this canto where no-one can see clearly, blinded as they are by the smoke of anger, also recalls scenes from *King Lear*, where anger causes blindness, literal or metaphorical and the resulting action is disastrous. The fact that this is the place where the wrathful purge themselves—as Lear does throughout the play—suggests some connection beyond coincidence. The striking verbal and structural parallel in the statements of Edmund and Marco Lombardo on the unwisdom of blaming evil on the stars, adds to the feeling that Dante's *Purgatorio* was in Shakespeare's mind at this time.

Certainly, as Shakespeare was writing this play, the notion of the purgatorial process preoccupied him. Wilson Knight in his essay "The *Lear* Universe" examines the way in which Lear must suffer to purge himself of his sin of injustice caused by excessive and destructive anger. The philosophy of the play is concerned with justice, human and Divine. Wilson Knight writes, "In *Macbeth* we experience Hell; in *Antony and Cleopatra,* Paradise; but this play (*King Lear*) is Purgatory."[12] If Shakespeare *had* read Dante's *Purgatorio* if would hardly be surprising if he were to glance at it again for ideas on the notion of the purgatorial process, and if he were following Dante's line of argument, he would turn to the canto where Dante considers the fate of the wrathful. And there he would find the argument on the reasons for the existence of so much evil on earth: a question asked by Dante (the Pilgrim) and by various characters in *King Lear*.

In this play, another interesting parallel with a passage from *Purgatorio* occurs. It was noted by Cary, as usual without comment, and also by Reginald Saner in his paper, "Gemless Rings". Dante has reached the sixth cornice of Purgatory, the circle of the Gluttons. Amongst a group he recognises Forese Donati, who had died only five years earlier. Forese Donati had been a friend of Dante, brother of Dante's great enemy, Corso Donati, and brother also of Piccarda Donati. Dante's wife, Gemma Donati, was a kinswoman of this Donati family. When Dante meets Forese, this latter has suffered much for his gluttony and is in the circle of the *golosi* (gluttons) in Purgatory. His appearance is much changed, and Dante comments:

> Parean l'occhiaie anella sanza gemme:
>
> *Purgatorio* XXIII.31

[The sockets of their eyes seemed rings without gems.]

The simile is a strange one—eye sockets like a ring without the gem—and drew the attention of both Cary and Reginald Saner to a similar line in *King Lear*. The passage occurs near the end of the play when Edgar is recounting how he met his father Gloucester, cruelly blinded by Regan and her husband Cornwall, and now wandering hopelessly. Edgar, in the guise of "Poor Tom", has offered to be his guide:

> ... in this habit
> Met I my father with his bleeding rings,
> Their precious stones new lost:
>
> *King Lear* V.3.187–9

Saner observed that, as well as the similarity of the image, there is also a very similar context:

The note of pathos which informs the episode (Dante's meeting with Forese) derives from Dante's compassion for the wretches who file past, and his shock at seeing Forese so piteously altered from his former state. In this very contrast we find an emotional parallel to the experience of Edgar as he describes the miserable condition in which he first saw his blinded father, with Gloucester nearly as woefully altered as Forese.

Thus the dramatic moment in which Shakespeare uses "the bleeding rings" image in *Lear* in entirely appropriate for a recollection of a similar moment in the *Purgatorio*. Such being the case, the parallel is not merely verbal—striking as is the literal similarity—but emotional.[13]

Saner goes on to discuss some of the arguments concerning the purgatorial aspect of *King Lear*, comments scathingly on "eighteenth century Enthusiasts" who claimed that Shakespeare may have read Dante, and concludes:

I should like to suggest that the context in *Lear* is very similar to the context where the "bleeding rings" verse occurs in the *Purgatorio*, and that this fact, along with the unusual image involved, make the parallel I have pointed out seem more than purely coincidental.[14]

This is interesting as a number of the parallels I and others have found, have this same quality—the parallel context as well as the parallel idea itself, which supports the theory that Shakespeare was familiar with Dante's work.

Saner was not however, prepared to accept that Shakespeare may have read Dante and was highly critical of those who tried to establish this. He did, however, concede that Shakespeare may have known some "passages or episodes" from Dante and concluded:

Nevertheless, I do think it a real parallel, in a double sense, and believe it to be the closest thing to a Dante borrowing yet discovered in Shakespeare.[15]

There is an odd factor here, which Saner did not mention. The simile itself is rather confusing. In the case of Forese Donati and his fellow-sufferers, what Dante sees is a group of people who have been starved. Their eye sockets are clearly delineated and inside them, the eyes are so sunken that they seem to have almost disappeared—like rings (*anelle*) without gems (*gemme*). If we think generally of circular shape with its centre—something of great value and beauty—missing from the space inside, the simile seems apt. But if we try to carefully visualise this image, it is not accurate. On a ring, a finger ring, the gem is set only on one point of the circumference. If the gem is missing, the space inside the ring is exactly as it was even when the gem was in place. But Dante's simile implies that the gem is *inside* the circle of the ring, as the eye is inside the socket. Ciardi,[16] one of the translators, realises this and translates the phrase as "Their eye-pits looked like gem-rims minus gem."

If Shakespeare were seeking an image to describe Gloucester's eyes after he has been blinded, he would surely try to visualise something which is circular and lacking the valuable object which had previously occupied this enclosed space—and indeed the Arden (2) footnote[17] explains "rings" as "sockets, without the jewels which were his eyes." Here the word "rings" is explained as though it were just a shape—circular—and not a finger-ring as is suggested by the words "precious stones". Perhaps we are meant to visualise some other item of jewellery, such as a brooch or button with the central jewel missing from a circular setting, for example.

Caroline Spurgeon believed that Shakespeare was interested in the setting of jewels and drew "several well-known images from the way in which the beauty of a precious stone is enhanced by its background or foil."[18] She added that the brooch seems to have been out of fashion in Shakespeare's time, and as evidence, cites from *Richard II*, V. 5. 66:

... love to Richard, he says
is a strange brooch in this all-hating world.

She explained that this meant that love is a most precious but unfashionable thing. She also cited Parolles' comment from *All's Well,* Act I, Scene 1, 166 ff, "Virginity, like an old courtier, wears her cap out of fashion: richly suited, but unsuitable; just like the brooch and the toothpick which wear not new". However, whether the brooch was in or out of fashion does not alter the fact that it existed and could be used in the creation of an image.

Dante, however, used the idea of a ring with a precious stone on another occasion in *Purgatorio* V. At the end of Canto V, amongst those who have died so suddenly that they have had no chance to repent, is a spirit who identifies herself as Pia. In a few lines of touching brevity, she identifies her murderer:

> Siena me fe'; disfecemi Maremma:
> salsi colui che 'nnanellata pria
> disposando m'avea con la sua gemma.
>
> Purgatorio V.134–6

[Siena made me, Maremma unmade me, as he knows who with this ring had plighted me to him in wedlock.]

She died at the hands of the man who "ringed" her (*'nnanellata*) before he disposed of her with "his jewel" (*la sua gemma*). Singleton's translation did not mention the jewel, although the word is clearly there in the original Italian. Ciardi translated the lines as,

> Siena gave me birth, Maremma death.
> As he well knows who took me as his wife
> with jewelled ring before he took my life.
>
> Purgatorio V.141–3[19]

The word *'nnanellata* is clearly the verb from the noun *anello* (modern spelling) and the jewelled ring is equally clearly a wedding ring to be worn on the finger. This would seem to indicate that the same words virtually, used in *Purgatorio* XXIII, *annella sanza gemme*, also refer to a jewelled finger ring.

Shakespeare also used a similar image on another occasion. In the famous dream in *Richard III*, Clarence describes the "inestimable stones, unvalu'd jewels" he sees on the ocean floor:

> Some lay in dead men's skulls; and in those holes
> Where eyes did once inhabit, there were crept,
> As 'twere in scorn of eyes, reflecting gems,
> That woo'd the slimy bottom of the deep,
> And mock'd the dead bones that lay scatter'd by.
>
> *Richard III* I.4.29–32

Here, the description is a literal one—and physically accurate. The eyes as jewels form an image which appealed to Shakespeare, and here it is used with great effect to create a certain rather terrifying beauty.

While Cary also notes this parallel, he notes that both Petrarch and Chaucer used the idea of the gemless ring. Both of these writers had certainly read Dante—and may have found the idea there, or from another source, or even independently. Petrarch uses the image in his sonnet *Lasciata hai, Morte,* where he describes the effects of Laura's death on the world. It is as though the world is now without the sun, *senza fior prato o senza gemma anella* (field without flower, ring without gem) (Francesco Petrarca, *Canzoniere,* Garzanti, Italy, Sonnet CCCXXXVIII). But the context is not similar and the gemless ring here is not related to eyes. Petrarch uses the image merely to convey the idea of the loss of something infinitely beautiful and valuable. Chaucer also uses a similar idea in *Troilus and Creseide,* V—"O ring of which the rubie is outfall"—but again he is not speaking of eyes. It seems more likely that if Shakespeare is borrowing the image, he is borrowing it from Dante.

But the fact that Shakespeare has used the same inaccurate simile as Dante in his "bleeding rings" image suggests that he already had this simile in mind when he came to describe the blinded Gloucester, and used it without thinking. If the simile were exact in its particulars, we could allow that both great poets may have chanced upon it independently. The fact that it is not, suggests that one writer followed the other, borrowing the error along with the effectiveness. Again, no one suggests that this passage from *King Lear* was written by anyone other than Shakespeare, so we can assume that if it is a borrowing from Dante, it is Shakespeare's.

III

Measure for Measure (1604)

> *... enskied and sainted.*
> *Measure for Measure*, Shakespeare

Macbeth appeared in 1606, *King Lear* in 1605 and *Measure for Measure* in 1604. Did Shakespeare use the *Divina Commedia* in this play too? In fact the *Enciclopedia Dantesca* commented that:

> At most he had some knowledge of *Inferno*, perhaps in the period when he was writing *Measure for Measure*.[20]

Might there be some evidence here? Certainly if the *Enciclopedia Dantesca* thought so, that seemed promising.

The title itself, *Measure for Measure,* from *Matthew,* VII.2: "With what measure ye mete, it shall be measured to you again", suggests another version of Dante's *contrapasso,* and the play is concerned with judgment and punishment throughout. Frank Kermode saw "something of the Dantesque pattern"[21] in the endings in *Measure for Measure,* perhaps because of the aptness of the final judgments.

In this play I found one example of a parallel between the two writers which, I am convinced, goes well beyond the possibility of coincidence. This parallel was not mentioned by any other writer on the subject. It is, I believe, virtually incontrovertible evidence that Shakespeare did, in fact, borrow from Dante. The similarity between a passage in which the playwright develops his character Isabella, and a passage from *Paradiso*, illustrates the way in which Shakespeare seems to have used an idea from Dante to give depth and motivation to his own creation and to arouse sympathy for her.

The source stories for *Measure for Measure* are Cinthio's *Hecatommithi* and *Epitia* (a posthumous drama, and a reworking of the earlier novel) and Whetstone's *Promos and Cassandra* and *Aurelia*. Cinthio's tale (in Italian) was published in 1565. His story had been adapted from a letter written in 1547 describing an event which occurred in a town outside Milan. The letter is in Latin and is translated and printed in the Appendices of *Measure for Measure* (Arden 2). Cinthio's tale was also the source for Whetstone's play (in English), published in 1578, which was, in turn, a source for Shakespeare's play, first published in 1623 but performed probably in 1604.

Shakespeare has used this "borrowed" plot, adapting it for various reasons. The female protagonist (named Epitia in *Hecatommithi*, and Cassandra in *Promos and Cassandra*) is a young, unmarried woman. She places a very high value on her virginity, or "honour". She is very beautiful and extremely eloquent and rational, as is Shakespeare's Isabella. The young woman in all three versions of the story is pleading for the life of her brother, who is condemned to death for an illicit sexual relationship. The "ruler" (a temporary appointee by the missing real authority) to whom she has taken her story, is fascinated by her, but his admiration soon turns to lust. Despite the fact that he aspires to deliver absolute justice to the offending brother, he offers liberation only on the condition that the woman will surrender to his will.

In his Introduction to *Measure for Measure,* the editor, J. W. Lever, comments on the elements of the play which were Shakespeare's contribution to the plot:

The most important innovation, however, was the presentation of Isabella as a novice of the strict order of St Clare. No "romantic" solution, such as Cinthio and Whetstone had relied on, was to be admitted. Even the natural affections of kinship, the chief motivations in these writers' renderings were brought into conflict with the moral rectitude to which Isabella aspired. Accordingly, lust was set over against abstinence, brothel against convent, mercy against justice, nature against spirit, with the life of a young husband and father in the balance.[22]

That Isabella is a nun makes her moral dilemma more intense and more moving than that faced by Epitia or Cassandra. After all, these two are promised marriage to the "ruler" if they surrender to his wishes, and this, it seems, at least restores their "honour". But if Isabella were to surrender, she could not make her vow of chastity in the knowledge of what she has done. Shakespeare has seen and used the theatrical potential of this situation.

In Act I, Scene 4 there is the intriguing use of a curious word. Isabella, who is a novice and appears in the novice's habit, is about to take her vows. She is told by Lucio, who comes with news of her brother:

> I hold you as a thing enskied and sainted
> By your renouncement, an immortal spirit,
> And to be talk'd with in sincerity,
> As with a saint.
>
> *Measure for Measure* I.4.34–7

The word "enskied", which we are told in the footnote of the Arden (2) edition means "placed in heaven", is "a Shakespearean coinage"[23] and it may recall, to the reader of Dante, a very similar Dantean coinage. In *Paradiso* III, Piccarda Donati is telling Dante of the woman who formed the order of nuns to which she herself belonged—Saint Clare of Assisi:

"Perfetta vita e alto merto inciela
donna più sù", mi disse, "a la cui norma
nel vostro mondo giù si veste e vela,
perché fino al morir si vegghi e dorma
con quello sposo ch'ogne voto accetta
che caritate a suo piacer conforma.
Dal mondo, per seguirla, giovinetta
fuggi'mi, e nel suo abito mi chiusi
e promisi la via de la sua setta.

Paradiso III.97–105

["Perfect life and high merit enheaven a lady more aloft," she said to me, "according to whose rule, in your world below, are those who take the robe and veil themselves that they, even till death, may wake and sleep with that Spouse who accepts every vow which love conforms unto His pleasure. From the world, to follow her, I fled while yet a girl, and in her habit I clothed me and promised myself to the way of her order."][24]

The passage is important for several reasons, not least because the word *inciela* is the exact Italian equivalent (except for the tense—*inciela* is present, "enskied" is past) of Shakespeare's "enskied". A footnote tells us:

inciela: neologismo dantesco che ha questa sola occorrenza nel poema. È verbo parasintetico con prefisso *in-* analogo ad altri usati da Dante (*imparadisare, immillarsi*), ... In esso non c'è solo l'idea del luogo ("mettere in cielo"), ma anche quella di una gerarchia di beatitudine, rafforzata da *più sù*.[25]

[inciela: Dantean neologism which has only this occurrence in the poem. It is a parasynthetic verb with the prefix *in-* analagous to others used by Dante (*imparadisare, immillarsi*), ... In it is not only the idea of place ("put in heaven"), but also the idea of a hierarchy of blessedness, reinforced by *più su*.][26]

How curious that Shakespeare and Dante should "coin" exactly the same word! And even more curious, that they should use it in almost exactly the same context! Piccarda Donati was speaking of Saint Clare, now in heaven and sainted. Piccarda herself had joined that Order, but was forced to return to the world because her brother, Corso Donati, had decided that she should renounce her vow of chastity and be married for his own political advantage. Dante meets Piccarda in Paradise in the first sphere of the Moon. Here are the inconstant—souls who have made holy vows and then broken them. Piccarda has been forced to break her vow by her brother.

And now, Isabella, also about to enter the Order of Saint Clare, is about to be asked by *her* brother Claudio to renounce her vow of chastity so that he may be saved from the punishment for the crime he has committed. If she were to accept Angelo's proposition, she too would, by Dante's code of justice, be in this same sphere of the Moon.

Even more compelling, later in the play, Angelo (the "ruler") is speaking to Isabella, attempting to persuade her to surrender her virginity to him in return for the promise of her brother's life. Early in the conversation, Isabella is quite unaware of his intentions and he tells her that she is either "ignorant" or "crafty". She protests:

> Let me be ignorant, and in nothing good,
> But graciously to know I am no better.

and Angelo continues,

> Thus wisdom wishes to appear most bright
> When it doth tax itself: as these black masks
> Proclaim an enciel'd beauty ten times louder
> Than beauty could, display'd.
>
> *Measure for Measure* II.4.76–81

The unusual word "enciel'd" is not printed in all editions. An alternative is "enshield" or "enshell'd"—the sound of which in both cases suggests an Italian pronunciation of "enciel'd". The First Folio gives "enshield", and in the footnote to the Arden (2) edition it is explained thus:

> enciel'd: "enshield", emended variously to "enshielded", "enshell'd". The verb "ceil" or "ciel" (commonly spelt with initial s) meant to shade as with a canopy or screen. ... The "en" prefix was a Shakespearean formation: cf. "enskied", I.4.34.[27]

Again we have another Shakespearean coinage—and this time almost identical with Dante's word *inciela*, which Singleton translates as "enheaven". Cary,[28] Longfellow,[29] and Ciardi[30] translate it as, respectively, "inshrine in heaven" and "in-heaven" and "enshrine a lady hereabove". If "enciel'd" has the meaning of "shaded" or "shielded", as the Arden footnote suggests, then the sentence is tautological and reads, "as these black masks/proclaim a shielded (or masked) beauty ten times louder/than beauty could, display'd". The "black masks" are probably the nuns' veils.[31] Angelo's cynical view is that in the same way as a person assumes a kind of false modesty in denying his own wisdom, and thus hopes to appear wiser, so too the nun in her veil hopes, by apparently concealing it, to emphasise her "enciel'd" beauty.

But if the word "enciel'd" means "enheavened", then the sentence takes on a clearer meaning—that the nuns' veils enhance a saintly or "enheavened" beauty more effectively than any open display of it would do. He is speaking in general, but in fact he is speaking in particular about how Isabella's veil has affected his perception of her saintly beauty, earlier commented on by Lucio. The effectiveness of the image lies in the contrast between "black masks" (with connotations of evil and deceit) and "enciel'd beauty" (saintly goodness). And if "enciel'd" means "enskied" then the contrast is as stark and hence as effective as Angelo means it to be.

In the source stories, the protagonist (called Epitia or Cassandra) as mentioned earlier, is not a nun. Perhaps because Isabella's fate, at this point in the play, has reminded Shakespeare of Piccarda Donati, he has made her one of the "Clarisse" (Poor Clares), like Piccarda, to maximize the magnitude of her sacrifice and the pathos of her fate. It also has the effect of emphasising her purity (in contrast to the lechery of Angelo) and her puritanism (parallel to that of Angelo). With this portrait in mind he has used the word that he found so effective in Piccarda's (or Dante's) description of Saint Clare. He uses firstly a translation (enskied) of Dante's word. Then, perhaps because the English word "sky" does not have the religious connotations of *cielo* (English uses "heaven" in such cases), and because it is quite harsh in sound, he changes the word to the gentler, softer sounding "enciel'd".

Edward Armstrong pointed out that with Shakespeare "often the sounds of words rather than their meanings provided associations which brought them from the store house of memory to the point of the pen",[32] and this example is typical of the way Shakespeare used ideas from other writers—here he has used an identical word, and a parallel situation, both of which serve to evoke the same emotions. The thought process here is exactly as described by Armstrong. "If, when he sat down to write a play, the theme recalled the mood in which another play, or more often, merely some incident or characterization in it, was conceived, the imagery of the earlier play tended to return to his mind."[33]

Another quality is shared by Isabella and Saint Clare as described by Piccarda. For all Isabella's obsessive virginity, she speaks with an almost sexual passion of the value that she puts on this quality.[34] When Angelo informs her that there is only one way she can save her brother's life, and asks her:

What would you do?

she responds,

As much for my poor brother as myself;
That is, were I under the terms of death,
Th'impression of keen whips I'd wear as rubies,
And strip myself to death as to a bed
That longing have been sick for, ere I'd yield
My body up to shame.

Measure for Measure II.4.99–103

More demure is the description quoted earlier of Saint Clare and her followers, who

... fino al morir si vegghi e dorma
con quello sposo ch'ogne voto accetta
che caritate a suo piacer conforma.

Paradiso III.100–2

[even till death, may wake and sleep with that Spouse who accepts every vow which love conforms unto His pleasure.]

The element of sexuality in both passages serves perhaps to accentuate the importance of the vow of chastity to both these women who have chosen to devote themselves to God. The footnote[35] to the passage from Dante comments that the phrase *si vegghi e dorma* is intended to convey the idea of spending day and night with Jesus—but the combination of the words *dorma* (sleeps) and *sposo* (bridegroom or spouse) puts a sexual slant on the relationship. This is not at all unusual, sexual imagery was often used for the relationship between nuns and Christ, examples of which can be seen in the passionate sermons of Bernard of Clairvaux, who associated Mary with the bride of the Song of Songs and who gave some eighty-six sermons on this subject between 1135 and 1153.[36] Dante (the Poet) had this image in mind when he wrote Piccarda's description of Saint Clare. Piccarda is perhaps also subconsciously comparing the life she had chosen as a nun with the grim reality of what happened when:

Uomini poi, a mal più ch'a bene usi,
fuor mi rapiron de la dolce chiostra;

Paradiso III.106–7

[Then men, more used to evil than to good, snatched me
from the sweet cloister.]

In *Measure for Measure* when Isabella comes to Angelo to plead for her
brother's life, she says with an unconscious seductiveness:

I am come to know your pleasure.

Angelo responds (aside),

That you might know it, would much better please me,
Than to demand what 'tis.

Measure for Measure II.4.31–4

The sexual connotations of the word "pleasure" would titillate the
audience as they do Angelo. The same word *piacer* (pleasure) occurs in the
passage from Dante. Piccarda explains how Christ, *quello sposo, ogne voto
accettal che caritate a suo piacer conforma*. Piccarda has taken the vow of
chastity and Isabella is about to, and yet both see their virginity in strangely
sexual terms.

In these two passages, there is surely more than coincidence at work.
The situations of the two women, Isabella and Piccarda, are parallel. Both
are nuns (Isabella a novice) and both in the order of Saint Clare. Each is,
because of her brother, in a position where she must renounce her vow
of chastity for his selfish ends. Shakespeare has made changes from his
sources, and by making Isabella a nun, he brings the parallel with Dante
closer. Both women describe their virginity in sexual terms. To this point
we could still allow coincidence. The words "enskied" and "enciel'd",
however, take us past the likelihood of chance. Their use also demonstrates

that if Shakespeare *had* access to a copy of *Paradiso*, it was in the original Italian. The variation in the spelling of "enciel'd", along with the similarity in pronunciation of these variations, suggest too that Shakespeare had heard the word spoken by an Italian speaker. There is no suggestion that this passage may not be the work of Shakespeare himself, so if this is a "borrowing", it attests to Shakespeare's personal knowledge of the *Divina Commedia*—or at least *Paradiso* III.

There is another passage in this play which is reminiscent of Dante's *Inferno* and this is probably the one that prompted the writer for the *Enciclopedia Dantesca* to concede that Shakespeare may have been familiar with Dante's work. Early in the play Isabella is visiting her brother Claudio who is facing the death penalty for an illegal sexual offence. He gives a description of how he imagines the afterlife:

> Ay, but to die, and go we know not where;
> To lie in cold obstruction, and to rot;
> This sensible warm motion to become
> A kneaded clod; and the delighted spirit
> To bath in fiery floods. Or to reside
> In thrilling region of thick ribbed ice;
> To be imprison'd in the viewless winds
> And blown with restless violence round about
> The pendent world:
>
> *Measure for Measure* III.1.117–25

This passage certainly has the "feel" of Dante's *Inferno* almost as though Claudio (or Shakespeare) had read it, but the last three lines are very specific in that they describe exactly how

> La bufera infernal, che mai non resta,
> Mena li spiriti con la sua rapina:
> Voltando e percontedo li molesta
>
> *Inferno* V.31–3

[The hellish hurricane, never resting, sweeps along the spirits
with its rapine; whirling and smiting, it torments them.]

The "viewless winds" are very like *la bufera infernal, che mai non resta*,
and this is Dante's punishment for those who have allowed their passions
to override their reason, as Claudio has done. His sin is also the sin of
Francesca and Paolo, and to be swept "round about the pendent world"
would be, in Dante's system, precisely what Claudio deserves.

In the fifth circle, Dante (the Pilgrim), meets Francesca of Rimini.
She, with her lover Paolo, are perhaps the most famous lovers in Italian
literature and Dante is much moved by her tale. But in life they have been
swept away by the tempest of their passion and so now in Inferno this will
be their fate—the fate of the incontinent. Claudio too, has had an illicit
relationship with Juliet who is now pregnant and so he seems to believe that
this fate is exactly what would await him in the afterlife. He, like the souls
in the fifth circle, will be swept around in the howling gale for all time.

Early in the play there is another image which also suggests
Shakespeare's familiarity with Dante's work. The Duke, who is about to
delegate his ruling power in the city of Vienna to Angelo, is giving him
some advice:

> Heaven doth with us as we with torches do,
> Not light them for themselves; for if our virtues
> Did not go before us, 'twere all alike
> As if we had them not.
> *Measure for Measure* I.1.32–5

The image is a vivid one. The idea is that Angelo's virtues are obvious to all
who know him, and this is as it should be. If others are not aware of our
virtues then we might just as well not have them. We reveal them not for
ourselves, but for the use of others.

The same image appears also in *Purgatorio*:

Facesti come quei che va di notte,

Che porta illume dietro e se non giova,

Ma dopo se fa le persone dotte,

Purgatory XXII.67–9

[you were as one who leads through a dark track

holding the light behind—useless to you,

precious to those who followed at your back][37]

Statius gives credit to Virgil for his conversion to Christianity. He describes how Virgil, giving light to those who came behind him, saved Statius himself. If Virgil is the symbol of human reason then this makes sense.

It is the same vivid image but with a different purpose. Shakespeare may have found the image in Dante and used it differently, or he may have found it elsewhere. We cannot claim it as a "borrowing" but it may have been one of the passages in which the writer for the *Encyclopedia Dantesca* heard an echo of Dante's work.

Another such "echo" occurs in *Measure for Measure* when the Duke, in his disguise as a Franciscan friar is admonishing Pompey for the way in which he makes a living from the earnings of a prostitute. In language filled with disgust and repulsion, he tells Pompey:

... Say to thyself

From the abominable and beastly touches

I drink, I eat, array myself and live.

Canst thou believe thy living is a life,

So stinkingly depending?

Measure for Measure III.2.22–6

By listing these necessary human actions, "I drink, I eat, I array myself and live" he is attempting to show that this is only one part of the human condition—that there is much more to life than the merely physical. He wants Pompey to see that his "living" is not a "life". We are forced to think of another side of life, the moral or the spiritual, a side of which the Duke feels Pompey to be totally ignorant.

The *Enciclopedia Dantesca* in its entry under "Shakespeare", draws our attention to a very similar passage in *Inferno*:

> "Io credo" diss'io "che tu m'inganni;
> Che Branca d'Oria non morì unquanche,
> e mangia e bee e dorme e veste panni".
>
> Inferno XXXIII.139–41

> ["I believe you are deceiving me," I said to him, "for Branca d'Oria is not yet dead, and eats and drinks and sleeps and puts on clothes."]

Interestingly, although Cary had not noted this parallel, he noted instead a passage in *The Tempest* which he finds similar to these same lines from *Inferno*. Miranda, seeing Ferdinand for the first time, cries:

> ... But 'tis a spirit.

And Prospero answers,

> No, wench, it eats and sleeps, and has such senses
> As we have, such.
>
> The Tempest I.2.414–16

The three passages have in common a list of human daily functions, with slight variations—slightly different actions, in a different order and in a different person. But on close examination, there is a strong parallel in context, associated images and emotional response. The lines from *Inferno* are spoken by Dante (the Pilgrim) himself. He has descended to the third circle (Ptolomeo) of Cocytus—the lowest level of Hell and reserved for those guilty of betrayal. Here are to be found some of the great traitors—

in particular, in this circle, those who have broken the ties of hospitality. Their heads emerge in part from the ice in which they are permanently imprisoned, their tears freezing in their eye-sockets.

Dante is asking about the identity of one he sees there. The other speaker is Frate Alberigo, one who, in his time on earth, had invited some members of his family to dinner, and then, at a certain signal, had them all murdered. He explains to Dante that the other head in the ice belongs to Branca d'Oria, guilty of the same kind of betrayal as himself. Dante is puzzled, as he knows that Branca d'Oria is still alive at the time in which the journey to Inferno is taking place.[38] For this reason, Dante insists on the fact that back in the world of the living, Branca d'Oria is still present, giving evidence of this: *mangia, e bee e dorme e veste panni*. But this is a list of physical activities, the significance of which is to make the point that Branca d'Oria may be physically "alive" on Earth although his spirit is here in Inferno, suffering all the torments that he has earned for his betrayal. And so the significance of the list is exactly as it is in *Measure for Measure*, where the Duke too, wishes to differentiate the physical from the spiritual.

The passage from *The Tempest* is also to suggest that life has two aspects—the physical with its basic needs, and the spiritual. Miranda has just seen Ferdinand. In her life (or at least her memory) until now she has seen only her father Prospero, and the beast-like Caliban. When she sees Ferdinand suddenly inexplicably present in her small world, she can only assume that he is "a spirit". Her father has to inform her that this attractive young man is a real physical presence. Prospero uses the neuter pronoun because Miranda has used it, but he insists that "it eats and sleeps, and hath such senses /As we have, such."

The verbal parallel in *Inferno* and *Measure for Measure* is much closer than that in *Inferno* and *The Tempest*. But what is constant is that in every case the list of physical activities is used to distinguish between man as an animal, and man as a spiritual being. In the case of the first parallel, there are other common ideas. Throughout Canto XXXIII, there is a pervading atmosphere of bestiality, disgust and horror. Earlier in the canto, we meet Ugolino and hear the appalling tale of his starvation with his children, with its ghastly implication of cannibalism. Here, in Antinora, Ugolino gnaws eternally at the bloody head of the man who betrayed him, Archbishop Ruggieri. The canto is the most dramatic and pathetic of all *Inferno*, but at the same time we are filled with revulsion at the thought of what must have happened in that terrible tower. The traitors are, in Dante's view, the worst of all sinners, and his images are devoted to conveying to the reader all his own disgust and contempt. In *Measure for Measure* the Duke's disgust is every bit as evident in his use of language. The words "abominable", "beastly", and "stinkingly" leave us in no doubt as to how he feels about this exclusively physical side of Man.

In *The Tempest,* too, there is also this element of the repulsive, the bestial, the man who is all animal. Earlier in the same scene, Miranda and Prospero have been confronted by Caliban, who enters cursing:

> As wicked dew as e'er my mother brush'd
> With raven's feather from unwholesome fen,
> Drop on you both! a south-west blow on ye,
> And blister you all o'er.
>
> *The Tempest* I.2.323–6

Prospero describes him as "A freckled whelp hag-born—not honour'd with /A human shape" (I.2.283–4) and "A thing most brutish" (I.2.357). Something in Shakespeare's thought process seems to link physical acts with bestiality and brutishness, and makes him insist that there *is* another side to man. No sooner has he confronted us with Caliban, than he presents Ferdinand in contrast, but Prospero reminds Miranda that the spiritual being also has its share of the physical. It seems that if Shakespeare did read Dante's tale of Branca d'Oria and Frate Alberigo, the concept of the spiritual and the physical being separable has made a deep impression on him. He has remembered Dante's listing of the physical acts of life which the body performs, but he also wishes to remind his audience that this is not all—and in fact this is nothing unless there is also the spiritual.

Lorenzo Mascetta-Caracci also noted this parallel between Dante's lines from *Inferno* XXXIII and the two passages from Shakespeare. He had already claimed that:

> non mancano casi di riscontri nelle opere dei due sommi, nei quali l'imitazione da parte del grande drammaturgo non può mettersi in dubbio.[39]
>
> [There is no lack of cases of similarity in the works of the two great masters, in which imitation on the part of the great dramatist cannot be in doubt.]

There are a number of parallels in *Measure for Measure* and Dante's *Divina Commedia* but there is also the general atmosphere of the play—which is gloomy and preoccupied with judgment and punishment. There are prisons, death sentences, decapitation, blackmail, injustice and deceptions and the nasty bed trick. It is similar to the atmosphere of *Inferno* where people sin and pay for this in the afterlife. Fortunately Shakespeare has managed to evaluate the relative gravity of various sins and to apportion the appropriate punishment in this life.

But certainly in this play one feels the influence of Dante more than in any other. The "enskied and sainted" description of Isabella is too close to Dante's (Piccarda's) description of Saint Clare to be merely coincidence. So too, Shakespeare's freshly coined word "enskied" is an exact translation of Dante's own coinage *inciela*. Added to this is the exactly similar situation faced by Isabella as faced by Dante's Piccarda—each must sacrifice her vow of chastity for the sake of a self-centred brother. To claim this parallel as coincidence is not possible.

IV

Troilus and Cressida (1602)

> *And appetite, an universal wolf,*
> *So doubly seconded with will and power,*
> *Must make perforce an universal prey,*
> *And last eat up himself.*
>
> *Troilus and Cressida*, Shakespeare

In the play *Troilus and Cressida* (c.1602), Shakespeare gives to his Ulysses a philosophy rather like Dante's own. It is concerned in part with the idea of natural order and the chaos that results when this order is disturbed. This thesis is presented by Ulysses in a speech which is far too long from the theatrical point of view. Clearly Shakespeare is more interested here in the ideas than in the dramatic impact. Briefly, Ulysses outlines the disastrous effects which result from disruption of the natural order. Virgil Whitaker[40] in his *Shakespeare's Use of Learning*, traced these ideas to three sources, Sir Thomas Elyot's *The Governour*, "An Exhortation concerning Good Order and Obedience to Rulers and Magistrates" from the first book of Homilies, and Richard Hooker's *Of the Laws of Ecclesiastical Polity*. Ulysses' speech concludes with a description of the end result of disorder:

> Then everything includes itself in power,
> Power into will, will into appetite;
> And appetite, an universal wolf,
> So doubly seconded with will and power,
> Must make perforce an universal prey,
> And last eat up himself.
>
> *Troilus and Cressida* I.3.119–24

Whitaker commented:

One idea in Ulysses' speech is not to be found in any of the immediate sources quoted. That is the reference to "appetite, an universal wolf" which must at last "eat up himself".[41]

One possible source for the idea could be Cesare Ripa's *Iconologia*, first published in Rome in 1593. For each personification there was a verbal description of the allegorical figure which Ripa proposed to embody that particular concept, and also of the symbolic background. Reasons were given, usually from classical literature, for the inclusion of these symbols and figures. In the personification of *Avaritia*, the description tells us that Greed is a pale, thin elderly woman, and it goes on to further describe and justify this. Also mentioned in the description is a wolf, which is "traditionally considered a voracious and avid beast. His leanness indicates his insatiability."[42] Neither the 1593 nor the 1602 edition was illustrated and the descriptions were in Italian. *Troilus and Cressida* was probably written in 1602, so Shakespeare, if he used this book, would have been using the Italian description without an illustration.

The 1603 edition however, of which an expanded version was printed in Italian in 1611, gives a rather more detailed version and mentions Dante's use of the image:

> La magrezza del lupo nota l'insatiabile appetito dell'avaro, e l'inconveniente tenacità della robba, che possiede. Onde Dante nel primo capitolo parlando dell'Inferno cosi dice:
>
> > Et ha natura si malavagia, e ria,
> > Che mai non empie la bramosa voglia
> > Et dopo 'l pasto ha più fame, che pria.[43]
>
> [The thinness of the wolf signifies the insatiable appetite of the miser, and the inconvenient tenacity of the things which he possesses. So that Dante in his first chapter of *Inferno* says: "And she has a nature so vicious and malign that she never sates her greedy appetite and after feeding is hungrier than before."]

This edition was probably too late for Shakespeare, and it does not mention the other element which seems to be exclusive to Dante and Shakespeare—the self-consuming aspect of the wolf. Shakespeare seems to have had access to many Italian books, and it also seems that he had some considerable knowledge of the Italian language. If we accept for the moment these two assumptions, it is possible that the "universal wolf" may have come from this source, and equally possible that it may have come from Dante, where the symbol is developed much more fully, and along the same lines as Shakespeare's (or Ulysses') argument in the play.

Images of appetite and images of animals pervade the entire play, and here, they have been combined. Vivian Thomas quoted from Raymond Southall:

> Ulysses' contention that "appetite", is "a universal wolf" touches the very quick of Shakespeare's conception of the spirit of capitalism as a force which reduces life to the mere satisfaction of the appetites.[44]

By "the spirit of capitalism" presumably he means a philosophy where the guiding principle is the desire to possess: "appetite". This is very close to Dante's avaricious, the hoarders and the wasters, and indeed it is on this fifth cornice in Purgatory[45] that Dante, deploring *il mal che tutto 'l mondo occupa* (XX.8) (the sin which rules the world), declaims:

> Maladetta sie tu, antica lupa
> che più che tutte le altre bestie hai preda
> per la tua fame sanza fine cupa!
> *Purgatorio* XX.10–12

> [Accursed be you, ancient wolf, who have more prey than all the other beasts, because of your hunger endlessly deep!]

But the image of the ravenous wolf, of course, can be seen first in

Dante's *Inferno*, where, Dante, at the beginning of his journey is confronted by three beasts, the third of which is:

> ... una lupa, che di tutte brame
> sembiava carca nella sua magrezza,
> e molte genti fe' già viver grame,
>
> Inferno I.49–51

[... a she-wolf, that in her leanness seemed laden with every craving and had already caused many to live in sorrow]

In Dante, the three beasts which block his path originated from the Bible, *Jeremiah*, V, 6. The symbolism of the beasts is Dante's own, and they are generally seen to represent the three great sins, lust, pride and avarice. Many commentators interpreted the wolf (a she-wolf) as:

> l'avarizia ... (da intendersi, in ampio senso, come *cupidigia*, che è secondo la definizione scolastica "inordinatus appetitius cuiuscumque boni temporalis") era senza dubbio nella sua mente la causa più profonda della corruzione sociale.[46]
>
> [avarice ... (to be understood, in its widest sense, as greed, which is according to the scholastic definition, "a disordered craving for anything is but a fleeting pleasure") was without doubt in his mind the most profound cause of social corruption.]

In Canto VII, Virgil addresses Pluto, the monster which guards the circle of the avaricious,

> ... "Taci, maladetto lupo;
> consuma d'entro te con la tua rabbia.
>
> Inferno VII.8–9

[Silence, accursed wolf! Consume yourself inwardly with your own rage.]

Di Salvo interpreted this to mean, *consumati dentro te stesso e con te consuma la tua rabbia*.[47] Virgil seems to be advising the *lupo* to "eat up himself"! The rather striking and unusual idea of the wolf consuming itself seems to be exclusive to Dante and Shakespeare. Di Salvo went on to add:

> "Lupo" è allusivo all'avarizia intesa come avidità, inappagata e inappagabile, di ricchezze, l'avidità che conduce l'uomo morale alla maledizione. Ma "lupo" allude anche alla lupa grama che impedisce a Dante la salita al colle.[48]
>
> ["Wolf" is allusive to avarice, understood as greed, unsatisfied and insatiable, for riches, the greed which leads the moral man to damnation ... But "wolf" alludes also to the hungry wolf which impedes Dante's ascent of the hill.]

Again we see the idea of insatiable appetite which leads to moral corruption, both ideas included in Shakespeare's "universal wolf" image.

La lupa is described again by Virgil, in response to Dante's cry for help in *Inferno* I.93–102, and we see that Shakespeare's symbol parallels Dante's in a number of ways. Firstly, Virgil explains to Dante that no-one escapes the hunger of the wolf: *non lascia altrui passar* (she lets no one pass). Shakespeare makes the same point when he describes appetite as "an universal wolf" which must "make perforce an universal prey".[49] It is a phrase reminiscent of a line in *King Lear,* where Albany berates Goneril for her appalling treatment of her ailing father. He recounts her cruelty, expresses his horror and also his belief that retribution will come, concluding

> It will come
> Humanity must perforce prey on itself,
> Like monsters of the deep.
>
> *King Lear* IV.2.47–9

The second common idea is that of the insatiability of the beast: *dopo 'l pasto ha più fame che pria* (after the meal it is hungrier than before). By a projection of this concept, we understand that eventually, the beast must consume itself—since nothing else remains to consume, a point which Shakespeare states explicitly—the wolf must at last, "eat up himself". Dante goes on to say *molti son li animali a cui s'ammoglia*, which Sapegno interpreted as:

> Molti sono gli uomini a cui il vizio rappresentato dalla lupa s'apprende ... Si può intendere anche che la cupidigia va sempre unita con molte altre colpe.[50]
>
> [Many are the men whom the vice represented by the wolf ensnares. One understands also that greed is always united with many other sins.]

The first of these interpretations, that many are caught in this vice, Shakespeare covers with the use of the adjective "universal". The second, that greed is united with many other vices, is perhaps implied by the concept of insatiability: everything is consumed by "appetite", and that would include such concepts as order, justice etc., the absence of which would lead to *molte altre colpe*. But Dante lives in hope of the coming of the "Veltro", which *la farà morir con doglia*. By inference, the "Veltro" must have the qualities which will overcome the results of *l'avarizia* and *la cupidigia*. Sapegno wrote:

> Per combattere e vincere la lupa occorre un veltro, e cioè un cane da caccia ben addestrato e veloce. E poichè nella lupa è rappresentata l'avarizia o la cupidigia, come causa fondamentale del disordine civile e morale dell'umanità, il Veltro dovrà rappresentare, nella mente di Dante, un azione di riforma promossa da Dio, che perseguiti la cupidigia *per ogni villa*, cacciandola dovunque essa si annidi, e ristabilendo

nel mondo tutto, e particolarmente nell'Italia, l'ordine e la giustizia.[51]

[To fight against and to defeat the wolf, a hound is necessary, and that is a hunting dog well trained and fast. And since the wolf represents avarice and greed, as the fundamental cause of civil and moral disorder in humanity, the hound must represent, in Dante's mind, a reform action promised by God, which pursues greed everywhere, hunting it wherever it hides, and re-establishing order and justice in the whole world, particularly in Italy.]

Sapegno also gave a second interpretation which he felt was perhaps more likely than the one given above, but it involved the causes of ecclesiastical corruption—a subject into which Shakespeare would have been unwise to venture. Dante blames *avarizia* for the corruption of the Church and tells Pope Nicholas III when he meets him in *Inferno* XIX.104–5,

… la vostra avarizia il mondo attrista,
calcando i buoni e sollevando i pravi.

[… your avarice afflicts the world, trampling down the good and exalting the bad.]

Shakespeare uses the image of the wolf on other occasions. In *King Lear*, Edgar, in his guise as Tom, lists the sins he has committed in the past, one of which is as "the wolf in greediness" (III.4.91). The footnote in the Arden (2) edition tells us that "The Seven Deadly Sins were often figured under the names of animals" so the image may have been a common one familiar to both Dante and Shakespeare. In *The Merchant of Venice*, Graziano says to Shylock at the trial that he is almost persuaded that Pythagoras was right in his theory that animal souls can invade humans:

... Thy currish spirit
Govern'd a wolf, who, hang'd for human slaughter,
Even from the gallows did his fell soul fleet,
And, whilst thou lay'st in thy unhallow'd dam,
Infus'd itself in thee; for thy desires
Are wolfish, bloody, starv'd and ravenous.

The Merchant of Venice IV.1.133–8

Shylock is certainly avaricious, but here Graziano is referring to his insistence on his pound of flesh. The qualities of the wolf here listed are largely the same as those of Dante's *lupa*. Whitaker[52] points out that *The Merchant of Venice* seems to reflect the trial of Dr Lopez and Marlowe's *Jew of Malta,* and that the name "Lopez" is derived from Latin *lupus* for wolf.

J. E. Hankins was also interested in this image of the "universal wolf", and presented his own theory of its origins:

[H]ere I am concerned with the allegory of the beast. There is a threefold allegory: personal, political, and cosmic. In a person the concupiscible appetite, when unrestrained by will and reason, will indulge in such excesses as lead to his destruction. In a state the disregard of established order of rank by self-willed individuals can lead only to anarchy and loss of political identity. In the cosmos if the planets could wander at will without control by the sun, the world would return to chaos. Appetite, if unrestrained, will lead to destruction on any level. It may be compared to a violent and voracious wolf, cosmically, a wolf with power to destroy the universe.[53]

Hankins heard here an echo of Ragnarok, as it was described in Norse Mythology. The account appeared in the Prose Edda.[54] In this tale:

First two wolves devour the sun and the moon, destroying the source of light. Then the greatest wolf, Fenris (or Fenrir), breaks his chain and goes forth to battle the gods, accompanied by the Midgard Serpent. The opposing forces destroy each other, and Asgard, the home of the gods, is likewise destroyed ... [T]he Norse image is that of a wolf; and Shakespeare's image is that of "an universal wolf" that makes "an universal prey" Fenris and his companion wolves seem to be a possible source for this image.

Hankins went on to comment in an endnote that he was "not sure where Shakespeare could have read this legend".[55]

He pointed out that there was a continual exchange of influences between Scandinavian and French literatures throughout the Middle Ages, or that there could have been an intermediate version in Latin or French which Shakespeare could have known, or that the cosmic wolves may have been in oral tradition.

But the similarity in thought here between Shakespeare and Dante is very close, and it seems more likely that Shakespeare has in fact, borrowed Dante's *lupa* simply because the notion of the wolf as avaricious, insatiable, ultimately self-destructive and the principal cause of social disintegration, occurs in the work of both authors. In the Scandinavian tale the only parallel seems to be the destructiveness of the wolf. While it cannot be established that Shakespeare could have read this tale, it is possible to establish the accessibility of the *Divina Commedia* to him.

In Vivian Thomas's book on Shakespeare's "problem plays", a long list of sources for *Troilus and Cressida* was given, followed by the claim:

To this list of sources and influences should be added ideas drawn from Boethius and Dante.[56]

But there was, disappointingly, no discussion of this and no further reference to Dante in the book. König, too, in his paper "Shakespeare und Dante", commented that:

> Zunächst mag die Wölfin im Eingange von Dante's Gedicht (*Inferno* I.49) die Anregung zu dem fast etwas gezwungen scheinenden Bilde in *Troilus und Cressida*.
>
> [The she-wolf in the beginning of Dante's poem (*Inferno* I.49) could very well have served as model for Shakespeare's image in *Troilus and Cressida*.]

and that *dass Dante's Bild hier grade in der Bedeutung aufgefasst ist* (Dante's image is captured in its true meaning),[57] but he offered no further discussion on the matter. Given the appearance of the wolf in the emblem books and the apparently wide currency for the idea of the wolf as a symbol of avarice in the Seven Deadly Sins, it may be that Shakespeare's image was not a borrowing from Dante—but his development of the symbol is remarkably similar to Dante's.

V
Hamlet (1601)

Thus conscience doth make cowards of us all.
Hamlet, Shakespeare

It seems from the plays we have already considered that in these early years of the 17th century, Shakespeare was preoccupied with some of the great moral problems of life. He is deeply concerned with the question of loyalty and betrayal. He is also concerned with the question of justice and punishment. The system of government also interested him. Was there some incident in his life—perhaps personal, perhaps political—that drove him to ponder on these matters? Certainly they were dealt with in some detail in the *Divina Commedia* where these subjects are dramatised and where opinions or even solutions to the questions are offered.

As far as we know from the accepted biography of Shakespeare there was little to bring him to such disturbing subjects. It was true that his son Hamnet had died in 1596 and heartbreaking though this must have been, it does not seem likely that this kind of family tragedy could conjure up thoughts of the great issues of Man's destructive relationships with Man. The plays from these years all have a similar reflective and pessimistic atmosphere. And in *Hamlet* (1601) there is a very real sense of gloom and moral confusion.

In *Hamlet*, in the most famous speech by the most famous of Shakespeare's characters, is a fascinating parallel with Dante noticed by James Russell Lowell. Writing in 1868, Lowell drew his readers' attention to two passages in Dante which, he claimed, "contain the exactest possible definition of that habit or quality of Hamlet's mind which justifies the tragic turn of the play, and renders it natural and unavoidable from the beginning".[58] Lowell did not suggest that Shakespeare had borrowed the idea from Dante, nor did he investigate the similarity other than to look at the common meaning.

The first passage he cited was from *Inferno* II. Lowell considered only three lines, but in the lines following these, the parallel is even more marked. Dante (the Pilgrim) has asked Virgil to lead him to *la porta di San Pietro*—the gates of St Peter which are the Gates of Paradise—and Virgil has agreed. But as the dark descends at the beginning of Canto II, Dante is not so sure. The prospect of entering the underworld is daunting. Other people have journeyed there before him, Paul, for example, and Aeneas, but Dante protests:

> Io non Enea, io non Paulo sono;
> me degno a ciò ne io ne altri crede.
>
> *Inferno* II.32–3

[I am not Aeneas, I am not Paul; of this neither I nor others think me worthy.]

Dante (the Poet) explains:

> E qual è quei che disvuol ciò che volle
> e per novi pensier cangia proposta,
> si che dal cominciar tutto si tolle,
> tal mi fec'io in quella oscura costa,
> perchè, pensando, consumai la 'mpresa
> che fu nel cominciar cotanto tosta.
>
> *Inferno* II.37–42

[And like one who unwills what he has willed and with new thoughts changes his resolve, so that he quite gives up the thing he had begun, such did I become on that dark slope, for by thinking on it I rendered null the undertaking that had been so suddenly embarked upon.]

Virgil, his guide, sees the problem and replies:

> l'anima tua è da viltate offesa;
> la qual molte fiate l'omo ingombra
> si che d'onrata impresa lo rivolve,
> come falso veder bestia quand'ombra.
>
> *Inferno* II.45–8

[Your spirit is beset by cowardice, which oftentimes encumbers a man, turning him from honourable endeavour, as false seeing turns a beast that shies.]

Even in the first three lines of this passage (37–9), the parallel is evident. Lowell wrote:

> Dante was a profound metaphysician, and as in the first passage (*Inferno* II.37–42), he describes and defines a certain quality of mind, so in the other (*Purgatory* V.16–18), he tells us its result on the character and in life, namely,

indecision and failure—the goal farther off at the end than at the beginning. It is remarkable how close a resemblance of thought, and even of expression, there is between the former of these quotations and a part of Hamlet's famous soliloquy.[59]

Consider the second part of Hamlet's "To be, or not to be ..." soliloquy:

> Thus conscience does make cowards of us all,
> And thus the native hue of resolution
> Is sicklied o'er with the pale cast of thought,
> And enterprises of great pith and moment
> With this regard their currents turn awry
> And lose the name of action.
>
> *Hamlet* III.1.83–8

Dante's comment concerning the way in which someone who wishes to "undecide" something already decided will introduce new thoughts (*novi pensier*) to change his intentions (*cangia proposta*) equates exactly to the effects of "the pale cast of thought" on the "native hue of resolution". Virgil's *l'anima tua è da viltate offesa* equates to "conscience does make cowards of us all" except that Virgil's comment is a personal observation and Shakespeare's is a generalisation. The remark *l'onrata impresa lo rivolve* equates exactly to "enterprises of great pith and moment ... turn awry". The two passages express virtually identical ideas.

It is possible of course that two great minds could have very similar views on the retarding effect of thought on action—and even that they might, by chance, and despite the fact that they are written in different languages, happen upon very similar language, imagery and point of view. For example, Dante's word *viltate* (cowardice) and Shakespeare's "cowards", or Dante's *[i]'mpresa* (enterprise) and Shakespeare's "enterprises" are exact parallels.

In both cases the idea of changing one's mind as a result of thought is presented as a negative. Both poets see this as a shift from what was "an enterprise of great pith and moment" or *an 'mpresa che fu nel comincia cotanto tosta* to a state of inaction. In neither case is it suggested that it may be advisable to think about the decision before taking extreme and irreversible action.

To this point, we can conclude only that both poets concurred on the cause and effect of procrastination, but they may have done this independently. If we consider the context in which both passages occur, however, there is another even more striking parallel—not noted by Lowell.

Dante (the Pilgrim) is deciding whether to cross into the unknown of the afterlife. He stands on *quella oscura costa* (II.40), *perchè, pensando, consumai la 'mpresa* (II.41). Singleton's translation given above seems to lose some of the elements of the parallel, but Ciardi's comes much nearer:

> so I hung back and balked on that dim coast
> till thinking had worn out my enterprise,
> so stout at starting and so early lost.[60]

Hamlet too, as he considers whether "to be, or not to be," stands on the edge of "The undiscovered country from whose bourn/No traveller returns". He too, in contemplating the alternative to living, is forced to consider the afterlife, facing the "dread of something after death". While we can accept that a consideration of lack of resolution may interest both poets, it would be rather an odd coincidence if both of them had broached this idea because both characters are faced with precisely the same decision—to enter or not to enter the next world, which is Hell in each case. Hamlet has already wished that "the Everlasting had not fixed/His canon 'gainst self-slaughter (I.2.131–2). He is therefore aware that what he is contemplating is against Divine Law and would incur the punishment of Hell.

The terms in which Hamlet considers this are so similar to Dante's that it is difficult to believe that the parallels in the circumstances of the passage, as well as in the passage itself, can *all* be attributed to coincidence.

There are various long footnotes in the Arden (2) edition of *Hamlet* on the sources of many of the ideas in this soliloquy. All of these are possible, and Shakespeare's ideas can usually be traced to multiple sources. But the real point of similarity for this particular parallel with Dante is the idea of hesitation and the way in which thinking prevents immediate action and weakens resolve. The editor of the Arden (2) edition, Harold Jenkins, traces a number of parallel expressions back to Belleforest, though he says there are few, since "they could hardly be expected to travel across the linguistic gap".[61]

On the meaning of the word "conscience", the Arden (2) edition gave two interpretations. The first was "as in ordinary modern usage, the inner voice of moral judgment." The second was "consciousness, the fact or faculty of knowing and understanding." The editor presented both cases, but pointed out that the first of these two meanings "does not so naturally lead on: the faltering of resolution as a result of 'thought'(1.85) cannot easily be attributed to the recognition or fear of wrongdoing but rather to what Hamlet later calls 'thinking too precisely on th'event' (IV.4.41)".[62] Certainly Dante's concern is with the result of thinking too much, rather than with any kind of moral judgment.

C. S. Lewis, on the other hand, accepted the first meaning, and believed conscience here means "nothing more or less than a 'fear of hell'".[63] This is also literally what causes Dante (the Pilgrim) to hesitate before he enters Inferno. In either case, then, the parallel exists. In both works, the passage is crucial. For Hamlet, this speech is at the centre of his experience and his character. For Dante, the course of the action in the *Divina Commedia* depends on the decision he makes here. Unlike Hamlet, he makes the decision to proceed, since Virgil tells him that he has, unlike Hamlet, the assistance of Divine Love (Beatrice).

The other similarity noted by Lowell is in *Purgatorio* V. Dante (the Pilgrim) is in Ante-Purgatory. This is the circle of the unshriven—in particular those who have died violently and have not had time to repent. Some of the spirits there immediately discern from the fact that Dante casts a shadow, that he is not a spirit and that he can therefore return to the world of the living. They importune him, anxious to tell him their stories and so, they hope, to win prayers from those back on earth and thus shorten their own time in Purgatory. Virgil is concerned that Dante should not loiter and explains to him that time here is important. He advises Dante:

> sta come torre ferma, che non crolla
> già mai la cima per soffiar di venti;
> ché sempre l'omo in cui pensier rampolla
> sovra pensier, da sé dilunga il segno,
> perché la foga l'un de l'altro insolla".

Purgatorio V.14–18

[Stand as a firm tower which never shakes its summit for blast of winds; for always the man in whom thought wells up on thought sets back his mark, for the one thought weakens the force of the other.]

Lowell cited only lines 16–18, and they are, in fact, an extension of the idea of how thought can weaken resolve—distractions can cause one to lose sight of the goal. Virgil's intention is to keep Dante's mind focused on the fact that he is there to repent, and that distractions such as conversing with the other spirits there, only delay this process.

These lines add little to the previous descriptions of lack of resolution in *Inferno* II. What is interesting here, is that two scenes later, after Hamlet has dealt with some new ideas (Ophelia, the discussion with the players, and the play itself), he will discover the King praying—and reject the idea of killing him while he is in a state of grace. In fact, Hamlet's father has suffered the fate of the unshriven—to be "sent to my account / With all my imperfections on my head"—and like some of the characters in *Purgatorio* V he had been murdered before he could repent his sins. Later in the play, Hamlet tells Horatio how he had made arrangements for Rosencrantz and Guildenstern to be "put to sudden death, / No shriving time allow'd" (V.2.46–7).

Hamlet's father had died violently and unshriven and from what he tells us, he is in Purgatory. The Ghost speaks of the "sulphurous and tormenting flames" to which he must soon render himself up. Like the spirits in Dante's Purgatory, he is "[d]oomed for a certain term" to suffer the consequences of dying unshriven, but unlike them he is also:

... for the day, confin'd to fast in fires,

Till the foul crimes done in my days of nature

Are burnt and purg'd away.

Hamlet I.5.11–13

In Dante's *Purgatorio* the spirits who endure tormenting flames are those who have reached the edge of the Earthly Paradise. There, the last sin, that of lust, must be purged from them, and this is achieved at the wall of fire, through which everyone must pass. None of the spirits in *Purgatorio* is inciting revenge, as is the Ghost in *Hamlet*—and indeed this would be contrary to the whole repentant mood of those who have this second chance to reach Paradise. Clearly, the Purgatory of which the Ghost speaks is not Dante's Purgatory—and while those still living in Dante's world hoped to be able to shorten the time spent in Purgatory by their loved ones, prayer was all they could offer to achieve this. But as Stephen Greenblatt[64] points out, by the time that *Hamlet* was written, the doctrine of purgatory had been outlawed by the reformist Church of England. Catholicism was persecuted, so how did Shakespeare manage to insert such a crucial reference into his play and escape the attentions of the authorities? Greenblatt comments that Shakespeare had a "remarkable gift for knowing exactly how far he could go without getting into serious trouble".

The idea of dying unshriven is clearly much on Hamlet's mind, and one wonders if Shakespeare, having read *Purgatory* V and the restatement by Virgil of the dangers of irresolution has, like Dante, associated the idea of the debilitating effect of thought on resolution with those who have died violently and unshriven—since these are precisely the spirits who are in this canto. There are other fascinating examples of this same way of associating ideas. Shakespeare sometimes links two ideas in a way which is unusual—except to the reader of Dante, who has already seen the same two ideas linked in exactly the same way in the *Divina Commedia*.

The two lines at the beginning of this last passage (V.14 to Lorenzo Mascetta-Caracci,[65] show a strong resemblanc passage in *The Taming of the Shrew*. Petruchio is about to m for the first time. Baptista warns him, "be thou armed for some unhappy words" and Petruchio answers,

> Ay, to the proof; as mountains are for winds,
> That shakes not though they blow perpetually.
> *The Taming of the Shrew* II.1.140–1[66]

In the passage from *Purgatorio* V the image is similar, except that "mountains" have been substituted for a tower, and in both cases the lines are a simile to demonstrate how firm the person facing the difficulty is resolved to be. Mascetta-Caracci cited this parallel as evidence of Shakespeare's knowledge of Dante, but he did not expand on this claim. Verbally, the similes are alike in their reference to strong winds, but the most convincing argument is perhaps the fact that it seems likely that Shakespeare was familiar with the lines immediately following this simile in this canto of *Purgatorio* and may therefore, have remembered this useful image for strength of resolution to utilise when he needed it, as he does for Petruchio.

The parallel between Hamlet's lack of resolution and that of Dante (the Pilgrim) is an interesting one but not conclusive in itself as a borrowing. In fact Michele Renzulli, writing in 1925, noted Lowell's parallel in a footnote. He clearly did not see it as evidence of Shakespeare's knowledge of Dante, as he concluded at the end of his chapter on the knowledge demonstrated by Elizabethan writers—of which Shakespeare is one—"we do not find a single line which reminds us even distantly of Dante".[67]

What is most persuasive, however, is the parallel of context. Both Hamlet and Dante (the Pilgrim) stand on the verge of a momentous decision, and that decision is whether to enter the next world or not. The "next world", in both cases, is Hell: in Hamlet's case because he is contemplating suicide and he knows this is forbidden by Divine Law, and in Dante's case, because that is where Virgil is offering to take him. This kind of similarity occurs so frequently in the passages where parallels appear, that it becomes increasingly difficult to attribute all of these to chance. There seems to be no question that this passage from *Hamlet* is

Shakespeare's own work and so, if it is evidence of familiarity with Dante's work, it is Shakespeare's own familiarity.

Fear of the afterlife in *Hamlet* is not limited to the protagonist. Even Claudius, that "smiling, damned villain", expresses his desire to repent, perhaps more from his fear of punishment than from any real regret for what he has done. Rationally, he argues:

> May one not be pardoned and retain th'offence?
> In the corrupted currents of this world
> Offence's gilded hand may shove by justice;
> And oft 'tis seen the wicked prize itself
> Buys out the law. But 'tis not so above:
> There is no shuffling, there the action lies
> In its true nature; and we ourselves compell'd,
> Even to the teeth and forehead of our faults,
> To give in evidence.
>
> *Hamlet* III.3.56–64

While Claudius is disturbed by the guilt he feels, he does not wish to give up what "th'offence" has won for him, the throne and Gertrude. He recognises that in "the corrupted currents" of his life, the reward for the offence "buys out the law". The power of his position presumably puts him above suspicion. But he also knows that "above", this will not be the case. There, the truth will be clear and there will be "no shuffling". While we may not approve his morality, we must applaud his faith!

The ideas expressed here are strongly reminiscent of those expressed by Guido da Montefeltro in *Inferno* XXVII, which were considered in relation to his placement as an Evil Counsellor, earlier in this book. No other writer has mentioned this similarity. This man was a great soldier and also known for his foxlike cunning and shrewdness. At a certain time in his life he decided to join the Franciscan Order, but his strategic skills were well-known to those in power, and the Pope of that time, Boniface VIII, sent for Guido to give advice on how his longstanding enemy, the powerful

Colonna family, could be defeated. At first Guido said nothing, aware that
that both the request and any answer he might give, were an abuse of the
sacred vows both he and the Pope had taken. But when the Pope promised
him absolution *in advance* for any sin that Guido might commit, Guido
gave advice which he knew was immoral:

> lunga promessa con l'attender corto
> ti fara triunfar nell'alto seggio.
>
> *Inferno* XXVII.110–11

> [long promise and short observance is the road
> That leads to the sure triumph of your throne.]

The advice achieved the desired result.

He thought such a stratagem would "buy out the law", in this case
Divine Law. However, when death came, and Saint Francis arrived to
take Guido to Paradise, they were suddenly interrupted by one of the *neri
cherubini* (black angels) who pointed out that this soul was his and that
Guido had failed to understand that:

> ... assolver non si può chi non si pente
> né pentére e volere insieme puossi
> per la contradizion che nol consente'.
>
> *Inferno* XXVII.118–120

> [... he who repents not cannot be absolved, nor is it possible
> to repent of a thing and to will it at the same time, for the
> contradiction does not allow it.]

Unpleasantly sarcastic, the black angel adds:

> ... Forse
> tu non pensavi ch'io loico fossi'!
>
> *Inferno* XXVII.122–3

[Perhaps you did not think that I was a logician!]

Clearly, here too "there is no shuffling"!

Guido da Montefeltro, like Claudius, is intelligent and shrewd. He has, like Claudius, knowingly committed a sin, and as with Claudius, his repentance is of a dubious nature. Both men are hypocritical: Claudius in that he wants absolution for his sin, but only along with the fruits of this same sin, and Guido in that, shrewd as he is, he knew always that he was committing a sin, but wished to enjoy the rewards he would receive for his pragmatic advice. Both men fear the consequences of their sin in the next life.

Both men confess, Claudius because he thinks he is alone, Guido because:

> ... di questo fondo
> non tornò vivo alcun, s'i'odo il vero,.
> sanza tema d'infamia ti rispondo.
> *Inferno* XXVII.64–6[68]

[... since from this depth no-one has ever returned alive, if what I hear is true, I answer you without fear of infamy.]

The perception that each of these men has of his own moral standing is very similar. Claudius admits his fault, wants absolution, but is rational enough to know that he cannot have this and continue to enjoy "my crown, mine own ambition, and my queen." Guido, recounting his experience in retrospect to Dante (the Pilgrim), recalls how the black angel, logician that he was, pointed out that it is impossible to repent and commit the same action simultaneously. Both men see the rationality of their fate.

Interestingly in *Henry VIII*, Queen Katherine on her deathbed, speaking of Cardinal Wolsely and accusing him of many misdeeds, concludes:

His promises were, as he then was, mighty;
But his performance, as he is now, nothing:

Henry VIII IV.2.44–5

There is here an echo of Guido da Montefeltro.

But although the parallel here is close, it is not conclusive evidence of a "borrowing". If we have already accepted that Shakespeare had read Dante, we could feel that Shakespeare's ideas here may have been influenced by this knowledge of *Inferno* XXVII. Otherwise, the similarity, taken in isolation, could perhaps be attributed to the similar rational way of thinking of both characters.

VI

Antony and Cleopatra (1607)

He which is was wish'd, until he were ...

Anthony and Cleopatra, Shakespeare

The plays we have so far considered were written in the years from 1601 to 1606. Perhaps those written immediately after *Macbeth* will also show some evidence of Shakespeare's knowledge of Dante's work. In 1607, Shakespeare wrote *Antony and Cleopatra.* In this play is an interesting parallel which is an observation on the nature of both personal and political loyalty. It must have been a subject that troubled Shakespeare and very early in the play we see Antony disturbed by his own shifting personal emotions and loyalty. He is living with Cleopatra in Alexandria, but having just heard the news of his wife's death in Rome, he comments:

There's a great spirit gone! Thus did I desire it:
What our contempts do often hurl from us,
We wish it ours again; the present pleasure,
By revolution lowering, does become

The opposite of itself: she's good, being gone;
The hand could pluck her back that shov'd her on.
I must from this enchanting queen break off:

Antony and Cleopatra I.2.117–24

We see here an introduction to the idea of changing loyalties on a personal level. Antony is initially saddened by this news but also surprised that although "this is as I desire it," he regrets the death of Fulvia. Because she is "gone", he feels he "could pluck her back again". He gives an excellent description of the strangely pendulum swing of emotions and loyalties.

Then, in Act I, Scene 4, we see a comment on the shift in political loyalty. Caesar has just received news that many people are deserting him to support Pompey. He responds:

I should have known no less:
It hath been taught us from the primal state
That he which is was wish'd, until he were;
And the ebb'd man, ne'er loved till ne'er worth love
Comes dear'd, by being lack'd. This common body,
Like to a vagabond flag upon the stream,
Goes to, and back, lackeying the varying tide,
To rot itself with motion.

Antony and Cleopatra I.4.40–7

Caesar claims to have learned early that the allegiance of the "common body" is to the person coming into power, until he is actually in power. Then, when that person loses power, he is not supported until he is no longer deserving of support, when their loyalty returns because they miss him. The image of the "vagabond flag" being washed to and fro in the constantly turning tide, illustrates again the pendulum swing of loyalty. The flag, representing the object of loyalty, "rot[s] itself" or disintegrates, as does the loyalty of its followers.

This passage is concerned with the ebb and flow of popularity and allegiance in politics—and so (to the reader of Dante) the mention of a "vagabond flag" takes the mind straight to the *insegna* (standard, ensign) of *Inferno* III.52–69, where Dante (the Pilgrim) describes those who have never allied themselves with any particular cause:

> E io, che riguardai, vidi una insegna
> che girando correva tanto ratta,
> che d'ogne posa mi parea indegna;
> e dietro le venia sì lunga tratta
> di gente, ch'io non averei creduto
> che morte tanta n'avesse disfatta.
>
> Questi sciaurati, che mai non fur vivi,
> erano ignudi, stimolati molto
> da mosconi e da vespe ch'eran ivi.
> Elle rigavan lor di sangue il volto,
> che, mischiato di lagrime, ai lor piedi
> da fastidiosi vermi era ricolto.
>
> Inferno III.52–69

[Looking again I saw a banner that ran so fast, whirling about, that it seemed it might never have rest, and behind it came so long a train of people that I should never have believed death had undone so many ... These wretches, who never were alive, were naked and were much stung by gadflies and wasps there, which were streaking their faces with blood that mingled with their tears and was gathered by loathsome worms at their feet.]

In Dante's account, these souls have no name: *misericordia e giustizia li sdegna* (Mercy and Justice disdain them). Dante does not single out any of them by name as he does with so many other sinners. They are referred to as *ignavi*, which is translated variously as "opportunistic", "lazy" or "lukewarm" and they are those who have failed to commit themselves to any cause in life. Here in Hell they are forced to follow the symbol of a cause, *una insegna* (a flag or banner), which represents nothing in particular. This was, after all, what they chose in life. They are tormented by painful physical goads, *mosconi* (flies) and *vespe* (wasps) and the resultant *sangue* (blood) and *lagrime* (tears), which they had conserved so carefully in life, now flow freely for the *vermi* (worms) which feed on them. In Dante's time *si credeva che nascessero spontaneamente dalle cose imputridite*[69] (they believed that these grew spontaneously from rotting materials). The opportunists must run for all eternity. They have no place here as they had no place in life. They must follow the flag which should symbolise a cause, but which constantly changes direction.

Surprisingly, the Arden (2) footnote gives the meaning of "flag" as "a common species of iris".[70] Other editions support this, some extending the idea to a reed or water plant. There is no reason given, however, as to why the word may not be taken in its more usual and literal sense, as a banner. According to the Lexicon,[71] Shakespeare uses the word "flag" as a noun ten times only in his plays. On four of these occasions, he uses it in the sense of "banner" or "standard". On five, he uses it in the sense of an "ensign by which signs are made". On this occasion *only*, he allegedly uses it in the sense of "the water-plant, Iris".

If Shakespeare uses the word "flag" in the sense of a flower, one wonders why. If it is floating in the water, it is dead, and will rot with or without the action of the tide. And why has he chosen specifically the iris? Would an iris be growing near the mouth of a tidal river in what must be salt water? Is a dead iris a suitable symbol for the object of loyalty?

It may be that the "stream" and the "tide" are both metaphorical— since Shakespeare has used the word "ebb'd" (I.4.43) to describe the man whose popularity has waned. The word "stream" is used on a number of occasions by Shakespeare to denote a crowd, and perhaps that is its meaning here. In the following passage:

... The rich stream
Of lords and ladies, having brought the queen
To a prepar'd place in the chair, fell off
A distance from her.

Henry VIII IV.1.63–6

the word "stream" is used to describe the crowd of "lords and ladies" in the procession of people who have come to see the coronation of Anne Bullen. There is, again, the notion of shifting allegiances—the ebb and flow of loyalty. Immediately before the procession after which Anne Bullen is escorted into the abbey, we have been informed of the plight of Queen Katharine, who, since her divorce, "remains now sick" (IV.1.34). Both women come to experience rapid changes in popularity in their own lives.

Similarly in *Coriolanus,* in a scene where various people discuss whether or not Coriolanus will be appointed Consul, and opinions fluctuate wildly, Sicinius says:

... To th' Capitol
Come, we will be there before the stream o'th' people;
And this shall seem, as partly 'tis, their own,
Which we have goaded onward.

Coriolanus II.3.259–62

Again, the word "stream" is used to describe a crowd of the common people, and as in *Antony and Cleopatra,* the subject under discussion is the matter of changing loyalties and the way that allegiance can so easily be shifted. In each of these cases where Shakespeare uses "stream", he sees a kind of faceless moving force which ebbs and flows and can easily be persuaded to change its allegiance and follow the "tide".

If this is the case, in the passage from *Antony and Cleopatra,* it may be that the words "ebb'd", "stream", and "tide" are all part of the same metaphor for people who act *en masse,* the crowd in which there is no individuality—it is like a "stream" which flows one way or the other simply because it is driven by the "tide" of public opinion—forcing those in the stream into "lackeying the varying tide".

Shakespeare's image is, however, ambiguous, depending perhaps on the punctuation, which, with a slight variation, could change in meaning. Its meaning could also change with the interpretation of the word "flag". We could read it as printed in the First Folio:[72]

> ... This common bodie,
> Like to a Vagabond Flagge upon the Streme,
> Goes too, and backe, lackeying the varrying tyde
> To rot itselfe with motion.

This would mean that it is the "vagabond flag" which moves "too and backe" in the tide and which, as a result of this motion, "rot[s] itselfe". The flag image is thus a simile to describe the ultimate destruction of the flag (iris) and the "common body" which resembles it. It is a strange comparison. The "iris" is already dead if it is floating. The crowd is not dead. It is active.

Or, if we punctuate slightly differently,[73] and interpret the "flag" as a flag with the usual meaning, the image could be interpreted in a different way. Consider the following:

> ... This common body,
> Like to a vagabond flag, upon the stream
> Goes to and back, lackeying the varying tide,
> To rot itself with motion.

In this case, it is the "common body" which is "upon the stream", and which "goes, to and back," "like to"—or *as though towards*—"a vagabond flag". The "flag" is clearly something to follow, a symbol of allegiance, but it is "vagabond", wandering randomly in different directions so that the allegiance is never fixed, but at the mercy of the "tide". The result of this mindless "lackeying" for the "common body" is "to rot itself", just as in Dante, "the lukewarm are depicted eternally rushing to and fro after an aimlessly dodging banner ... tormented by flies and wasps."[74] They are covered in blood and pus which feed worms and maggots—which promote "rot".

If we read the image in this way, the problems with the "flag" image are resolved, and the whole concept takes on a fuller meaning. The apparently arbitrary choice of the iris, to float to and fro until it rots on the stream, is replaced by the meaningful symbol of a "flag" or banner, which is "vagabond" and which, in the context of an observation on the shifting nature of allegiance, is remarkably apt and resonant. If we are discussing loyalty, a flag (or banner) is exactly the right symbol for the entity to which we give our allegiance. A dead flower is not.

This interpretation is satisfying in the sense that the image has the qualities of economy and aptness which we associate with Shakespeare. It is interesting to note too, that, to the reader of Dante, the image is already established in the mind, so that to interpret the "flag" as a flower seems absurd and the "stream" seems to be the huge crowd (*Inferno* III.55–7) Dante meets in this circle.

This is, of course, an unconventional interpretation of Shakespeare's "vagabond flag" but it is more rational than the accepted view. I interpreted it in this way as the image of Dante's *ignavi* was already in my mind when I read Shakespeare's views on the ebb and flow of popular loyalty.

VII

Cymbeline (1609)

Is't enough I'm sorry?
Cymbeline, Shakespeare

About 1609, Shakespeare wrote *Cymbeline.* In this play there is a different kind of parallel, interesting for the combination of ideas, rather than for the similarity of the ideas themselves. The strange and quite detailed episode in Shakespeare which appears to be closely related to a passage in the *Divina*

Commedia, is the scene in *Cymbeline,* Act V, Scene 4, often referred to as the "Vision".

In Shakespeare's plot,[75] Posthumus, a Roman, has believed a false tale concerning the infidelity of his wife, Imogen. As a result he orders her death and believes that this instruction has been obeyed. At the beginning of Act V, Scene 4, he has been captured by English soldiers and is in the charge of a gaoler who leaves him alone to soliloquize on his condition. Repentant, he sees Death, "th'sure physician", as a way to freedom from the fetters of his conscience.

In the ensuing speech, he speculates on the nature of repentance:

> ... Is't enough I'm sorry?
> So children temporal fathers do appease;
> Gods are more full of mercy. Must I repent?
> I cannot do it better than in gyves,
> Desir'd more than constrain'd: to satisfy,
> If of my freedom 'tis the main part, take
> No stricter render of me than my all.
>
> *Cymbeline* V.4.11–17

The Arden (2) footnote[76] to this passage tells us:

> Ingleby with acknowledgements, comments: "in this speech Posthumus is made to employ the language of the early divines in distinguishing the three parts (primary, secondary and *main*) of Repentance, as the condition of Remission of Sins. 1. Attrition, or sorrow for sin: "Is't enough I am sorry?" 2. Penance: which was held to convert attrition into contrition, or godly sorrow: "Must I repent?" 3. Satisfaction: "Must I satisfy?" And he contends that as he has fulfilled the former requirements, he is willing to fulfil the last—to pay his debt for having taken Imogen's life, by giving his own."

To the reader of Dante, this passage (with the accompanying footnote) immediately recalls the description of the three steps at the entrance to Purgatory in *Purgatorio* IX:

> Là ne venimmo: e lo scaglion primaio
> bianco marmo era si pulito e terso,
> ch'io mi specchiai in esso qual io paio.
> Era il secondo tinto più che perso,
> d'una petrina ruvida e arsiccia,
> crepata per lo lungo e per traverso.
> Lo terzo, che di sopra s'ammassiccia,
> porfido mi parea si fiammeggiante,
> come sangue che fuor di vena spiccia.
>
> *Purgatorio* IX.94–102

[We then came on, and the first step was white marble so polished and clear that I mirrored myself in it in my true likeness; the second was darker than perse and was of a stone rugged and burnt, cracked in its length and in its breadth. The third, which lies massy above, seemed to me of porphyry as flaming red as blood that spurts from a vein.]

The entrance to Purgatory is a physical representation of the ritual of the Roman Catholic confessional and the three steps which Dante sees symbolize the three acts of perfect confession. The first step, made of *bianco marmo* (white marble), is polished and shiny like a mirror. According to Sapegno,[77] it represented the first stage of repentance in which the penitent recognised his sin. The second step, made of *una petrina ruvida e arsiccia, crepata* (rough, dark and cracked stone), symbolized confession; the dark colour was the colour of shame and the rough, cracked surface suggested that within, as well as on the surface, shame was felt. The third step, made of *porfido ... come sangue* (porphyry ... like blood), symbolized satisfaction; the idea of the warmth of love which was ignited in men and led them to repent the sins committed. Some of the old commentators (Lana, Buti and Landino) reversed the order of the first two.

The similarity here between Shakespeare's and Dante's view of the rites and significance of confession is not at all surprising: both poets express well-known and accepted medieval theories on the subject and this parallel is not a matter of Shakespeare "borrowing" from Dante. But what is fascinating here is that Shakespeare, after writing about the ritual of repentance, then goes on to describe the "Vision"—the descent of Jupiter on the eagle—so strangely similar to the dream of the eagle which occurs in Dante's canto (*Purgatorio* IX) on the subject of repentance.

At the end of his speech on penitence, Posthumus falls asleep, and the "Vision" begins. As Posthumus sleeps, around him circle various "apparitions", his father, his mother and two brothers, all of whom are dead. They give some information on the circumstances of their deaths and question Posthumus on his treatment of Imogen. At the end of this strange ritual, the brothers appeal to Jupiter for justice. The stage direction tells us:

> In thunder and lightning, Jupiter appears sitting upon an eagle: he throws a thunderbolt. The Ghosts fall on their knees.[78]

Such scenes were common on the Elizabethan stage, although it seems that "the earlier plays tended to allow their gods to walk on like any mortal; the first of Shakespeare's gods to fly was Jupiter on his eagle in *Cymbeline*."[79]

Jupiter speaks angrily to the "apparitions" but concludes:

> ... Be content
> Your low-laid son our godhead will uplift:
> His comforts thrive, his trials well are spent:
> > *Cymbeline* V.4.102–4

Jupiter leaves behind a "tablet" (a single sheet, richly bound) which is to be laid upon the breast of Posthumus and then departs on the eagle, "to my palace crystalline". Sicilius describes how the eagle "stoop'd, as to foot us," and then departed with Jupiter:

> The marble pavement closes, he is enter'd
> His radiant roof.
>
> *Cymbeline* V.4.120–1

The ghosts vanish and Posthumus wakes. Sleep, he feels, has been kind in giving him a family in his dream. The dream has, in fact, anticipated reality and the family reunion of Act V, Sc. 5, where Imogen is reunited with her two long-lost brothers. Posthumous is left dazed and bewildered. He reads the mysterious message left for him and concludes:

> 'Tis still a dream: or else such stuff as madmen
> Tongue, and brain not: either both, or nothing,
> Or senseless speaking, or a speaking such
> As sense cannot untie. Be what it is,
> The action of my life is like it, which
> I'll keep, if but for sympathy.
>
> *Cymbeline* V.4.146–51

The dream, though a dream, has told a truth. He has been lifted out of his despair and, shortly after, is freed from the manacles and eventually reunited with Imogen.

The dream of the eagle, of course, is already familiar to the reader of Dante. On Dante's journey through Purgatory, he completes the early stages on foot in the company of his beloved guide, Virgil. But in the flowering valley of the negligent rulers (*Purgatorio* VIII), when night falls, Dante (the Pilgrim) is overcome by sleep and at dawn, the hour when dreams are most likely to come true, he dreams of the eagle. He describes how:

in sogno mi parea veder sospesa
un aguglia nel ciel con penne d'oro,
con l'ali aperte e a calare intesa;

Purgatorio IX.19–21

[I seemed to see, in a dream, an eagle poised in the sky, with
feathers of gold, its wings outspread, and prepared to swoop.]

He thinks of others who have been carried off, Ganymede, for example,
and then:

... mi parea che, rotata un poco
terribil come folgor discendesse,
e mi rapisse suso infine al foco.

Purgatorio IX.28–30

[Then it seemed to me that, having wheeled a while, it
descended terrible as a thunderbolt and snatched me upwards
as far as the fire.]

This image of course recalls the tale of Jupiter in Ovid's *Metamorphoses:*

The king of gods was once fired with love for the Phrygian
Ganymede, and when that happened Jupiter found another
shape preferable to his own. Wishing to turn himself into a
bird, he none the less scorned to change into any save that
which can carry his thunderbolts. Then, without delay,
beating the air on borrowed pinions, he snatched away the
shepherd of Ilium, who even now mixes the winecups, and
supplies Jove with nectar, to the annoyance of Juno.[80]

In Dante's dream the eagle swoops and carries him up to the sphere of
fire, where the scorching heat wakens him. He is dazed:

... e diventa' ismorto,
come fa l'uom che, spaventato, agghiaccia.

Purgatorio IX.41–2

[I grew pale, like one who is chilled with terror.]

He imagines that Achilles, too, must have awakened in the same way:

li occhi svegliati rivolgendo in giro
e non sappiendo là dove si fosse,

Purgatorio IX.35–6

[Turning his awakened eyes about him and not knowing where he was.]

He awoke to find himself on the island of Sciro, where his mother had taken him while he slept.

But Virgil reassures Dante. While this latter had slept, Virgil tells him, Dante (the Pilgrim) *had* been transported through the air by Lucia, symbol of God's Grace, to the gates in Purgatory, where he is soon to see the three different coloured steps. The dream of the eagle has been for him, as it was for Posthumus, true in a symbolic sense. Dante has been transported by the Grace of God, just as Posthumus has been uplifted (metaphorically) by "our godhead", Jupiter.

The parallels are close. Both Posthumus and Dante (the Pilgrim) are on a journey of penitence: Posthumus on his own account, Dante as part of his other-world experience of Purgatory. Both men describe the three stages of repentance, Posthumus in his soliloquy before he falls asleep and Dante in his explanation of the symbolism of the three stone steps, which he sees when he awakens from the dream. Both men dream of the eagle, which appears, hovers, descends and re-ascends. Both eagles are supernatural: one bears Jupiter on its back, the other has *penne d'oro* (golden feathers) and carries Dante into the sphere of fire. Jupiter descends "in thunder and lightning", Dante's eagle descends *terribil come folgor* (terrible as a thunderbolt).

Both dreamers awake in a daze: each of them finds that his dream was, in a sense, real. Posthumus finds the "tablet", which is real. Dante finds that he *has* been lifted to the Gate of Purgatory. Both men have been uplifted by a supernatural force, Posthumus metaphorically by the god Jupiter from the depths of guilty despair, Dante literally, from the flowering valley to the gate of Purgatory, by the Grace of God, represented by Lucia. Both men are now close to redemption.

The symbol of the eagle is used throughout *Cymbeline,* as it is in the *Divina Commedia.* Imogen, speaking of her husband, tells her father "I chose an eagle" (I.2.70). The Frenchman in Act I, Scene 5 says of Posthumus, "I have seen him in France: we had very many there could behold the sun with as firm eyes as he." The reference to the eagle's ability to "behold the sun" concerns the notion that the eagle could look into the sun directly without blinking, an idea also accepted by Dante.

There were three qualities traditionally associated with the eagle during the Renaissance—keen vision, royalty and the ability to gaze into the sun. As Peggy Munoz Simonds[81] pointed out, Posthumus has none of these qualities (except perhaps the last, though the Frenchman does not seem to find this exceptional), but she went on to suggest another well-known myth about the eagle which could be applied to Posthumus and which Shakespeare may have known from Renaissance emblem books. It had originated as an early Christian story written by Physiologos in Greek as early as the second century, and involved "the spiritual fall, reform and regeneration of humanity",[82] which is essentially the story of Posthumus in the play.

Physiologos was attempting to explain David's promise in Psalm 103 that "your youth will be renewed like the eagle's" and to consider the sin, fall and ultimate renewal in the myth of the eagle. The first part of the myth is when the sinner becomes aware of his sin. The second part is the flight to the sun, which burns away what is no longer required. The third part is when the eagle falls and plunges into a fountain of pure water and is restored and made new again—which may be seen as the cleansing effect of repentant tears. Simonds related these three stages to Posthumus and found parallels.

The Imperial Eagle was the standard and symbol of Rome and Dante uses this throughout *Paradiso* VI, where he describes the expansion of the Roman Empire in terms of the flight of the Eagle. Justinian traces its flight from its legendary origins to the time of Caesar, to the peace missions of Augustus and to the overthrow of the Lombards by Charlemagne. He describes how the Eagle governed the world:

> ... sotto l'ombra de le sacre penne
> governò 'l mondo lì di mano in mano
> e, sì cangiando, in su la mia pervenne.
>
> *Paradiso* VI.7–9

> [... beneath the shadow of its sacred wings, from hand to hand, until by succeeding hand it came into mine.]

The colourful and dramatic metaphor of the Eagle is sustained throughout almost the entire canto, and it evokes all the majesty, beauty and power that was Rome.

Shakespeare uses the same image exactly. In *Cymbeline* the Roman Soothsayer says:

> I saw Jove's bird, the Roman eagle, wing'd
> From the spongy south to this part of the west,
> There vanish'd in the sunbeams, which portends
> (Unless my sins abuse my divination)
> Success to the Roman host.
>
> *Cymbeline* IV.2.348–57

Later in the play, the Soothsayer tells Cymbeline:

> ... For the Roman eagle,
> From south to west on wing soaring aloft,
> Lessen'd herself and in the beams o' the sun
> So vanish'd; which foreshow'd our princely eagle,

Th'imperial Caesar, should again unite
His favour with the radiant Cymbeline,
Which shines here in the west.

Cymbeline V.5.471–7

Thus, the symbol of the Eagle (the Justice of the Empire) is what, in his dreams, brings Dante (the Pilgrim) to the gates in Purgatory, from whence he will progress to the Earthly Paradise and from there to Paradise itself. In the sixth sphere of Jupiter (*Paradiso* XVIII), Dante sees the spectacular lights which first spell out a message,[83] and then form themselves into the shape of an Eagle. In Canto XIX the Eagle announces that it is a symbol of Divine Justice, which none may question.

Shakespeare too has associated Jupiter with the Eagle (as had Ovid—a source for both Dante and Shakespeare), with Divine Justice (as Ovid had not). For Posthumus, his only hope for justice is from a supernatural force. His dream-family lists his sufferings and his dream-mother asks:

Since, Jupiter, our son is good,
Take off his miseries.

Cymbeline V.4.85–6

The dream Jupiter, sitting upon an eagle, announces his intention to intervene and later in the scene, Posthumus is freed.

It is not surprising that Shakespeare used the traditional symbol of the Eagle for the ever-expanding Roman Empire, with all its associated images of spreading wings, rapid flight, talons, thunderbolts, power, and the ability to look into the sun. But this symbol, if Shakespeare had read *Purgatorio,* would certainly have reminded him of the Dantean eagle dream and associated with it, in the same canto, the entrance to Purgatory. If he had also read *Paradiso*, then he would certainly be aware of the Eagle as the symbol of Divine Justice.

The image of the Eagle which swoops to the ground and then rises again into the heavens may well have been suggested by any of a number of biblical passages which, in discussing the sources of Dante's dream, Erich Auerbach lists.[84] Shakespeare too, would have had access to the same biblical images—as he also would have had to Ovid's tale of Ganymede. We cannot therefore claim that Dante's eagle is the source for Shakespeare's. But the many parallels in the two dream episodes suggest some close association of ideas.

The parallels with Dante's dream are persuasive as evidence of Shakespeare's knowledge of Dante, particularly in the juxtaposition of the eagle dream and its associated symbolism with the detailed exposition of the theory of true repentance. Dante (the Pilgrim) arrives at the Gates in Purgatory *only* because he is raised there by Lucia, symbol of Divine Grace and represented in his dream by an eagle. Posthumous is able to repent *only* because in his dream, Jupiter, borne by an eagle, promises that "Your low-laid son our godhead will uplift". Both men have required supernatural assistance in the form of an eagle to achieve justice and salvation. The two ideas, the eagle dream and the nature of repentance, are closely related in Dante, and less obviously so in the emblem books. Whilst the link between them in Shakespeare may have been made because of the link between the eagle and renewal in the emblem books, it seems likely that Shakespeare also recalled the detail and dramatic effect with which this link had already been made in *Purgatorio*.

It may be that even if this pairing of ideas is evidence of the writer's knowledge of Dante, the writer of this part of *Cymbeline* may have been a collaborator, and in fact the authenticity of the "Vision" has been questioned on a number of grounds. The editor of the Arden (2) edition, J. M. Nosworthy, in his introduction, claimed that it is the necessity of the Vision which argues most powerfully for its authenticity. He wrote of how

> it follows upon four and half Acts of bad faith, cruelty, violence and revenge which have brought physical, mental and spiritual confusion upon whole armies as well as upon individuals, and is succeeded by a scene of less than five hundred lines which wins significant order out of this chaos.[85]

He believed that only supernatural intervention could resolve the discord and that the Vision is therefore essential to the play and not an addition or the work of a collaborator.

Harold Bloom, too, singled out this scene for its strangeness. He found it "awful, but I think deliberately so".[86] He described the verse here as "doggerel" and commented, "something buffoonish breaks loose in Shakespeare, and Jupiter descends to a verbal music that sets a new, all-time low in divine epiphanies".[87] He quoted the lines spoken by Jupiter as he descends on the back of the eagle (V.4.93–113) and commented:

> There is no way Shakespeare, keenest of ears, does not apprehend the absurdity of this. The puzzle is insoluble, if we insist on taking this seriously. But it is certainly an outrageous parody of the descent of any god from a machine, and we are expected to sustain it as travesty.[88]

But perhaps the puzzle can be solved. It may be merely Shakespeare connecting the idea of contrition with the dream of the descending eagle which he recalled from *Purgatorio* IX, and sensing that the dream would make a dramatic moment on stage. Perhaps too, it may have been a way of utilizing some state-of-the-art stage machinery which would delight and astound any audience—and, Ian Wilson suggests, sending up "what Jonson, Inigo Jones and their crew of Whitehall ladies had been creating with their masques, this demanded a crane, windlass and counterweight concealed high in the "heavens" backstage whenever *Cymbeline* was staged. An expensive investment in equipment, this was surely introduced into the script only with the consensus of his fellows that such a contrivance was what the increasingly sophisticated theatrical audience now expected."[89] Bloom, like Nosworthy, does not dispute that this scene is the work of Shakespeare, and if the parallel with Dante is in fact a "borrowing", then again we can probably attribute this knowledge of Dante to Shakespeare himself.

Interestingly, the image of an eagle carrying off a child in its talons was the emblem on the crest of the Derby family, of which Ferdinando Stanley, Lord Strange was a member. Various members of this family are shown in a very favourable light in Shakespeare's historical plays, and it is Ferdinando who is thought to have been the patron of the acting company of which Shakespeare was supposedly a member until about 1594.

Of Ferdinando Stanley at a tilt, George Peele wrote the following description in 1590:

> The Earl of Derby's valiant son and heir,
> Brave Ferdinand Lord Strange, strangely embarked
> Under Jove's kingly bird, the golden Eagle,
> Stanley's old crest and honourable badge,
> As veering 'fore the wind, in costly ship,
> And armour white and watchet buckled fast,
> Presents himself, his horses and his men,[90]

The date given for *Cymbeline* is 1609, by which time Ferdinando had been dead for 15 years, his death having occurred under extremely suspicious circumstances. His younger brother, William Stanley, had succeeded to the title Earl of Derby. Interestingly, Peter Levi[91] points out that the epitaphs on the Stanley tomb at Tong were attributed to Shakespeare by Dugdale in his *Visitation to Shropshire* (1664). One is to Sir Edward Stanley, who died in 1603 and the other to his father Sir Thomas Stanley, who died in 1576. The likely date of the tomb is 1612. These two epitaphs are printed in Levi's book and they certainly are strongly reminiscent of Shakespeare in themes and language.

The history of William Stanley, his aristocratic background, the family interest in, and patronage of the theatre, his reported interest in "penning commodyes for the commoun players"[92] his education at Oxford, his travels to France and the court of Henri IV, his travel to Italy and his interest in the language, his detailed knowledge of the law, his interest in music, in the occult and the supernatural, all lead to all manner of interesting speculation and it would take an entire book to investigate where this information could lead us. Again, it is not the subject of this book, but the image of the eagle certainly seems to have fascinated Shakespeare.

VIII
The Tempest (1611)

Being once perfected how to grant suits,
How to deny them; whom to advance, and whom
To trash for over-topping; new created
The creatures that were mine; I say, or changed them
Or else new formed them; having both the key
Of officer and office, set all hearts
To what tune pleased his ear;

The Tempest, Shakespeare

In *The Tempest* (1611) and in the same scene (I.2) as the phrase "it eats, it sleeps ..." (discussed in Evidence III) occurs, Erato Hills, in a brief comment in the August issue of *Notes and Queries*[93] in 1878, pointed out a parallel which had not been noted by any other writer on the subject. Had he looked further, he would have found some quite compelling evidence that it probably was a "borrowing", as there were also other ideas in the play strongly reminiscent of Dante. The parallel passages he noted were in *The Tempest* (I.2.83–7) and *Inferno* (XIII.58–61). In the *Inferno* passage, Dante (the Pilgrim) is in the wood of the suicides, where the spirits of those who have taken their own lives have become thorny trees. The dreadful Harpies feed on the leaves of the trees and when they do, the trees bleed. Only while the blood flows are the trees able to speak and one of the souls there, Pier della Vigna, speaks to Dante, revealing much of his character and recounting how events brought him to this place:

Io son colui che tenni ambo le chiavi

del cor di Federigo, e che le volsi,

serrando e diserrando, si soavi,

che del secreto suo quasi ogn'uom tolsi:

Inferno XIII.58–61

[I am he who held both the keys of Frederick's heart, and turned them, locking and unlocking, so softly that from his secrets I kept almost every one.]

He had been in a relationship of exclusive confidentiality with the Emperor Frederick II, and the image of holding both the keys to Frederick's heart immediately suggests the papacy, and perhaps the fact that Pier della Vigna was to the Emperor as the Pope is to God. He goes on to explain how, faithful though he was to his office to the point of sacrificing his sleep and later his life, envious courtiers turned public opinion against him. Eventually he was imprisoned and blinded, finally taking his own life.

The presentation of the character is sympathetic, and clearly Dante (the Poet) believed that della Vigna was innocent. Later evidence, given in a footnote, tells us that he was not.

The parallel passage in *The Tempest* occurs when Prospero is recounting to Miranda how they had come to the island. He describes how the "government I cast upon my brother" while he himself went off to pursue his "secret studies". The once trusted brother then usurped power in Milan, driving them out of the city. Antonio,

Being once perfected how to grant suits,

How to deny them; whom to advance, and whom

To trash for over-topping; new created

The creatures that were mine; I say, or changed them

Or else new formed them; having both the key

Of officer and office, set all hearts

To what tune pleased his ear;

The Tempest I.2.79–85

Eventually the brother Antonio "did believe /He was the duke" and forced Prospero and his infant daughter to leave the city.

The parallel in the image of the keys as a way of assuming power is striking, especially to those who know the symbolism of the keys in the Roman Catholic Church. In the case of Dante, Sapegno[94] suggests that the source for this image was from an epistle by Nicola della Rocca, and referred specifically to Pier della Vigna: "tamquam imperii claviger, claudit, et nemo aperit; aperit, e nemo claudit"; and Sapegno points out " e questa, a sua volta, è variazione di un testo biblico, Isaia, XXII, 22" (and this, in its turn, is a variation on a biblical text, Isaiah XXII, 22):

> And the key of the house of David will I lay upon his shoulder; so he shall open, and none shall shut; and he shall shut and none shall open.

Although the account of Pier della Vigna is sympathetic, the image of the keys suggests a kind of devious and manipulative power which is not appealing in either case. But more striking than the verbal parallel is the parallel of context. In each case, power is given by a ruler to someone he holds in close confidence and trust. In each case, that person then assumes even greater power, Antonio to the extent of turning the people against the legitimate ruler, Prospero, and expelling him from the city. In the case of Pier della Vigna, his power engenders envy in the courtiers, who then have him imprisoned and tortured to the point where he must take his own life.

While the keys as a symbol of power could have been arrived at independently by both writers, what is more interesting is the parallel of context. It is not an exact parallel, in that in *Inferno* XIII, the person who now holds the keys is the one who suffers, whereas in *The Tempest*, the person who entrusted the keys[95] to another is the sufferer. But the common factors of the key symbolism, the willing transfer of power by a ruler, the too-willing acceptance of that power, and the resultant suffering again suggest more than coincidence. It seems that Erato Hills had indeed discovered a "borrowing" and certainly he did not deserve the reply which he received from F. J. Furnivall[96] in the November issue of *Notes and Queries* of the same year. On this particular parallel Furnivall wrote:

> That Shakespeare's musical key, by which Prospero set hearts to what tune he liked, can be Dante's key, by which Frederick's heart was unlocked, I cannot anyhow perceive. Surely Erato Hills doesn't unlock his drawer with his wife's harp or piano tuning key.[97]

But the "key" in the early part of Prospero's speech is a "key /Of officer and office" and at this point still a "key" in the same sense that Dante has used the word. Furnivall, like Toynbee and Saner, was very resistant to any suggestion of Shakespeare borrowing from Dante. Certainly he seems to have spent little time investigating the possibility of a "borrowing" in *The Tempest,* where there are a number of ideas which recall aspects of *Inferno* XIII.

The lines from *Inferno* XIII were spoken by the spirit of Pier della Vigna who, because he has taken his own life, is now a thorny tree in the wood of the suicides. The description of these trees recurs throughout the canto, so there is mention of gnarled and tangled branches, thorns, roots, leaves, twigs and trunks. Interestingly, in the lines immediately following the tale of Prospero's fall from power, is an image of a tree. He describes his brother thus:

> ... that now he was
> The ivy, which had hid my princely trunk,
> And suck'd the verdure out on't.[98]
>
> *The Tempest* I.2.85–7

Did Shakespeare, having used Dante's key symbol, recall the images of the Pier della Vigna and the wood of the suicides and see Prospero's brother (ivy) who "suck'd the verdure" from Prospero (princely trunk) as rather like the Harpies who fed on the bleeding trees in Canto XIII?

But this parallel does not end here. König[99] noted (although he did not note the previous parallel) a similarity between the punishment of Caliban and his two friends in *The Tempest* and the punishment of the two squanderers in *Inferno* XIII. He did not elaborate on this, but the parallel is a continuation of the images mentioned in the preceding paragraphs and is worth looking at in some detail.

Throughout *The Tempest* it seems that the images of *Inferno* XIII are present in Shakespeare's thoughts. Once he has recalled the trees in the wood of the suicides, they appear again in Prospero's account of the circumstances in which he acquired the services of Ariel. It seems that the mother of Caliban, the witch Sycorax, as a punishment for Ariel's disobedience (so Prospero reminds Ariel),

> ... did confine thee,
> By help of her more potent ministers,
> And in her most inimitable rage,
> Into a cloven pine.
>
> *The Tempest* I.2.274–8

Sycorax died, leaving Ariel "imprison'd" in the "cloven pine", where he remained a dozen years. There he languished, "vent[ing]" his groans". Fortunately, Prospero recounts:

> ... it was mine art
> When I arriv'd and heard thee, that made gape
> The pine, and let thee out.
>
> *The Tempest* I.2.291–3

Again we are reminded of Dante's wood of the suicides, where the souls of those who have taken their own lives or who have squandered their worldly goods, have become tree trunks. Feeding on these trees are the ghastly Harpies, and in *The Tempest*, Act III, Scene 2, after thunder and lightning, Ariel enters, "like a harpy; and claps his wings upon the table". His role in this guise is to punish the enemies of Prospero. When he vanishes, Prospero says:

> Bravely the figure of this harpy has thou
> Perform'd, my Ariel.
>
> *The Tempest* III.3.83–4

Certainly this "harpy" evokes none of the fear and loathing we feel for Dante's monstrous creatures:

> Ali hanno late, e colli e visi umani,
> piè con artigli, e pennuto il gran ventre;
> fanno lamenti in su li alberi strani.
>
> *Inferno* XIII.13–15

> [They have broad wings, and human necks and faces, feet with claws, and their great bellies are feathered; they make lament on the strange trees.]

The punishment for the "varlets" is again familiar. Ariel tells us:

> . . they my lowing followed through
> Tooth'd briers, sharp furzes, pricking goss and thorns,
> Which entered their frail shins.
>
> *The Tempest* IV.1.179–81

They too, like the suicides, are subjected to the *stecchi con tosco* (poisoned thorns) and *rami ... nodosi e 'nivolti* (gnarled and warped branches). At the end of Act IV, the stage direction tells us:

> A noise of hunters heard. Enter divers Spirits in shape of hounds, and hunt them about. Prospero and Ariel setting them on.

Prospero tells Ariel:

> Let them be hunted soundly: At this hour
> Lie at my mercy all mine enemies:
>
> *The Tempest* IV.1.264–5

The entire episode has all the essential factors from *Inferno* XIII, where Dante describes the fate of Lano da Siena, a famous squanderer:

> E poi che forse li fallia la lena,
> di sé e d'un cespuglio fece un groppo,
> Di retro a loro era la selva piena
> di nere cagne, bramose e correnti
> come veltri ch'uscisser di catena.
> In quel che s'appiattò miser li denti,
> e quel dilaceraro a brano a brano;
> poi sen portar quelle membra dolenti.
>
> *Inferno* XIII.122–9

[And perhaps because his breath was failing him, he made one knot of himself and of a bush. Behind him, the wood was full of black bitches, eager and fleet, like greyhounds loosed from the leash. On him who had squatted they set their teeth and tore him piecemeal, then carried off those woeful limbs.]

The combined factors of the spirit which can speak imprisoned in the tree, the Harpies, the thorny trees, the attacking hounds, not to mention the earlier images of the keys and the trees, are all essential features of *Inferno* XIII. They are not, however, all ideas exclusive to Dante. The spiky, bleeding plants with the talking souls imprisoned within and also the Harpies occur in *The Aeneid,* Book III, and this was certainly Dante's source.[100] There is also a story in Boccaccio's *Il Decamerone*[101] involving wild dogs hunting down and killing a young girl in the forest. When the young protagonist of the story tries to rescue her from the dogs and also from another young man pursuing her, the latter recounts how, because of her coldness to him in life, and because of his consequent suicide, their punishment is to eternally re-enact this chase until he kills her with the knife which he had used to take his own life, and feeds her heart to the dogs. As in Dante's story, and Shakespeare's, the pursuit by the vicious dogs is a punishment.

Shakespeare may well have had access to all these sources (*The Bible, The Aeneid, Il Decamerone*) but it is unlikely that he would have combined, by chance, exactly the same factors in his play *The Tempest* as Dante has used in his *Inferno* XIII. We must conclude that these parallels mentioned above, because of their number, are almost certainly evidence of "borrowing". The similar context for the image of the keys is not strikingly so, but it is there. Perhaps Shakespeare, in telling the story of Prospero's self-induced loss of power, has remembered Pier della Vigna and the image of the keys and turned to Dante to re-read the relevant canto. In it, he has found the thorny, talking trees with the spirits imprisoned inside them, the Harpies, and the vicious attacking hounds which punish those who deserve this fate—all grist to his mill.

It seems that something has recalled the terrifying images of *Inferno* XIII to Shakespeare's mind as he was writing *The Tempest,* and even though these parallels do not completely fulfil the requirements stipulated to justify a claim of a genuine "borrowing", they qualify (like the passages from *Cymbeline)* on the grounds that the *combination* of parallel factors makes any claim of coincidence unsound. The image of the keys contributes to the portrait of Prospero, while the other elements taken from *Inferno* XIII are more relevant to the creation of atmosphere and setting. They show the constant "borrowing" of elements from this one canto, and re-enforce the idea that Shakespeare was writing *The Tempest* with all the components of it in his mind.

IX

Richard II (1595)

Eating the bitter bread of banishment.

Richard II, Shakespeare

The parallels between the works of Dante and Shakespeare that we have considered to this point have been chosen for the following reasons. The idea expressed in each is very similar, perhaps in plot, in theme or in tone. More importantly, many of the parallel passages appear in a similar context. Sometimes too, there is even a similarity in vocabulary, despite their different languages. I have also selected passages which are long enough to demonstrate some or all of these requirements. Interestingly, they have all come from plays written between 1601 and 1609.

But there are other apparently similar passages from Shakespeare noted by a variety of writers, some of which are quite brief and so can perhaps be attributed to coincidence. Other apparently parallel passages are not so similar but have the same feel about them and may remind the reader of Dante. Most of these passages are from plays written earlier than those we have considered to this point

In *Henry VI*, Part III (1591) is a passage which is strongly reminiscent of the famous opening lines of *Inferno*. The play was also called *Richard, Duke of York,* and in the First Quarto (1595), it was titled *The True Tragedy*—though in this last-mentioned version, the passage we are about to consider had been omitted.[102] In Act III, Scene 2, Richard, Duke of Gloucester (later, Richard III) and son of the Duke of York, soliloquizes on his rather remote chance of inheriting the throne, and on the misfortune of his physical deformity. This speech gives us a number of insights into his character and it is a passage in this key speech which brings Dante to mind. Richard tells us, rather bitterly:

And I, – like one lost in a thorny wood,
That rents the thorns, and is rent with the thorns,
Seeking a way, and straying from the way;
Not knowing how to find the open air,
But toiling desperately to find it out,
Torment myself to catch the English crown.

Henry VI, Part III, III.2.174–9

The parallel with Dante is not strikingly close, but there are several common factors and a certain similarity of context. The opening lines of the *Divina Commedia* are well known and it may just be that Shakespeare had heard about them or perhaps had glanced at them fleetingly—or that the image is his own independent creation. Dante begins:

Nel mezzo del cammin di nostra vita
mi ritrovai per una selva oscura
che la diritta via era smarrita.
Ah quanto a dir qual era è cosa dura
esta selva selvaggia e aspra e forte
che nel pensier rinova la paura!
Tant'è amara che poco è più morte;

Inferno I.1–7

[Midway in the journey of our life, I found myself in a dark
wood, for the straight path was lost. Ah, how hard it is to tell
what that wood was, wild, rugged, harsh; the very thought of
it renews the fear! It is so bitter that death is hardly more so.]

Both passages, Shakespeare's simile and Dante's metaphor are, of course, a description of losing one's way in life and losing sight of the goal. Both are in the first person, and both characters are desperate to see a path ahead. In both cases the forest is almost impenetrable, "thorny" and blocking out "the open air" in the case of Richard, *oscura* (dark) and *selvaggia* (wild) in the case of Dante. In each case the speaker is afraid and tormented—Richard is "toiling desperately" and "rent with thorns". Dante (the Poet) finds *nel pensier rinova la paura* (the memory brings back the fear) and *tant'è amara che poco è più morte* (so bitter it is that death could hardly be worse).

The parallel is not compelling as evidence of Shakespeare's knowledge of Dante's work, but Shakespeare's image still recalls Dante's famous opening lines. It does not fulfil the criteria previously established for a "borrowing", but it is interesting that one of the earliest indications (1591) that Shakespeare may have known something of Dante, is a passage which reminds the reader of Dante's very first image in the opening lines of *Inferno*.

In *Richard III*, written about 1593, several writers have heard echoes of Dante. Clara Longworth de Chambrun[103] directed our attention to the famous account of Clarence's dream[104] in the play, which she believed was the first direct allusion to Dante's *Inferno* in Shakespeare:

> Oh then began the tempest of my soul!
> I passed methought, the melancholy flood
> With the grim ferryman that poets write of
> Into the kingdom of perpetual night.
>
> *Richard III* I.4.54–7

Dante had described Charon, the ferryman who took the lost souls across the Acheron to Inferno, thus:

> Ed ecco verso noi venir per nave
> un vecchio, bianco per antico pelo,
> gridando: "Guai a voi, anime prave!
>
> Non isperate mai veder lo cielo:
> i' vengo per menarvi all altra riva
> nelle tenebre etterne, in caldo e 'n gelo.
>
> *Inferno* III.83–7[105]

[There, steering toward us in an ancient ferry
came an old man with a white bush of hair,
bellowing: "Woe to you depraved souls! Bury

here and forever all hope of Paradise:
I come to lead you to the other shore,
into eternal dark, into fire and ice.]

Inferno III.79–84[106]

Certainly there are some common elements in the two passages. It is the same character, Charon, "the grim ferryman" who is taking the lost souls across the Acheron (the "melancholy flood") to Inferno. He is angry, condemnatory of his passengers, and refers to their destination as "perpetual night" or *tenebre eterne*. It seems that Shakespeare is writing with Dante's *Inferno* in mind. Dante's source for this scene was Virgil's *Aeneid* but Clara Longworth claimed that this did not refer only to the *Aeneid*, because Clarence speaks of "poets"[107] in the plural.

She was not the only one to be reminded of Dante in this passage. Frank Kermode[108] described Clarence's account of his dream as "his great scene—perhaps the first in Shakespeare to deserve that accolade." Kermode commented on the influence of Seneca on this scene and then remarked that the effect of the passage was "extraordinarily like Dante".[109] He quoted the lines following the previous passage:

The first that there did greet my stranger soul
Was my great father-in-law, renowned Warwick,
Who spake aloud, "What scourge for perjury
Can this dark monarchy afford false Clarence?"
And so he vanish'd. Then came wand'ring by
A shadow like an angel, with bright hair
Dabbled in blood; and he shriek'd out aloud,
"Clarence is come: false, fleeting, perjur'd Clarence,
That stabb'd me in the field by Tewksbury!"

Richard III I.4.48–56

Kermode continued:

> It is easy enough to see why this passage so impressed T. S. Eliot by "its use of infernal machinery." He claims that "the best of Seneca has here been absorbed into English," and contrasts the speech with one from Marlowe's *Dido* in order to demonstrate that it does something Marlowe could not do: "the phrase 'What a scourge for perjury ...' has a concision which is almost classical, certainly Dantesque." Steeped in Dante as he was, Eliot could not miss this echo. It is very unlikely that Shakespeare read Dante, and it is certain that he read Seneca, yet it is true that the passage sounds more like *Inferno* than Seneca.[110]

Shakespeare's brief sketches of Hell, this first in *Richard III,* are always reminiscent of Dante's *Inferno* and they appear with increasing frequency and detail in later plays.

An early play in which I believe Shakespeare seems to have used material from the *Divina Commedia* to develop a character is *Richard II* (1595) The image is perhaps one of the most moving and well known in the *Divina Commedia* and is to be found in *Paradiso* XVII. Here, Dante (the Pilgrim) meets his ancestor, Cacciaguida, who reveals to him the fact that he will be exiled from his beloved Florence. Since the fictive time of Dante's journey is 1300, and the time of writing is sometime later, then the prediction is, of course, true. Dante wrote his great work while actually in exile. Cacciaguida tells him:

> Tu proverai sì come sa di sale[111]
> lo pane altrui, e come è duro calle
> lo scendere e 'l salir per l'altrui scale.
>
> *Paradiso* XVII.58–60

[You shall come to know how salt is the taste of another's

bread, and how hard the path to descend and mount by
another man's stairs.]

The image captures all the misery of homesickness and the longing
for those things to which we have grown so comfortably and pleasantly
accustomed. At the same time it seems to recreate the uneasiness of the
guest who is perhaps aware that he has outstayed his welcome and who
returns reluctantly to the confines of his room, or departs awkwardly,
knowing that his hosts will savour his absence.

Tuscan bread is usually made without salt and it seems that the
explanation of this goes back to the 12th century when Pisa raised the tax
on salt to extort more money from Florence. The Florentines responded
by making their bread without salt—as they still do today. Dante in
exile, of course would probably be unpleasantly aware of this. Much more
complicated explanations of this are given in the footnote, where "salt" is
translated often as "bitter".

In *Richard II*, when Bolingbroke returns from exile, he lists his
grievances and the reasons why Bushy and Greene are to be executed. At
the end of this speech, he describes his exile when he

> ... sigh'd my English breath in foreign clouds,
>   Eating the bitter bread of banishment,
>
> *Richard II* III.1.20–1

The footnote in the Arden (2) edition tells us that the reference to "Eating
... bread is Biblical phraseology: Noble[112] cfs. 1 Kings, xxii, 27." The biblical
reference, as given by Noble, reads:

> feede him with bread of affliction and with water of trouble.[113]

The *OED*[114] gives as one meaning of "bitter" the phrase "full of affliction"
and points out that Shakespeare used the word "bitter" in this sense in
Titus Andronicus:

Nor can I utter all our bitter griefe,

Titus Andronicus V.3.89

There is therefore a parallel of idea in that both Shakespeare's "bitter bread", and the biblical phrase "bread of affliction" are perhaps metaphorical descriptions of the sufferings of Bolingbroke and Micaiah respectively.

The instruction in the biblical source is given by the king of Israel and refers to Micaiah who is about to be imprisoned. Prison does not equate to banishment in that the suffering involved is of a different type—deprivation rather than alienation. In the biblical quotation there is also the "water of trouble", and perhaps we can assume that this is a very strict prison diet of bread and water exclusively and it is part of the punishment. But a starvation diet is not Bolingbroke's complaint at all. The previous line, "sigh'd my English breath in foreign clouds" makes it clear that his concern was with being in a foreign country. The "bitter bread of banishment" is a complaint about exile—not about hunger. And while "bitter bread " may well equate to "bread of affliction" and both describe an experience of suffering, it is the association of the idea of unpalatable (or just different) bread with exile which makes the expression seem closer to Dante's image than to the biblical reference.

As in the previous parallels cited, the wider context and emotional response are also similar. Bolingbroke has been exiled unfairly. He was in a position of some privilege and authority:

Myself—a prince by fortune of my birth,
Near to the king in blood, and near in love,

Richard II III.1.16–17

and then was suddenly, apparently to avoid unnecessary bloodshed, banished for ten years "upon pain of life". Presumably out of sympathy for Gaunt, this sentence was commuted to six years. Bolingbroke is a self-proclaimed patriot:

Then, England's ground, farewell: sweet soil, adieu,

My mother and my nurse that bears me yet!

Where'er I wander boast of this I can,

Though banished, yet a true-born Englishman.

Richard II I.3.306–9

Dante too, in the Florence of 1300, had held a position of privilege and authority. He had been appointed as one of the city's seven priors and in retrospect, Dante himself saw that the decisions he made at this time were responsible for his later misfortunes. Florence was divided into Guelphs and Ghibellines, which then split further into factions, causing constant disruption in the city. While Dante was in Rome on a diplomatic mission, his enemies passed a decree of banishment against him, confiscated his possessions, and proclaimed that should he return he would be burned alive. Like Bolingbroke, he was passionate about his city state—Florence— and although he is scathing about many of the people and practices there, it is clear that he misses his home with all the intensity of a lover separated from his mistress. Unlike Bolingbroke, he died in exile in 1321.

Again, there are several parallel ideas. The "bitter bread"[115] reference in *Richard II* would remind any reader of Dante of the famous image in *Paradiso* XVII.[116] Both men are great patriots who suffer much in their absence from their beloved home. Both men are exiled by a ruler (or ruling power) threatened by the capability of the man they banish. If Shakespeare were searching for words to express the misery of exile, it would be astonishing if he re-created by chance part of Dante's haunting image. It is more likely that he recalled what he had already read and admired—and used it again.

Lorenzo Mascetta-Caracci[117] saw another parallel in *Richard II* with Dante on the subject of exile. In Act I, Scene 3, after Bolingbroke has been banished by Richard, Gaunt tries to make his son see banishment in a more positive light. Bolingbroke is not to be persuaded and argues that the mind does not have the power to deceive itself to this extent. Anticipating his exile, he cries:

O, no. The apprehension of the good
Gives but the greater feeling to the worse.

Richard II I.3.300–1

Mascetta-Caracci saw this as Shakespeare's translation of the sad complaint of Francesca da Rimini:

... "Nessun maggior dolore
che ricordarsi del tempo felice
nella miseria ..."

Inferno V.121–3

[There is no greater sorrow than to recall, in wretchedness, the happy time.][118]

The parallel is not verbally close, but the *sentiment* is very similar. Mascetta-Caracci commented that the phrase "the apprehension of the good" is *una formola dantesca* and quoted:

Ciascun confusamente *un bene apprende*
nel qual si quieta l'animo, e disira;

Purgatorio XVII.127–8

[Each one apprehends vaguely a good wherein the mind may find rest and this it desires.]

Mascetta-Caracci expanded this idea no further. Considered alone, the parallel is not convincing as evidence of Shakespeare's knowledge of Dante, and as Mary Augusta Scott pointed out, the idea is present in Chaucer, who may himself have found it in Dante:

For, of fortunes scharp adversite
The worste kynde of infortune is this,
A man to han ben in prosperite,

And it remembren, when it passed is.

Troilus and Criseyde lib.III.CCXXVI[119]

She also noted that the same idea appeared in an old play, *The Misfortunes of Arthur,* by Thomas Hughes, 1587:

> Of all misfortunes and unhappy fates
> Th'unhappiest seemes to have been happy once:[120]

Cary also commented on how often this passage from Dante has been imitated (Chaucer in *Troilus and Cressida,* Marino in *Adone,* Fortiguerra in *Ricciardetto* and Leigh Hunt in his *Story of Rimini*). He noted too that:

> The original, perhaps, was in Boetius *de Consol, Philosoph,* "In omni adversitate fortunae infelicissimum genus est infortunii fuisse felicem et non esse." 1. 2. pr. 4. Boetius and Cicero *de Amicitia,* were the two first books that engaged the attention of Dante, as he himself tells us in the *Convito,* p. 68.[121]

The notion seems to have been a common one, but perhaps considering the other parallels in *Richard II* on the loneliness of exile and the sadness of happiness remembered in a time of suffering, it may be that Dante's images were in Shakespeare's mind and that the famous lines of Francesca were recalled here.

There is another unusual image in *Richard II* which is concerned with political ethics. At the beginning of the final act, Richard is on his way to the Tower. The Queen awaits his passing in the street and is able to speak to him. She addresses him as:

> ... Thou most beauteous inn,
> Why should hard-favour'd grief be lodged in thee,
> When triumph is become an alehouse guest?

Richard II V.1.13–15

The notion of "grief" being lodged in a "beauteous inn" (Richard) is striking and Cary notes that Dante uses a very similar image in *Purgatorio* VI. Dante (the Pilgrim) has just encountered the spirit of Sordello, who, like Dante's guide, Virgil, is from Mantua. The two compatriots embrace, their common birthplace prompting a mutual affection. This causes Dante (the Poet) to think about patriotism and so begin his invective against Italy, torn by internal strife and lacking the firm hand of a strong ruler:

> Ahi, serva Italia, di dolore ostello,
>
> nave sanza nocchiere in gran tempesta,
>
> non donna di province, ma bordello!
>
> *Purgatorio* VI.76–8
>
> [Ah, servile Italy, hostel of grief, ship without pilot in great tempest, no mistress of provinces, but brothel!]

Here, the *ostello*, where grief lodges, is Italy—not the lady of the provinces, but of a *bordello* (brothel).

In both passages there is a strong contrast, a device always popular with Shakespeare. He (or the Queen) contrasts the "most beauteous inn" (Richard) with an "alehouse" (Bolingbroke). Dante contrasts his *donna di province* with the lady of a *bordello* But the parallel goes beyond the image of "grief" lodged at an "inn". In both passages the image is part of an address in the second person by an erstwhile loving admirer to a less-than-impressive-at-the-moment beloved: Isabel to her husband Richard, now deposed, and Dante to his beloved Italy, now in a state of constant internecine conflict. In both cases, the discussion which follows the image concerns conflict and internal disruption[122] where there should be harmony, and this is a result of ineffective or illegitimate rule. Shakespeare's Richard talks of how, when

> The mounting Bolingbroke ascends my throne,
>
> The time shall not be many hours of age

More than it is, ere foul sin gathering head
Shall break into corruption;

Richard II V.1.56–9

Dante asks

Cerca, misera, intorno da le prode
le tue marine, e poi ti guarda in seno,
s'alcuna parte in te di pace gode.

Purgatorio VI.85–7

[Search, wretched one, round the shores of your seas, and
then look within your bosom, if any part of you enjoy peace.]

The image of "grief" lodging at an inn is a strange one, and it is difficult to imagine that Shakespeare arrived at it independently, especially as the mode of address is identical to Dante's, the context is similar and both images successfully use contrast to gain their effect.

The Arden (2) edition of *Richard II* notes that parts of Act V of the play are much influenced by Daniel's *Civil Wars*,[123] and suggests that one such scene where this influence is evident is where we see the grief of Queen Isabel in the street watching as Richard passes on his way to the Tower. The stanza which corresponds to Shakespeare's dialogue for Isabel on this occasion reads:

O dost thou thus returne again to mee?
Are these the triumphs for thy victories?
Is this the glory thou doest bring with thee,
From that unhappy Irish enterprise?
O have I made so many vowes to see
Thy safe returne, and see thee in this wise?
Is this the lookt for comfort thou dost bring,
To come a captive that wentst out a king?[124]

She goes on then to swear her loyalty to Richard. While there is clearly some similarity between Daniel's version and Shakespeare's in the question form of Isabel's remarks and the contrast between Richard's earlier state and his present condition, the image concerning grief lodging in the "beauteous inn" is not there and not suggested. It is clearly Shakespeare's contribution to the scene, and it is so unusual that one cannot but feel that the image in Dante has impressed itself on Shakespeare's mind, and he has used it here to good effect.

X

A Midsummer Night's Dream (1595)

> *Tomorrow night, when Phoebe doth behold*
> *Her silver visage in the wat'ry glass,*
> *Decking with liquid pearl the bladed grass*
> *(A time that lovers' flights doth still conceal),*
> *Through Athens' gates have we devised to steal.*
>
> *A Midsummer Night's Dream*, Shakespeare

In strong contrast to the atmospheres established in *King Lear* and *Macbeth*, is the mysterious, magical setting of *A Midsummer Night's Dream* (c.1595). In this play, written about ten years before the tragedies previously considered, there also seems to be a number of parallels with Dante. Here, the moon presides over almost all the action and for this reason, the mind goes to Dante's *Paradiso* II and III—the Paradise of the Moon. So many images and ideas occur in these two cantos which are also evident in Shakespeare's play that it is difficult to imagine that this parallelism is mere coincidence. A very similar atmosphere pervades both works. The image of the moon is linked with the ideas of inconstancy, vows and chastity, all set in a pale white, watery transparency which gives to both works the sense of a mysterious, dreamlike, insubstantial existence lived by those under its beams.

The Arden (2) edition claimed that "any comprehensive source for *A Midsummer Night's Dream* is altogether unlikely".[125] It also quoted from A. H. Humphreys (ed. *Henry IV,* Part I, p. xxi) that literary sources "are, rightly speaking, the whole relevant contents of the writer's mind as he composes, and no account of them can be complete".[126] The reader of Dante may feel that *Paradiso* II and III were part of "the relevant contents of the writer's mind" as Shakespeare composed this play and were perhaps one of the sources not yet identified.

In *Paradiso* II and III Dante begins his journey with Beatrice through the many spheres of the heavens. At the speed of an arrow, the two fly to the first sphere, the moon, and pass into its substance like light into water. In Dante's description of the speed of his interplanetary flight, the image of archery is unusual—interestingly an example of *ysteron-proteron*[127] to describe the incredible speed with which he arrived:

> Beatrice in suso, e io in lei guardava;
> e forse in tanto in quanto un quadrel posa
> e vola e da la noce si dischiava,
> giunto mi vidi ove mirabil cosa
> mi torse il viso a sé;
>
>

Paradiso II.22–6

> [Beatrice was gazing upward, and I on her: perhaps in that time that a bolt strikes, flies, and from the catch is released, I saw myself arrived where a wondrous thing drew my sight to it.]

Reversing the steps of the flight of an arrow seems to hold our attention while we try to absorb the concept and to imagine the speed.

Shakespeare too uses the images of archery. In the opening scene Theseus is reminding Hippolyta that only four days remain before their wedding. He feels that the old moon is loitering. Hippolyta replies:

Four days will quickly steep themselves in night
Four nights will quickly dream away the time;
And then the moon, like to a silver bow
New bent in heaven, shall behold the night
Of our solemnities.

A Midsummer Night's Dream I.1.7–11

The moon, central to the theme, is presented in the opening lines:

Now, fair Hippolyta, our nuptial hour
Draws apace; four happy days bring in
Another moon: but O methinks, how slow
This old moon wanes!

A Midsummer Night's Dream I.1.1–4

Later in the play, Oberon uses the image of archery again; reminiscing to Puck, he recounts how he had seen Cupid in action:

That very time I saw (but thou couldst not)
Flying between the cold moon and the earth,
Cupid all arm'd: a certain aim he took
At a fair vestal, throned by the west,
And loos'd his love shaft smartly from his bow
As it should pierce a hundred thousand hearts.

A Midsummer Night's Dream II.1.155–60

In each case the action of shooting an arrow is described in terms of the different elements of the act—the bent bow, the released shaft, the flight and the strike. Shakespeare's description though presents these in the right order—while Dante's is reversed.

In the same canto (*Paradiso* II) as Dante uses the arrow image, he also asks Beatrice about the cause of the spots on the moon and wonders why people accept the popular medieval notion of Cain and the thornbush.

"Ma ditemei: che son li segni bui
di questo corpo, che la giuso in terra
fan di Can favoleggiare altrui"

Paradiso II.41–3

[But tell me what dark traces in the grain
of this bright body show themselves below
and cause men to tell fables about Cain?]

This is a reference to the tale that Cain, for his sin, had been imprisoned on the moon and condemned to carry a thornbush (under which he had tried to conceal the body of the brother he had murdered) for all eternity. Beatrice rejects this and gives her own explanation of the moonspots. She suggests an experiment with mirrors by which her own interpretation can be verified.

Shakespeare, too, refers to the fable of Cain in the part of the plot which concerns the artisans and their play. Quince, in his casting role, explains how the actor playing the role must appear:

Ay; or else one must come in with a bush of thorns and a lantern, and say he comes to disfigure or to present the person of Moonshine.

A Midsummer Night's Dream III.1.55.ff

Later, in the actual performance of their play, the Prologue explains:

This man, with lantern, dog, and bush of thorns,
Presenteth Moonshine.

A Midsummer Night's Dream V.1.134–5

There is no footnote in the Arden (2) edition to explain this allusion. The *New Variorum Edition* of the play, in a later similar reference (Act V, Scene 1, 255) seems to be quite unaware of its meaning:

As an illustration of the text the voluminous mass of folk-lore which has gathered around this "man" seems no more appropriate here than in Caliban's allusion to him in *The Tempest*. The zealous student is referred to the two or three folio pages in Halliwell *ad loc.* or to Grimm's *Deutsche Mythologie* there cited. From tender years every English-speaking child knows that there is a man in the moon, and is familiar with his premature descent and with his mysterious desire to visit the town of Norwich. Which is all we need to know of him here. Ed.[128]

Longfellow, in his translation of the *Divina Commedia* comments on Dante's first reference to Cain ("Caino e le spine") in *Inferno* XX.126:

The Man in the Moon is Cain with his Thorns. This belief seems to have been current too in England, *A Midsummer Night's Dream*, III, 1.

Longfellow's comment, however, gives no evidence that the belief was current in England other than in the quotation from Shakespeare's play. It may have been common knowledge[129] or Shakespeare may also have found it in one of the many other English or Italian books he read—or he may have even seen it in Dante.

In Canto III, Dante is about to respond to Beatrice's theory when he sees the vague outlines of several figures which he believes at first to be reflections in water. They are, however, actual spirits who have been sent to this sphere for the fault of inconstancy. They have broken holy vows. One of these spirits speaks to Dante, explaining that she was a nun in life, Piccarda Donati, a woman he had known (and who has been discussed in Chapter 2, III), and sister to his friend Forese Donati (also discussed in Chapter 2, II). She is in the lowest level of Paradise, but she is content with this as *'n la sua volontade è nostra pace* (in his will is our peace) (*Paradiso* III.85). She goes on to tell Dante how she had joined the Order of Saint

Clare,[130] but had been forced to break her vow of chastity by *Uomini poi, a mal più ch'a bene usi* (*Paradiso* III.106). She then introduces the figure next to her as the Empress Constance, who had also been a nun but had been forced to marry for political reasons. Piccarda finishes her story, begins to sing the Ave Maria, and,

> … cantando e cantando vanio
> come per acqua cupa cosa grave.
>
> *Paradiso* III.122–3

> [singing, and singing vanished, as through deep water some heavy thing.]

In *A Midsummer Night's Dream*, when Hermia asks what will be her fate if she refuses to marry Demetrius, Theseus tells her to consider whether:

> You can endure the livery of a nun,
> For aye to be in shady cloister mew'd,
> To live a barren sister all your life,
> Chanting fair hymns to the cold fruitless moon.
>
> *A Midsummer Night's Dream* I.1.70–3

Theseus leaves no doubt as to which course of action he recommends. Apart from the choice of words such as "endure", "mew'd" and "barren," he adds that a married life is comparable to "the rose distill'd", a single life to a rose which "withering on the virgin thorn,/Grows, lives, and dies, in single blessedness". Was Shakespeare thinking of the nuns in Canto III in the sphere of the Moon, Piccarda Donati and the Empress Constance? Hermia's choice is the same as that faced by these women—to live her life in the cloister, or to marry the man chosen for her by a powerful man of her family. Her third option is death, which was also presumably an option for the nuns in Dante's canto.

These women, Piccarda and the Empress Constance have broken their vows and so are inconstant. And these notions of broken vows and inconstancy are one of the themes of *A Midsummer Night's Dream*. Caroline Spurgeon claims that the moon "serves, as does the sun, for an emblem of steadfast constancy",[131] but it difficult to see on what evidence she bases this claim. The moon waxes and wanes, it is described by Shakespeare in this play as "wandering" and "watery", is the "governess of floods" and "controls not only the weather, but also the fiery shafts of love which at will she quenches in her 'chaste beams'".[132] The weather, floods and love are all notoriously unpredictable and erratic and so it is difficult to associate the controller of these with the idea of constancy. Juliet's comment seems rather more credible, when she says:

> O swear not by the moon, th'inconstant moon
> That monthly changes in her circles orb,
> Lest that thy love prove likewise variable.
>
> *Romeo and Juliet* II.2.109–11

and in fact the Shakespeare Lexicon gives a number of Shakespearean references where the moon is an image of change and inconstancy.[133]

The relationships in the play are almost all inconstant, as couples pair, separate, and re-pair, under the influence of enchantments and the moon. There is much talk of broken vows: Hermia swears "by all the vows that ever men have broke", Helena tells how Demetrius[134] "Hail'd down oaths that he was only mine". Puck observes that "fate o'er-rules, that one man holding troth/a million fail, confounding oath on oath." Lysander tells Helena "Look when I vow, I weep: and vows so born/In their nativity all truth appears." Helena responds:

> These vows are Hermia's: will you give her o'er?
> Weigh oath with oath, and you will nothing weigh:
> Your vows to her and me, put in two scales
> Will ever weigh; and both as light as tales.
>
> *A Midsummer Night's Dream* III.2.130–4

Vows, usually broken, permeate the play.

A very similar association of ideas occurs in an earlier comedy, *Love's Labour's Lost*. The four young men have vowed in the first scene of the play to devote themselves to the pleasures of the mind, and abstain from more worldly pursuits for a period of three years. This vow becomes difficult to keep when four young ladies arrive on the scene. By Act IV, Scene 3, there is some discussion of "betrayal" in the sense that the young men are, one by one, breaking their vow of abstinence. When the King asks Berowne

> Are we betray'd thus to thy overview?

Berowne answers:

> Not you by me, but I betray'd to you:
> I, that am honest; I, that hold it sin
> To break a vow I am engaged in;
> I am betray'd by keeping company
> With moon-like men, men of inconstancy.
>
> *Love's Labour's Lost* IV.3.72–7

Again there is the association of breaking vows, inconstancy and the moon. The footnote in the Arden edition comments on line 77, which it considers to be corrupt, and adds the fact that "the moon is a standard symbol of inconstancy in Shakespeare".[135] Something of the atmosphere of *Paradiso* II and III can be felt here too. Earlier in the scene there is the reference to the moon when the King reads the sonnet:

> Nor shines the silver moon one half so bright
> Through the transparent bosom of the deep
>
> *Love's Labour's Lost* IV.3.28–9

It is mentioned again by the King in line 226: "My love, her mistress, is a gracious moon." Vows, both heavenly and earthly, are considered by

Longaville in the sonnet he reads (IV.3.57–70) and "paradise" is named twice in the scene. Although one cannot find a close parallel, one is left with the impression again that Dante's *Paradiso* II and III were in Shakespeare's mind.

Although these cantos of Dante's *Paradiso* were not necessarily a source for the atmosphere Shakespeare creates in *A Midsummer Night's Dream*, the fact remains that the main ideas are present in both works. Of course it is not surprising that both writers should connect the idea of chastity with the moon, since Diana was the goddess of both, and it is also likely that both poets would associate the idea of a nun with the idea of chastity, since both lived in the Christian tradition, although Shakespeare's example of a nun's life as an alternative for Hermia is anachronistic, since she lives in Ancient Greece. Less likely is that both poets would have independently associated the moon with inconstancy and with broken vows.

But what actually gives Shakespeare's play the same *feel* as Dante's cantos on the moon, are the frequent images of water and the constant reference to the pale colours of this sphere. Shakespeare's scenes are dominated by the moon and the images are filled with words relating to water, liquids, coldness, pale colours and pale coloured jewels. The moon is "watery", its beams "chaste". It is "like to a silver bow", or like a "watery eye." It is "cold"; it is "fruitless". Demetrius' oaths of love for Helena were "hail", and "when this hail some heat from Hermia felt/so he dissolved and show'rs of oaths did melt" (I.2.244–5). When he turns from Hermia he describes "my love to Hermia /Melted as the snow (IV.1.164).

Lysander describes (I.1.209–11) how:

> Tomorrow night, when Phoebe doth behold
> Her silver visage in the wat'ry glass
> Decking with liquid pearl the bladed grass

he and Hermia will steal away. A number of elements in this beautiful image bring to mind Dante's description in *Paradiso* III.10–15:

Quali per vetri trasparenti e tersi
o ver per acque nitide e tranquille,
non si profonde che i fondi sien persi
tornan d'i nostril le postille
debili si, che perla a le nostre pupille,

Paradiso III.10–14

[As in clear glass when it is polished bright
or in a still and limpid pool whose waters
are not so deep that the bottom is lost from sight,
a footnote of our lineaments will show,
so pallid that our pupils could as soon
make out a pearl on a milk-white brow][136]

Both descriptions are of reflections—or at least appear to be so. Shakespeare's moon goddess, Phoebe, sees her image reflected in the water. Dante sees the spirits of the inconstant as though they were reflections in polished glass or limpid water. Both images use the common ideas of water, glass, and pearl. Both images create the sense of tranquillity and cold beauty. And in both, of course, is the omnipresent moon.

Dante's spirits disappear *cantando vanio /come per acqua cupa cosa grave (Paradiso* III.122–3)—they sink away like something heavy in deep water. The process of turning into liquid seems to interest both poets, Shakespeare with his image of Demetrius' love for Hermia, and Dante with the dematerialisation of his spirits.

Later in the play, a phrase "from heaven to earth, from earth to heaven" in Theseus's long speech at the beginning of Act V, Scene 1 again suggests Dante's rapid flight. But the whole speech is worth considering for the ideas suggested in it. Hippolyta has commented on the strangeness of the play they have seen, *Pyramis and Thisbe,* and Theseus replies that he cannot believe "These antique fables, nor these fairy toys." He elaborates on the idea:

The lunatic, the lover, and the poet.

Are of imagination all compact:

One sees more devils than vast hell can hold;

That is the madman: the lover, all frantic,

Sees Helen's beauty in a brow of Egypt;

The poet's eye, in a fine frenzy rolling,

Doth glance from heaven to earth, from earth to heaven;

The forms of things unknown, the poet's pen

Turns them to shapes, and gives to airy nothing

A local habitation and a name.

Such tricks has strong imagination,

That if it would but apprehend such joy,

It comprehends some bringer of that joy:

A Midsummer Night's Dream IV.1.6–20

On this speech, Harold Bloom commented that there were two voices, one of the "highly unimaginative" Theseus, and the other "perhaps is Shakespeare's own, half distancing himself from his own art, though declining also to yield completely to the patronizing Theseus."[137]

It could be explained in another way. Let us assume for a moment that Shakespeare *had* been reading Dante's *Divina Commedia* and was thinking of Dante as a poet, perhaps even also as a "lunatic" and a "lover". Certainly, Dante saw "more devils than vast hell could hold", though he does seem to accommodate them rather well in his *Inferno*. If we take the reference to "Helen's beauty" and the "brow of Egypt" to mean that the lover sees ultimate beauty in the girl he loves, be she ever so humble (the footnote in the Arden *Dream* interprets the "brow of Egypt" as "a gypsy's"),[138] then Shakespeare could be commenting on Dante's constant insistence throughout *Paradiso* on the ever-increasing beauty of Beatrice, which, by the end of Canto III, was blinding:

La vista mia, che tanto lei seguio

quanto possibil fu, poi che la perse,

volsesi al segno di maggior disio,

e a Beatrice tutta si converse;

ma quella folgorò nel mio sguardo

sì che da prima il viso non sofferse;

e ciò mi fece a dimandar più tardo.

Paradiso III.124–30

[My sight, which followed her so far as was possible, after it lost her, turned to the mark of greater desire and wholly reverted to Beatrice; but she so flashed upon my gaze that at first my sight endured it not; and this made me the slower with my questioning.]

Certainly, it is true to claim of Dante in these two cantos that:

The poet's eye, in a fine frenzy rolling,

Doth glance from heaven to earth, from earth to heaven;

And as imagination bodies forth

The forms of things unknown, the poet's pen

Turns them to shapes, and gives to airy nothing

A local habitation and a name.[139]

A Midsummer Night's Dream V.1.13–17

The Arden footnote on the phrase "bodies forth" explains that this means "embodies in forms which the mind's eye, ear, etc can take in; find (in T. S. Eliot's phrase) an 'objective correlative' for".[140] T. S. Eliot may have invented the term, but long before him Dante used the device with astounding effect in the *Divina Commedia,* particularly in *Inferno,* where every circle had a physical geography and climate to illustrate the particular sin for which the spirits there were being punished. In *Paradiso* too, the device is used, and is apparent in Cantos II and III, where the inconstant exist in a place devoid of clear definition or substance—representative perhaps of their inability to remain steadfast. The last four lines quoted apply exactly to what Dante has achieved in these cantos.

While none of the parallels or similarities considered here is, in itself, evidence that Shakespeare had read Dante and was using his ideas, the fact remains that in some of the plays, settings and atmospheres in the *Divina Commedia* are often recalled. Bradley, in his Lectures on *King Lear* is constantly reminded of the gloom, chaos and howling winds of *Inferno*. *Macbeth* recreates the same world of darkness and fear which characterises Dante's vision of Hell, and which is, in essence, Shakespeare's own vision of Hell. Almost in direct contrast is the pale, moonlit and silvery world of *A Midsummer Night's Dream,* where so many of the settings and images seem to recall Dante's *Paradiso* II and III and where Dante, like Shakespeare, deals with the themes of inconstancy and broken vows. The parallel lies in the collocation of ideas which suggests a connection between the two writers, similar to the link between Dante's *Inferno* XIII and *The Tempest*.

The similarities are numerous, and it is the cumulative effect of these parallels which gives strength to the argument. If we were to draw conclusions from this chapter alone, the result would probably be that the likenesses were a matter of coincidence. But adding these parallels to the other more specific examples in the preceding chapters, they may serve to tip the scales of belief. If Shakespeare *had* read Dante's work, it would be surprising if he did not find Dante's different worlds very useful as settings for his plays.

CHAPTER 3

Eliminating the Impossible

Read the greate poet of Itale,
That Dante hight, for he can devise
From point to point, not a word will he faile.
The Monk's Tale, Chaucer

In the preceding chapter, a number of parallels between the works of Dante and Shakespeare have been considered. These have been noted by various writers—English, American, Italian, French and German—as well as by the present (Australian) writer. Not all of these claim or even suggest that a parallel is evidence of Shakespeare's knowledge of Dante's work; indeed, some are anxious to insist that this could not possibly be the case. If they have noted only one or two parallels, they are careful to comment that these similarities may be attributed to coincidence. This is certainly true and it is possible to believe that many of the parallels noted, taken in isolation, may be attributable to coincidence.

But it is unlikely however that the parallels considered here where there is a similarity of vocabulary, idea and context could all be explained as coincidence. With such a degree of similarity, we would, by modern standards, be thinking in terms of conscious plagiarism. The fact that Shakespeare has written even a few passages in which the language, idea, and context are so very similar to passages from Dante, would certainly seem to suggest that the playwright had some considerable and quite detailed knowledge of Dante's work.

If this is so there are a number of inferences to be made. The first of these is that Shakespeare must have gained his knowledge of Dante either indirectly from the writing or the conversation of someone who was familiar with the Italian's work, or directly through reading the *Divina Commedia* himself. It will therefore be necessary to look at the work of anyone writing in English in Shakespeare's time or before, who demonstrated some extensive knowledge of Dante, and whose work could have provided Shakespeare with his knowledge of the *Divina Commedia*. We cannot know what Shakespeare may have learned in conversation, but it is difficult to accept that the detailed knowledge revealed even in these few "borrowings" could all have been remembered so accurately from an oral source.

If we cannot find the apparently Dantean ideas used by Shakespeare in other writing accessible to him, we must conclude that Shakespeare *himself* had read the *Divina Commedia*—or at least, parts of it.

The whole of the *Divina Commedia* was not translated into English until 1802, by Henry Boyd. Some parts of it had been translated earlier— for example William Hayley translated three cantos of *Inferno* in 1782— but even this was some 166 years after Shakespeare's death and, in any case, Shakespeare's apparent "borrowings" of material from the *Divina Commedia* are drawn from all three *cantiche* of the work, not solely from *Inferno*. Shakespeare, if he read Dante's masterpiece, must therefore have read it in the original Italian. He must also have read it with considerable care and often enough to be able to find the appropriate image or idea he required in each of the cases where it seems he has made a "borrowing". If he did read Dante in Italian, this would not be the only book he had read in this language and used as a source, as is demonstrated later in Chapter 4.

From this follows the idea that there must have been at least one copy of the *Divina Commedia* readily available to him in the period in which he wrote the plays where we find "borrowings". Either he had a copy in his possession, or he had easy access to a private library, probably belonging to an aristocrat, where he was able, over a period of about fifteen years, to come and go as he wished.

There were at the time many Italianate Englishmen. Many aristocrats had travelled to Italy and had some grasp of the language. Some had an Italian influence in their family background. Queen Elizabeth herself could read and write Italian. Many writers studied Italian as they knew this would give them a greater choice of source material for their writing. Let us consider those writers who may have known enough of Dante's work to provide Shakespeare with the knowledge he appears to have.

The greatest English writer to demonstrate a familiarity with Dante's work was Chaucer, who had travelled to Italy in 1372–73 and 1378–79. Paget Toynbee, in his introduction to his survey of Dante in English literature, believes that when Chaucer was travelling in Italy in 1378–79 he may well have acquired a copy of the *Divina Commedia*, and this may have been the first copy to reach England.[1] This is only speculation, but Toynbee gives a list of twenty-two different passages[2] from the *Divina Commedia* translated and used by Chaucer in his writing between 1380 and 1386. They are so numerous that it would be absurd to imagine that Chaucer was working purely from memory and without a copy beside him. (Cary comments on some twenty-four passages from Dante which he finds similar to passages from Chaucer. However, only eleven of these references occur in both lists and Cary is not discussing "translations").

Below is Toynbee's chronological list of English translations from Dante by Chaucer.

1380–82

Inf. II.127–9	in *Troilus and Cressida* II.967–9
Par. XXXIII.13–15	in *Troilus and Cressida* III.1261–3
Inf. III.112–14	in *Troilus and Cressida* IV.225–7
Par. XIV.28–30	in *Troilus and Cressida* V.1863–5

1382

Inf. II.1–3	in *Parlement of Foules* ll.85–6
Inf. III.19–20	in *Parlement of Foules* ll.169–70
Purg. XXVIII.14, 16–18	in *Parlement of Foules* ll.201–3

1384

Inf. II.7–9	in *House of Fame* II.15–18
Par. I.19, 22–26	in *House of Fame* III.19, 11–13, 15–17

1385–86

Inf. XIII.64–6	in *Legend of Good Women*, Prol., ll. 358–9
Inf. V.100	in *Legend of Good Women*, Prol., l. 503
Purg. XXI.31–2	in *Legend of Dido* l.181
Inf. VII.64	in *Legend of Ypermystra* l.77

1386–88

Purg. I.19–20	in *Knight's Tale* ll.635–6
Inf. V.100	in *Knight's Tale* l.903
Inf. XIII.40–4	in *Knght's Tale* ll.1479–82
Inf. V. 100	in *Man of Law's Tale* l. 600
Par. XXXIII. 16–21	in *Prioress's Tale*, Prol, ll. 22–6
Inf. XXXIII. 43–75	in *Monk's Tale* ll. 433–65
Inf. V. 56	in *Monk's Tale* l. 487
Purg. VII. 121–3	in *Wife of Bath's Tale* ll. 272–4
Inf. V. 100	in *Merchant's Tale* ll. 742
Inf. V. 100	in *Squire's Tale* l. 479
Par. XXXIII. 1–12, 16–21	in *Second Nun's Tale*, Prol., ll.36–44, 50

The above list, however, is a list of "translations" from Dante by Chaucer and therefore it does not include several passages in Chaucer which, although strongly reminiscent of Dante, could not be called "translations". One such passage cited in Toynbee's *Dante in English Literature*,[3] and also noted by Cary,[4] is Chaucer's description of the eagle in *The House of Fame* (ii, 21–31, 33–40, 76, 79–84).[5] This description has many features in common with Dante's dream in *Purgatorio* IX, and also with Shakespeare's eagle dream in *Cymbeline*. In Chaucer's version, there are the "fethres as of gold", "dint of thonder" and "grim pawes strong" which carry Chaucer "as lightly as I were a larke". There is also the reference to Ganymede in both versions, though not in Shakespeare's. The eagle explains to Chaucer that he dwells with Jupiter and does "al his comaundement". It is very close to Dante's version, and it is possible that Shakespeare may have "borrowed" from this for his eagle with Jupiter sitting upon its back.

Shakespeare's version, of course, was written for stage production and the "uplifting" in it is perhaps metaphorical rather than literal, although by the time *Cymbeline* was written, some very sophisticated stage machinery was available.[6] Shakespeare would have certainly read of the eagle in Chaucer, but the association of the dream with the definition of the nature of repentance suggests that Shakespeare had also read it in Dante. For Shakespeare there are often several sources for the same idea and it is not possible to establish with certainty which source is used here. The other passages cited by Toynbee as evidence of Chaucer's borrowing from Dante clearly are not the source of any other passages from Shakespeare which appear to have parallels in Dante.

Ann Thompson, in her study of the influence of Chaucer on Shakespeare, claimed that Shakespeare knew Chaucer's work unusually well and was influenced by it in different ways.[7] In *Measure for Measure*, it is interesting that she saw the influence of Chaucer in precisely the same passage where the influence of Dante has already been considered in Chapter 2, III. It is the passage where Claudio, facing death, imagines the world to which, as a sinner, he will be going,

> ... imprisoned in the viewless winds
> And blown with restless violence round about
> The pendent world.
>
> *Measure for Measure* III.1.125–7

She believed that this may have been inspired by Chaucer's:

> And breakers of the law, soth to saine
> And likerous folke, after that they ben dede,
> Shull whirle about the worlde, always in paine.
>
> *Parlement of Foules* 78–80

If Chaucer's image is the source, it is clear that Shakespeare has embellished this to form his own more detailed image. The ideas of "whirle" and "always in paine" are enlarged by describing the "viewless winds" and the "restless violence" and even adding the adjective "pendent" to Chaucer's "world" to create the sense of a world suspended in space. Shakespeare is perfectly capable of taking an image and making it his own, but is there not a closer affinity here with Dante's original?

> La bufera infernal, che mai non resta,
> mena li spirti con la sua rapina:
> voltando e percotendo li molesta.
>
> *Inferno* V.31–3
>
> [The hellish hurricane, never resting, sweeps along the spirits
> with its rapine; whirling and smiting, it torments them.]

The *mai non resta* equates exactly with "restless". The *voltando e percotendo* equates with "blown with ... violence round about". The notion of suffering contained in the words *rapina* and *molesta* is suggested throughout the three lines. And Shakespeare's image has almost the energy and force of Dante's, which Chaucer's—condensed as it is into one line—has not.

But the passage from Dante (*Inferno* V.31–3) is *not* one of those which Toynbee (or Cary) claimed had been used by Chaucer, though it certainly appears to be in this category. Even assuming that it was a source for Chaucer, it may be that Shakespeare, in embellishing it, by chance returned to an image very close to Dante's original. Or it may be that Shakespeare was himself inspired by the original.

Ann Thompson also claimed that there is evidence that Shakespeare used ideas from Chaucer's *Monk's Tale* in both *King Lear* and *Antony and Cleopatra*. Toynbee told us that Chaucer had used Dante's *Inferno* XXXIII, 43–75 in his *Monk's Tale*. These lines are part of the story of Ugolino, which Chaucer adapted to his own purposes. But Chaucer, at the end of the *Monk's Tale*, invites his readers to go to the original:

Whoso will hear it in longer wise,

Reade the greate poet of Itale,

That Dante hight, for he can devise

From point to point, not a word will he fail.

The Monk's Tale[8]

Since Shakespeare had read the *Monk's Tale,* then he must have read these lines. We can conclude from this that he certainly *knew of* Dante and may have taken Chaucer's advice.

If we assume that Shakespeare had read all of Chaucer's work and could therefore have read any of the references to Dante which Toynbee lists above, then we might expect to find among them some of the ideas which we have already found in Shakespeare's plays and which seem to be inspired by Dante.

In fact, the only "translation" from Dante by Chaucer listed by Toynbee, also occurring in Shakespeare, is the reference in *Cymbeline* to the eagle in Dante's *Purgatorio* IX. We must conclude then that Shakespeare's knowledge of Dante has not come from Chaucer.

Edmund Spenser (1552–96), had an excellent knowledge of Italian literature but he does not mention Dante by name. There are aspects of *The Faerie Queene* which are strongly reminiscent of Dante, for example the way in which Spenser is able to group together all kinds of diverse elements from his reading into one heterogeneous whole, and the habit of beginning a stanza with a simile so lengthy and detailed that the reader almost forgets the original subject. More specifically, Toynbee tells us:

> Judging from internal evidence, not a few critics and commentators ... maintain that in *The Faerie Queene* (1590–96), Spenser displays an intimate acquaintance with the *Divina Commedia*, and they quote numerous parallel passages from the two poems in support of this contention.[9]

Below is the list of parallel passages in *The Faerie Queene* and the *Divina Commedia*, collected by Upton, Todd, and others.

Book I: c.i 7, ll 2 ff. (*Inf.* I.1–3); c. i. 13, ll. 6–7 (*Inf.* XVII.1–2); c. i. 15, ll. 1–5 (*Inf.* XVII.25–7); c. i. 17, l.6 (*Inf.* XVII.14–15); c. i. 21, l. 5 (*Inf.* XXXIV.45); c. ii. 30, ll. 8 ff (*Inf.* XIII.28ff.) c. ii. 41, ll. 1 ff. (*Inf.* XVII.19ff.); c. iv. 16, l. 3 (*Inf.* XXVI.42); c. v. 33, l. 7 (*Inf.* V.16); c. viii. 31, ll. 1 ff. (*Inf.* XX.10–15); c. xi. 10, l. 1 ff. (*Inf.* XXXIV.46–50); c. xi. 34, l. 9 (*Purg.* XXXIII.143–4); c. xii. 4, l.9 (*Inf.* III.8).

Book II: c. iii. 40, ll. 1 ff. (*Inf.* XXIV.47–51); c. vi. 46, l. 6 (*Inf.* VIII.31); c.vii. 65, ll. 1. ff (*Purg.* XIX.118ff.); c. viii. 35, l.7 (*Purg.* V.14).

Book III: c. ii. 23, ll. 1–2 (*Inf.* V.100); c. iv. 3, l. 8 (*Par.* I.12); c. xi. 54, ll.1 ff. (*Inf.* III.1–9).

Book IV: c. i. 20, ll. 4 ff. (*Inf.* I.1ff.); c. i. 42, ll. 1 ff. (*Inf.* VII.22–3); c. iii. 46, ll. 2–3 (*Inf.* IX.89–90); c. xii. 34, ll. 6 ff. (*Inf.* II.127–9).

Book VI: c. vii. 42, ll. 1–2 (*Inf.* III.109); c. x. (*Purg.* XXX).

The references cited here from *Inferno* fall into several categories. Many of them are to particularly alarming monsters or characters from *Inferno*, such as Geryon, Caròn, Minos, Filippo Argenti in the mud, Lucifer and his wings, Lucifer's yellowish face, the soothsayers with their heads turned round, the voices within the flames, the *messo* with the wand, and the bleeding branches. Another type of reference is to well-known passages, such as the opening image of the *selva oscura*, the lines above the entrance to Inferno, ending, *Lasciate ogni speranza, voi ch'entrate*, the opening line of Francesca, *Amor, ch'a nullo amato amar perdona*, and the passage where Virgil scolds Dante to move more quickly up the cliff in Canto XXIV. Apart from this, there is an image in which Dante likens his wilting spirits to *fioretti* which wilt but then are renewed in the new day. There are four references only to *Purgatorio*. One is to Adriano V, face down in the dirt.

Two are to images, one of renewal, *come piante novelle/ rinovellate di novella fronda*, and one of firmness, *sta come torre ferma*.[10] The last reference is not specific, just to *Purgatorio* XXX, where Virgil disappears and Beatrice appears in the Earthly Paradise. There is only one reference to *Paradiso*, from Canto I, where Dante tells us that he will make what remains of his experience the subject of his poem.

Clearly, none of these references to Dante's *Divina Commedia* in Spenser's poetry—and *The Faerie Queene* is recognised as one of the sources of *King Lear*, so Shakespeare had certainly read it—could be the source for the "bitter bread" image of exile or the "beauteous inn" image in *Richard II*. Nor could the hesitation image in *Hamlet* as the protagonist decides "to be or not to be" originate here. Neither do we find there a source for the description of Isabella "enskied and sainted", Claudio's vision of Hell or the list of physical acts in *Measure for Measure* and *The Tempest*. There is nothing to bring to mind a source for the "gemless rings" image from *King Lear*, the river of blood or the types of treachery in *Macbeth*, or anything to suggest the combined ideas of repentance and the eagle dream of *Cymbeline*. Shakespeare's knowledge of Dante has not come from Spenser's work.

Thomas Sackville, later Lord Buckhurst (1536–1608), seems also to have had some knowledge of Dante. About 1563 he set off on a prolonged tour of Europe and spent several years in Italy. In 1591 he was elected Chancellor of the University of Oxford and in 1599 he succeeded Lord Burghley as High Treasurer of England. Toynbee tells us:

> About 1557 Sackville planned a poem on the model of Lydgate's "Falls of Princes", "in which" says Warton, "all the illustrious but unfortunate characters of English history, from the Conquest to the end of the fourteenth century, were to pass in review before the poet, who descends, like Dante, into the infernal region, and is conducted by Sorrow. Every personage was to recite his own misfortunes in a separate soliloquy." To this poem, the first volume of which appeared in 1559, with the title *A Mirror for Magistrates*, Sackville

contributes a poetical *Induction,* and the *Complaint of the Duke of Buckingham,* which however were not published until the issue of the second volume in 1563. The machinery and language of the *Induction* not unnaturally provoke comparison with the *Inferno,* which, as Courthope observes, led Pope to place Sackville as a poet in the school of Dante. During his long absence in Italy Sackville might well have become acquainted with the *Divina Commedia.*[11]

There are a number of phrases in this work, "a desert woode", "sweete remembrance of his pleasures past", "a loathsome lake", "the sighs, the sobs, the deepe and deadly groane" which certainly make us think of Dante, but the references seem to be to *Inferno* only and Shakespeare's borrowings are from all three books of the *Divina Commedia.* It is interesting to note that one of the copies of the *Divina Commedia* listed in the catalogue of the Bodleian Library for 1605 was "Purchased out of a sum of 100 pounds given to the Library in 1600 by Thomas Sackville, Lord Buckhurst (1536–1608), Chancellor of the University". We cannot know whether this particular book was purchased at the request of Sackville, but it may have been that whoever purchased it believed that Sackville would approve the choice. There does not seem to be, however, sufficient material from Dante in Sackville's work to provide Shakespeare with the knowledge he appears to have of the *Divina Commedia.*

Sir Philip Sidney (1554–86), had an excellent knowledge of Italy. He had spent two years in Venice and Padua from 1573 to 1575. He mentions Dante in his *Apologie for Poetry,* and in this work Beatrice is mentioned for the first time in English literature. But there is nothing in Sidney's work to provide a source for Shakespeare, although the mention of Dante's name, as in Chaucer, may have prompted Shakespeare to pursue his reading in this direction.

Ben Jonson (1573–1631) too, makes reference to Dante. In his play *Volpone,* the following exchange takes place:

Volpone:

                          The poet
As old in time as Plato, and as knowing,
Says that your highest female grace is silence.

Lady Would-Be:

Which o' your poets? Petrarch? or Tasso? or Dante?
Guarini? Ariosto? Aretine?
Cieco di Hadria? I have read them all ...
Here's *Pastor Fido*—

Volpone (*Aside*):

Is everything a cause to my destruction?

Lady Would-Be:

I think I ha' two or three o'them about me.

Volpone:

The sun, the sea will sooner, both stand still
Than her eternal tongue! nothing can scape it.

Lady Would-Be:

Here's *Pastor Fido*—

Volpone (*Aside*):

Profess obstinate silence,
That's now my safest.

Lady Would-Be:

All our English writers,
I mean such as are happy in th' Italian,
Will deign to steal out of the author, mainly;
Almost as much as from Montagnié—
He has so modern and facile a vein,
Fitting the time, and catching the court-ear.
Your Petrarch is more passionate, yet he,
In days of sonetting, trusted 'em with much:

Dante is hard, and few can understand him.
But for a desperate wit, there's Aretine!
Only his pictures are a little obscene.

Volpone, III.4.77–97[12]

The view expressed by Lady Would-Be concerning "all our English writers" who "will deign to steal out of the author" is of course, not necessarily the opinion of Jonson himself, but it was obviously the opinion of some at the time, and seems to be a direct reference to Shakespeare, particularly with the mention of Montaigne, whose ideas Shakespeare used freely even before Florio's translation was published. If it is a reference to Shakespeare, it seems to be claiming that he was one who was "happy in the Italian". The reference is not complimentary and seems to have the barb which is often to be felt in the comments of Ben Jonson on the subject of Shakespeare.

Shakespeare had performed in Jonson's *Everyman in his Humour* at the Globe in 1598. When the *First Folio* was published in 1623, it contained a glowing tribute to Shakespeare from Jonson, which concluded, "He was not of our age, but for all time!" According to the vicar of Stratford in the early 1600s, Shakespeare had died "of a fever" following a drinking bout with Ben Jonson and Michael Drayton.[13] Clearly, Jonson and Shakespeare knew each other and we might suppose that if Jonson were reading Dante, he might have mentioned the fact to Shakespeare. But Toynbee suggests that the comment by Lady Would-Be that "Dante is hard", might not be the result of Jonson's own experience, but rather taken from John Florio (a close friend of Jonson)[14] who had made a similar comment in the dedication to his *Worlde of Wordes* (1598):

> Bocace is prettie hard, yet understood; Petrarche harder, yet explained: Dante hardest, but commented. Some doubt if all aright.[15]

This view that the comment is Florio's is supported by Drummond, who informed us that Jonson "did neither understand French nor Italiannes".[16]

Certainly all of the poets mentioned in Lady Would-Be's speech above are named in Florio's list of his source books for his 1611 dictionary and it may be that the reference to Dante was also from Florio. But there is nothing of Dante in Jonson's work[17] that Shakespeare could have used as source material for the similarities we have noted.

John Florio was the English-born son of a Florentine protestant and was a prominent teacher of Italian and French in London in the last decades of the sixteenth century and the early decades of the next. He published his first conversation manual, *Firste Fruites* in 1578, and his second, *Second Frutes* in 1591. In the first of these there is some mention of Dante. In a section headed "Of the Superlatives", Florio comments on the way in which Dante uses the Italian word for "both" and cites a number of examples. His comment suggests that he has a copy of Dante's work before him. His Italian/English dictionary *A Worlde of Wordes* was published in 1598 and the revised edition, *Queene Anna's New World of Words* appeared in 1611. In this last, in the list of sources which appeared at the end, were included Dante's *Divina Commedia* and four different commentaries. In the 1598 edition, there were some references to Dante, but he was not mentioned in the list of sources, perhaps because it was published in the protestant reign of Elizabeth. However, by 1611 when the revised edition was printed, James I was on the throne and Florio was employed in his household.

Florio's greatest work was probably his translation of Montaigne's *Essays* and this, the dictionaries and the conversation manuals, were used extensively by Shakespeare. But nowhere in these works is any detailed knowledge of Dante to be found and they are clearly not the source of the images and ideas of Shakespeare which seem to be closely related to Dante. However, Shakespeare and Florio for a certain period moved in the same circles, and a closer examination of this Italian influence will be considered later in the next chapter.

Several other English writers in the sixteenth century also showed some knowledge of Dante. William Thomas wrote a dictionary in 1550 called *The Dictionarie for the Better Understanding of Boccace, Petrarche and Dante* which gave a number of words used by Dante with their English meanings.

The words alone could not have provided a source for Shakespeare for the quite complex images and ideas we are considering in his plays.

It seems, then, that Shakespeare could not have learned much about Dante from the work of other English writers. In fact, only the writings of Chaucer and Spenser demonstrate any real knowledge of the *Divina Commedia* and in the material they have used, with the exception of Chaucer's one line on the afterlife, and his own version of the dream of the eagle, there is no source for the other Shakespearean passages we have considered which seem to be derived from Dante.

There were also the many Italian writers whose works appeared in translation and to which Shakespeare seems to have had access. One of these was Ariosto, whose *Orlando Furioso* had been translated by Sir John Harington and published in 1591. The work is acknowledged as a source for Shakespeare, particularly for *Much Ado About Nothing* (1598).[18] Shakespeare may have used Harington's translated version—the sheer length of the Italian original is a daunting prospect—but an Italian version was listed among the Italian books available to Florio for the compilation of his 1611 dictionary, and many of the titles in this list were also used by Shakespeare.

In *Orlando Furioso* there is an amusing parody of Dante's *Divina Commedia*. Canto XXXIV begins with a description of the Harpies that hover round the cave which is the entrance to Hell. Here:

> ... l'aria ne senti percossa e rotta
> da pianti e d'urli e da lamento eterno:
> segno evidente quivi esser lo 'nferno.[19]
>
> *Orlando Furioso* XXXIV.4

> [... the air seemed shaken and shattered with cries and shouts of eternal lament; an evident sign that here was Hell.][20]

Harington translated these lines as:

> To harken at the same he waxèth bold
> And heard most woeful mourning, plaints, and cries

Such as from Hell were likely to arise.[21]

Dante had written:

> Quivi sospiri, pianti e alti guai
> risonavan per l'aere sanza stelle,
>
> *Inferno* III.22–3
>
> [Here sighs, cries and loud shrieks sounded in the air without stars.]

The similarity between Dante and Ariosto (in the original) is unmistakable and it is clear to the reader that this is a reference to Dante. It is interesting to note that Shakespeare, in *Macbeth,* has Ross say in his account of the state of Scotland, now under the rule of Macbeth and transformed into a kind of hell:

> … sighs, and groans, and shrieks that rent the air
> are made, not marked;
>
> *Macbeth* IV.3.168–9

The idea that these sounds have "rent" the air sounds closer to Ariosto's *rotta* than to Dante's original.

The parody continues and in the course of the canto, there is mention of the terrible stench, the insubstantiality of the spirits there, and even a conversation with one of them, a woman, Lidia, who recounts how spiteful she was in life to a man who loved her. Even her opening word, *Deh*, recalls the opening *Deh* of Dante's Pia, who, quite the opposite of Lidia, recounts with pathetic brevity the tale of her death at the hands of her husband (*Purgatorio* V.130–6). All of these ideas we encounter in Dante, though with minor differences. The character Astolfo then moves on to Purgatory, where the description again reminds us of Dante's Earthly Paradise with a crystal stream in which Astolfo washes himself, beautiful flowers and fruits, all atop a high mountain in the *terrestre paradiso.* Eventually he goes to the moon and later he is transported higher in the heavens by four horses and a chariot.

Ariosto certainly knew Dante's work well, and while there are some images very reminiscent of the *Divina Commedia,* none of them is among those we are considering as "borrowings" by Shakespeare. Few, apart from the one discussed above concerning the sounds heard in Hell, are as detailed as those Shakespeare seems to have used. If the playwright had read this work, whether in the original or in the rather loose, inaccurate and abbreviated translation by Harington, he would once again have been made aware of Dante's work. But we cannot conclude that the knowledge Shakespeare apparently has of Dante is via Ariosto.

If we cannot find Shakespeare's knowledge of Dante in the work of other writers, we are left then with the other alternative—that Shakespeare *himself* read the *Divina Commedia.* This depends on two assumptions, firstly that his command of the Italian language was sufficient for him to read and understand (perhaps with some assistance) the quite difficult Italian of Dante, and secondly, that there were one or more copies available to him to use quite frequently and consult when necessary.

CHAPTER 4

The Last Remaining Option

> *... All our English writers,*
> *I mean such as are happy in th'Italian*
> *Will deign to steal out of the author, mainly;*
>
> *Volpone*, Ben Jonson

Consider the possibility that Shakespeare was sufficiently proficient in Italian to read Dante's great work in the original. This is not extremely unlikely, given the generally pro-Italian climate of the Elizabethan Age, at least in matters secular. Mario Praz remarked that "[s]ince Italian books were widely read in the society in whose midst Shakespeare lived, there is nothing extraordinary in his acquaintance with Italian literature; rather the contrary would be surprising".[1] Learning foreign languages in Shakespeare's time, for the diplomat, the intellectual, the cultured, the traveller and the merchant dealing with other countries, was essential simply because English was not spoken outside England. In John Florio's *Firste Fruites* (1578) is the following dialogue:

> What thinke you of this English tongue, tel me, I pray you?
> It is a language that wyl do you good in England, but passe
> Douer it is worth nothing.
> Is it not used then in other countreyes?
> No, sir, with whom wyl you that they speake?
> With English marchants.

English marchants, when they are out of England, it liketh them not and they do not speak it.[2]

Because of this, Englishmen of a certain type and class made every effort to learn at least one other foreign language. To illustrate the effectiveness of this, we have only to consider that when Giordano Bruno came to England in 1583, where he stayed for two years, he did not find it necessary to learn English. He lectured at Oxford, where all instruction was in Latin, and he spied for Walsingham (if John Bossy's theory is correct), to whom he reported in letters written in an Italianized French. He lived in the house of Michel de Castelneau, the French Ambassador, who did not speak English and yet managed to do his job effectively, using Latin for his official correspondence. When Bruno, in one of his dialogues, was asked why he had not learned English, he answered (speaking of himself in the third person):

> Nothing tempts him or obliges him to do so; because all gentlemen of any rank with whom he holds conversations can speak Latin, Spanish or Italian. They are aware that the English language is used only in this island and they would consider themselves barbarians if they knew no other language than their own.[3]

John Florio himself had not been quite so fortunate. In his *Firste Fruites*, he recounts how:

> When I arrived first in London, I coulde not speake English, and I met about five hundred persons, afore I could find one that could tel me in Italien or French, where the Post dwelt.[4]

Queen Elizabeth was proud of her Italian and at the age of twelve had made a number of translations from English into Italian. She was described by Pietro Bizani as "a perfect mistress of our Italian tongue, in the learning of which signior Castiglione was her principal master".[5] Other aristocrats of the period who had learned Italian included the Earl of Surrey, Sir Thomas Wyatt, the seventeenth Earl of Oxford, Edward de Vere, the fifth Earl of Rutland, Roger Manners, the fifth and sixth Earls of Derby, Ferdinando Stanley and William Stanley, the third Earl of Southampton, Henry Wriothesley, and the Earl of Leicester. Two women, the Countess of Bedford, and Anne Cooke, the mother of Sir Francis Bacon, were also proficient in the language.

Powerful men at court, too, had mastered it, such as Lord Burghley, Sir Francis Walsingham, and Sir Robert Cecil. Lewis Einstein cited a case where a Venetian envoy reported that at a dinner given him by Cecil, at which the entire Privy Council was present, the conversation was conducted chiefly in Italian, "almost all of them speaking our Italian tongue or at least all understanding it".[6] Many writers had made it their business to study the language, since so much literary material was available to them from this source: Christopher Marlowe, Edmund Spenser, Sir Philip Sidney, John Lyly, Gabriel Harvey, William Thomas, and John Marston were all proficient in the language. The most important of all these for our present argument is Henry Wriothesley, the third Earl of Southampton, to whom Shakespeare dedicated his *Venus and Adonis* and *The Rape of Lucrece*, and of whom John Florio (who had been tutor to Southampton since 1591) had written in the dedication of his 1598 dictionary:

> I might make doubt, least I or mine be not now of any *further* use to your self sufficiencie being at home so instructed for *Italian* as teaching or learning could supplie, that there seemed no neede for travell, and nowe by travell so accomplisht, as what wants to perfection?[7]

Foreign languages were not on the curriculum of the schools or the universities, so there was a great demand for language teachers, of whom John Florio was one of the most famous.

Very obviously Shakespeare's interest in Italy and Italian literature is revealed in about 1593, when his first Italian-set plays, *Two Gentlemen of Verona* appeared, and a year later, *The Taming of the Shrew*. *Romeo and Juliet* appeared in 1595, *The Merchant of Venice* in 1596, *Much Ado About Nothing* in 1598, *All's Well That Ends Well* in 1602, and *Measure for Measure* and *Othello* in 1604. These plays are all set in Italy, except for *Measure for Measure* which is set in Vienna, but the characters all have Italian names and the source of the play is Italian, as are the sources of some other Shakespearean plays which are not set in Italy. We would have to assume that even though interest in Italian culture and literature was fashionable and widespread in England at this time, and other English writers borrowed from it (Sidney, Spenser, and Jonson), there may have been some special influence in Shakespeare's life which steered him so effectively in this direction.

From his earliest plays, he had access to a large selection of Italian literature which he used as source material. If we could establish that in any of these cases he was working from an untranslated original, we would have a good case for the argument that Shakespeare had some knowledge of Italian. Selma Guttman, in her comprehensive listing of Shakespeare's foreign sources, found twenty-seven Italian authors from whose work various writers believe Shakespeare borrowed material. For each of these works, she included information on whether a translation into English would have been available to Shakespeare. Her information was taken from works written between 1904 and 1940, dealing with English, French and German commentary concerning Shakespearean sources originally written in foreign languages. She considered only foreign sources which directly influenced works in Shakespeare's accepted canon. She commented that "some source suggestions herein recorded are implausible and far-fetched".[8]

Guttman included Dante in her list and the entry is as follows:

Since the general trend of criticism is exemplified by the annotation below, a list of the translations of Dante is omitted.

Kuhns, (L) Oscar, *Dante and the English Poets from Chaucer to Tennyson*, New York, 1904, pp. 70–9.

Although there are many alleged cases of Dante's influence on Shakespeare, these parallels are inconclusive or questionable.[9]

(She recorded, however, only one writer on the subject and one wonders to what "translations" she was referring.)

Below is a summary of the Italian sources she has listed:

Author	Title	English Version
Alberti	*Della tranquillità dell'animo*	may have read in MSS
Aretino	*Marescalco*	–
Ariosto	*I Suppositi*	Gascoigne (1572)
	Orlando Furioso	Harington (1591)
Bandello	*Novelle*	Fenton (1567)
Barberino	*Reali di Francia*	–
Berni	*Orlando Innamorato*	–
Boccaccio	*Il Decamerone*	Lydgate (1527)
		Painter (1566)
Boiardo	*Timone*	–
Castiglione	*Il Cortegiano*	Hoby (1561)
Cecchi	*L'Ammalata*	–
Cinthio	*Hecatommithi*	Whetstone (1578)
Dante	*La Divina Commedia*	–
Dolce	*Le Prime Imprese del Conte Orlando*	–
Doni	*The Bolognese Doctor & the Foolish Student*	–
Fiorentino	*Il Pecorone*	–
Fortini	*The Florentine Doctor & the Student*	–
Guazzo	*Dialoghi Piacevoli*	Pettie (1586)
Guicciardini	*Ore di Recreazione*	Danett (1593)
Machiavelli	*Il Principe*	Paterick (1577)

Masuccio	*Novelle*	–
Oddi	*I Morti Vivi*	–
Pasqualigo	*Il Fedele*	A. M. (1580)
Pescetti	*Cesare*	–
Petrarch	*Il Canzoniere*	many
Porto	*Romeus & Juliet*	–
Straparola	*Two Lovers of Pisa*	Tarleton (1590)
Tasso	*Amyntas*	Fraunce (1591)

Kenneth Muir, writing on Shakespeare's sources in 1977, listed nine of the Italian writers from Guttman's 1947 survey (Ariosto, Bandello, Boccaccio, Boiardo, Castiglione, Cinthio, Fiorentino, Pasqualigo and da Porto). He added to the list a further six possible sources:

Author	Title	English Version
Groto	*La Hadriana*	–
Gonzaga	*Gli Inganni*	–
Secchi	*Gli Inganni*	–
unknown	*L'Interesse*	–
unknown	*Gli Ingannati*	–
Nenna	*A Treatise on Nobility*	Jones (1594)

He was dubious about all of these sources. (The *Inganni/Ingannati* plays were also mentioned in Guttman's book, but without any authors.)

Murray J. Levith[10] in 1989 added to the list of possible sources, the following three Italian works:

Author	Title	English Version
Guarini	*Il Pastor Fido*	–
Sannazaro	*L'Arcadia*	–
unknown	*Il Sacrificio*	–

He gave no English version of any of these.

In 2001, Stuart Gillespie, in *Shakespeare's Books*,[11] listed many of the Italian authors mentioned above, and added a further five names:

Author	Title	English Version
Accolti	*Virginia*	–
Bruto	(A Manual)	*The Necessarie, Fit and Convenient Education of a Yong Gentlewoman.* (1598)
delle Colonne	*Historia Troiana*	*Historyes of Troye* (1474)
Mantuan	*Eclogues*(?)	*Eclogues* (1567)
Saviolo	fencing manual	*V. Saviolo his Practise* (1594–95)

But on the possible Italian sources listed by Guttman, she recorded several comments by other writers which led one to believe that Shakespeare was, in some cases, working from the Italian original. For example, many writers saw Ariosto's *Orlando Furioso* as one of the sources of *Othello*. Guttman reported from William Theobald,[12]

> Brandes is quoted to the effect that *Othello* III.4.71ff ("A sibyl ...") was derived from *Orlando Furioso* in the original, inasmuch as the phrase "prophetic fury" occurs in both *Othello* and the Italian of Ariosto but not in the translation of Harington.

Naseeb Shaheen gave another example from *Othello* which supported the theory that Shakespeare was writing from an Italian original, this time from Bandello. Shaheen claimed,

> The sensational device that Shakespeare uses of having Desdemona momentarily revive and exonerate Othello after having been apparently killed by him (V.2.80–125) is to be found only in Bandello. Only in Bandello does the maid (like Emilia) call for help. Only in Bandello do the neighbours break in and find the dead husband lying face downwards on

his almost dead wife. These events occur in neither Belleforest nor Fenton.[13]

When Shakespeare was writing his plays, there was no translation into English of Cinthio's *Hecatommithi*, seventh story, third decade, which was another tale which contained part of the plot of *Othello*. There was a French translation made in 1584, but Muir claimed that Shakespeare's play seemed to be closer to the Italian version than to the French. To illustrate this point he referred us to a phrase "as acerb as the coloquintida" (*Othello* I.3.350) where the First Folio had substituted the word "acerb" for the word "bitter". Muir claimed that:

> it is reasonable to suppose that Shakespeare wrote "acerb" and not "bitter" since no actor, compositor, or editor would be likely to substitute the rare word for the common. O. E. D. does not recognise the word till 1657.[14]

He wrote:

> The probability that Shakespeare read the Italian text is re-enforced by his use of the word "acerb"—which the Folio changed to "bitter"—for Cinthio tells how the love of his villain for Desdemona "turned to the bitterest hatred"—*in acerbissimo odio.*[15]

Mario Praz, too, gave yet another example to support this theory. The following lines spoken by Iago in *Othello,* he believed are almost a literal translation of Cinthio's moral, and they "could be, by the way, one of the proofs that Shakespeare knew Italian":[16]

> … thus credulous fools are caught,
> And many worthy and chaste dames, even thus
> All guiltless, meet reproach.
>
> Othello IV.1.45–7

Cinthio wrote:

> Aviene talhora che, senza colpa, fedele et amorevole donna, per insidie tesele da animo malvagio, et per leggerezza di chi più crede che non bisognerebbe, da fedel marito riceve morte.

> [It sometimes happens that without guilt on her part a faithful and loving woman, through a deceit engined by an evil soul, and the folly of some credulous person, is killed by a loyal husband.][17]

In reference to da Porto's *Romeus and Juliet*, Guttman summarized an argument of R. H. Moore,[18] who claimed:

> In four instances in which Shakespeare's characters deviate from Brooke's poem, *Romeo and Juliet* agrees with the original version of Luigi da Porto of which no known English or French translation was in existence. Although one may either ignore this indebtedness to da Porto or assume a lost intermediary play, Shakespeare had, probably, direct or indirect contact with Luigi da Porto's own version of the tale.

Ernesto Grillo devoted an entire chapter of his book to establishing that "Shakespeare must somehow or other have learned enough Italian to read and understand our writers".[19] He claimed that in some of the plays there are whole lines translated from the Italian without the slightest alteration:

> *Dramatis personae,* like Mercutio for example, cannot avoid the Italian linguistic forms which Shakespeare employs with great ability and success. The greeting between Hortensio and Petruchio (*The Taming of the Shrew* I.2.23–5) is exchanged in two or three lines of pure Italian.

Pet.	Signior Hortensio, come you to part the fray?
	Con tutto il cuore ben trovato, may I say.
Hor.	*Alla nostra casa ben venuto molto honorato signor*
	mio Petrucio.[20]

He went on to give several pages of similar examples, citing various Italian sources which were not at the time translated, for example *Il Pecorone* and *Hecatommithi*. Of the former, he wrote:

> This collection of short stories—*Il Pecorone*—was only published in Italy in 1558, and in Shakespeare's time existed solely in the original. The simple story of the Jew and the pound of flesh might be traced to other sources, but only in *The Merchant of Venice* and in *Il Pecorone* do we find that the debtor, Antonio, whose pound of flesh was demanded by the creditor, is liberated by the skilful defence and intercession of the Lady of Belmont, wife of the debtor's own friend. In every other detail, too, we note that Shakespeare faithfully followed the Italian original.[21]

Grillo found the influence of Giordano Bruno in *Hamlet*, even though none of Bruno's work had been translated into English. He had no doubt at all that Shakespeare's knowledge of Italian was extensive, but he did not mention the works of Florio, which would have provided Shakespeare with at least some of his Italian material.

Morton Luce, in his Introduction to the Arden (1) *Twelfth Night*,[22] threw a great deal of light on the *Inganni/Ingannati* plays mentioned by both Guttman and Kenneth Muir. *Gl'Ingannati*, he believed, provided much of the plot for *Twelfth Night*. He claimed that this play was published in 1537 in a volume titled *Il Sacrificio*,[23] *Comedia de gl'Intronati*. "[T]his" Luce claimed, "Shakespeare almost certainly consulted."[24] He also mentioned that the two plays both entitled *Inganni,* one by Secchi and one by Gonzaga, were bound up with a copy of *Gl'Ingannati* in a volume with three other

Italian plays "in one of which, *Il Viluppo*, di M.G. Parabosco, 1547, *Orsino innamorato* appears among the *Dramatis Personae*."[25] In the play *Inganni* by Gonzaga, Luce noted that a girl disguised as a boy is called *Cesare* which brings to mind Viola's choice of "Cesario" as her new name in her role as a boy. These parallels in names suggest that Shakespeare had probably seen this book of five Italian plays.

In a lengthy Appendix to this edition of *Twelfth Night*, where he noted a number of parallels between this and the Italian plays, Luce concluded "Shakespeare on occasion must seem to have had recourse to an Italian original; I will now add that if he consulted Bandello or Cinthio or Ser Giovanni in one instance, then why not on another?"[26] In the Introduction to the Arden (1) edition[27] of *Two Gentlemen of Verona*, Warwick Bond included a footnote in which J. L. Klein also claimed that Parabosco's *Il Viluppo* was a source used by Shakespeare. Klein concluded "there seems to have been no English translation".[28]

The number of untranslated Italian sources apparently used by Shakespeare is considerable, and it becomes almost impossible to deny him some familiarity with the language, even if on many occasions, he also had access to a translation into English or French. All Italian writers on the subject seem to accept that Shakespeare knew their language to some extent, and in 1911 the Italian writer Carlo Segre, arguing the case for Shakespeare's use of the untranslated work of Cinthio as a source for *Othello* and therefore his knowledge of the Italian language, commented rather acidly:

E perchè non avrebbe dovuto conoscerla, mentre intorno a lui la conoscevano tutte le persone di mezzana cultura, i suoi amici, i suoi protettori, i compagni istessi della sua carriera d'autore? Io sono verso di lui un po' più generoso di molti suoi compatrioti, e non esito a ritenere ch'egli, il quale penetrò nell'anima dell'antichità con una felicità d'intuito, che non potè essere soltanto istintiva, possedesse una facilità di apprendere almeno non inferiore a quella d'una folla di insipidi cortigiani, che hanno portato il proprio nome nella propria tombe.[29]

[And why would he not have known it, when around him all the people of average culture knew it, his friends, his patrons, his companions in his career as a playwright? I am, towards him, a little more generous than many of his compatriots, and I do not hesitate to retain that he who penetrated into the soul of antiquity with a felicitous intuition which could not have been solely instinctive, possessed a facility to understand at least not inferior to that of a crowd of insipid courtiers who have taken their names to their graves.]

Of those titles added by Muir, only Nenna's work had been translated into English. This translation was the work of William Jones and was published by Shakespeare's fellow Stratfordian, Richard Field, in 1595. Field had also published Shakespeare's *Venus and Adonis* in 1593. Kenneth Muir believed that this book was the probable source of the ideas on nobility and virtue used in *All's Well That Ends Well* (1602). The editor of a modern reprint of *A Treatise on Nobility* commented in the introduction that "Nenna is noteworthy not for its originality but rather for the way it summarizes the arguments on both sides ... from Aristotle, and the more recent Dante and Castiglione".[30] This same editor, Alice Shalvi, referred the reader constantly to Dante's *Convivio,* and in one part of the treatise, to the speech in *All's Well That Ends Well* concerning honour:

... Honours thrive
When rather from our acts we them derive
Than our foregoers.
All's Well That Ends Well II.3.35–7

She found very close parallels between the two works.

Since Nenna's treatise was available in English after 1595, Shakespeare's borrowing of ideas from it does not provide evidence for the claim that

Shakespeare knew Italian. And since the ideas concerned were initially presented in Dante's *Convivio* and *De Monarchia*, via Nenna's treatise, it does not suggest that Shakespeare had read the *Divina Commedia*, or indeed any of Dante's work. It *does* show that Shakespeare was aware of, and interested in Dante's ideas.

Clara Longworth de Chambrun presented an interesting argument on the Italian phrases used in Shakespeare's plays, claiming that all of them could be found in Florio's language manuals. She believed that Shakespeare's knowledge of Petrarch, Dante and Machiavelli was scattered throughout his work, but that his knowledge of the Italian language, at least the spoken language, was not great. She claimed that between the writing of *The Merchant of Venice* (1596) and *The Tempest* (1611), Shakespeare had learned that the accent on the name "Stephano" goes on the first syllable, and not the second.[31] This would indicate that he had heard the correct pronunciation from a competent Italian speaker. She also commented on the fact that Shakespeare was able to give us in the plays "une impression véritable d'italianisme, de culture italienne".[32] She believed that he must have listened to the conversation of someone who was extremely enthusiastic about the Italian culture and that "cet italianisant devait être Florio."[33]

Grillo was much more convinced of Shakespeare's grasp of the Italian language and claimed that Shakespeare's knowledge of Italian topography and customs was the knowledge of one who had lived there. "We have no hesitation," he wrote, "in affirming that on least one occasion he must have visited Italy."[34] He claimed that in *The Two Gentlemen of Verona* and *Romeo and Juliet* there was little evidence that the playwright had been to these two locations, but in later plays, *The Taming of the Shrew*, *The Merchant of Venice*, *Measure for Measure*, *Twelfth Night* and *Othello*, there were scenes which are purely Italian:[35]

> Here we find such definite characteristics, such vivid local colour and such wealth of precise and vigorous details that we are forced to conclude that Shakespeare must have visited Milan, Verona, Venice, Padua and Mantua.[36]

He gave a number of examples, just one of which should be sufficient to make the point:

> The local colour of *The Taming of the Shrew* displays such an intimate acquaintance not only with the manners and customs of Italy but also with the minutest details of domestic life that it cannot have been gleaned from books or acquired in the course of conversations with travellers returned from Padua. The form of marriage between Petruchio and Katharine, which was later recommended by Manzoni's loquacious Agnese to Renzo and Lucia, was Italian and not English. Some lines where the noble lord proposes to show Sly his pictures:
>
> > We'll show thee Io was a maid;
> > And how she was beguiled and surprised,
> > As lively painted as the deed was done.
>
> suggest that the poet may have seen Correggio's famous picture—*Giove ed Io*—which is quite possible if he visited the north of Italy in 1592–93, because from 1585–1600 the picture was exhibited to the public in the palace of the sculptor, Leoni, in Milan, where it was admired by numerous travellers.[37]

Grillo, however, was probably unaware of the fact that at Belvoir Castle, ancestral home of the Manners family, there was a copy of this painting in fresco on the ceiling of the Elizabethan Salon.[38] Roger Manners, Earl of Rutland, was a friend of Southampton, and through this connection, Shakespeare may also have seen this fresco. In an account book for 1613 at Belvoir Castle an entry was found recording payment to "Mr Shakespeare and Mr Burbadge" for making and painting an *impreso*—an emblem with a motto[39]—and Rutland therefore certainly knew Shakespeare. *The Taming of the Shrew* was written about 1594 but Shakespeare's acquaintance with

Rutland may well have begun at the same time as his acquaintance with Southampton and he may have visited Belvoir at this time. Grillo's argument was that books alone could not account for Shakespeare's knowledge, topographical, social and linguistic, of Italy, and he believed that sometime in the early 1590s, Shakespeare must have visited Italy. There is, however, no documented evidence of this.

Mario Praz, too, observed that while he did not see much evidence of real knowledge of Italy in *Two Gentlemen of Verona* and *The Taming of the Shrew, Romeo and Juliet* "displays a much stronger local colour".[40] He went on to note that there were a number of local allusions in which Shakespeare demonstrated great accuracy and that these were confined to an area including Venice, Verona, Padua, Mantua and Milan. The alternatives he saw were that Shakespeare had visited Italy, or that he had conversations with Italians at home. He rejected the first of these on the grounds that there was no evidence for it and claimed that Shakespeare:

> may have had frequent occasions to meet Italian merchants; the Elephant Inn, which he mentions with praise as being the one where it was "best to lodge" in the unknown Illyrian town of *Twelfth Night,* and being of course, nothing else but the inn called "The Oliphant" in Bankside, was patronised by Italians.[41]

But he pointed out that Shakespeare must have been in the same circles as John Florio, whose vocabulary had a prevailing Lombardo-Venetian character, and believed "that this may help us to understand why the local allusions in Shakespeare's Italian plays are limited to Venice and the neighbouring towns".[42]

Strangely, however, there is no record of John Florio ever having visited Italy, and although he was seen by Englishmen as an Italian, he was English-born, spent some time in Switzerland or Germany or France, and as far as we know, then returned to England. It would therefore seem unlikely that he would be in a position to give Shakespeare accurate information on local customs in Italy. Even if he relayed information he had heard from his father, it is difficult to believe that this would be so detailed that it would suggest a first hand knowledge on the part of Shakespeare.

It seems then, that Shakespeare's knowledge of Italian allowed him to work almost certainly in at least one case, *Othello*, and probably also in *Romeo and Juliet, The Merchant of Venice* and *Twelfth Night,* from Italian originals. Significant, too, is the fact that if he took some of his phrases from Florio's conversation manuals, as Clara Longworth de Chambrun believed, he may have been studying Italian, since that was their primary purpose.

CHAPTER 5

The Antique Book

Oh that record could with back-ward look
Even of five hundreth courses of the sunne,
Show me your image in some antique book,

Sonnet 59, Shakespeare

It remains only to establish that Shakespeare could have had access to a copy of the *Divina Commedia* which was, in Shakespeare's time already 300 years old and certainly an antique book. The most obvious place in which he could have found such a book would probably be in the library of some aristocratic house. The only evidence we have of any aristocratic connection is in his warm dedication of *Venus and Adonis* in 1593 to the Earl of Southampton and the even more affectionate dedication of *The Rape of Lucrece* to the same man one year later. These two pieces of writing are the nearest we have (apart from, perhaps, the sonnets) to autobiographical information on Shakespeare.

The dedication of *Venus and Adonis*, published in 1593, tells of a new relationship and suggests a social circle rather different from the milieu in which it is claimed Shakespeare lived in Stratford and the normal theatrical world which, as an actor, he would have found in London. We do not know, however, when he arrived in London, nor do we know where he had been in the years from 1585, when his twins were christened, to 1592 when the reference is made to "an upstart Crow" in Greene's *Groates-worth of Witte*, which is generally considered to be a reference to Shakespeare.

The dedication of *Venus and Adonis* reads:

To the Right Honourable
Henry Wriothesley, Earl of Southampton
and Baron of Titchfield

Right Honourable, I know not how I shall offend in dedicating my unpolished lines to your Lordship, nor how the world will censure me for choosing so strong a prop to support so weak a burden. Only if your Honour seem but pleased, I account myself highly praised, and vow to take advantage of all idle hours, till I have honoured you with some graver labour. But if the first heir of my invention prove deformed, I shall be sorry it had so noble a god-father, and never after ear so barren a land, for fear it yield me still so bad a harvest. I leave it to your Honourable survey, and your Honour to your heart's content which I wish may always answer your own wish, and the world's hopeful expectation.

Your Honour's in all duty,
William Shakespeare

The writer revealed a flattering respect for the Earl and a certain modesty and humility about his own writing which does not seem altogether genuine. Some of the expressions used were largely conventional and common enough in dedications of the time. Perhaps the expectation was partly for some kind of financial reward from his patron. Shakespeare also revealed his belief that the relationship would continue—as he intended to honour his patron with "some graver labour". A year later, in the dedication to *The Rape of Lucrece* the more explicit declaration of love made by the poet revealed that the relationship between himself and the Earl had developed considerably. It would seem that the poet was less tentative about the acceptability of his offering and at least in his own view, the relationship (perhaps only a literary relationship), was set to develop indefinitely.

This time he wrote:

> To the Right Honourable
> Henry Wriothesley, Earl of Southampton
> and Baron of Titchfield
>
> The love I dedicate to your lordship is without end: whereof
> this pamphlet without beginning is but a superfluous moiety.
> The warrant I have of your Honourable disposition, not the
> worth of my untutored lines, makes it assured of acceptance.
> What I have done is yours, what I have to do is yours, being
> part in all I have, devoted yours. Were my worth greater, my
> duty would show greater; meantime, as it is, it is bound to
> your Lordship, to whom I wish long life still lengthened with
> all happiness.
>
> Your Lordship's in all duty
William Shakespeare

The young man who inspired such devotion was nineteen years old in 1593 when Shakespeare dedicated *Venus and Adonis* to him. Henry Wriothsley had been Earl of Southampton since he was eight years old, his father having died in 1581. The young Earl had immediately become a royal ward in the care of Lord Burghley, who sent him, at the age of twelve, to St John's College, Cambridge and later, in 1588, to Gray's Inn. Burghley had plans for his young ward, and by the time Southampton was seventeen years old, Burghley was attempting to arrange a marriage between his own granddaughter, Lady Elizabeth Vere (daughter of Edward de Vere, Earl of Oxford, and later, wife of William Stanley, Earl of Derby) and a reluctant but extremely attractive Southampton. One of Burghley's motives may have been the desire to eliminate the Catholic tendencies in the young man.

In 1590, Southampton's tutor, Swithin Wells, had been dismissed from his post. He had been caught at a Mass at Holburn and was hanged in December 1591. To replace him, Burghley appointed John Florio, probably also as a spy in the Southampton household, again to discourage any Catholic tendencies. Somewhere in these years, Shakespeare must have met Southampton and begun writing his enigmatic (and, to some, deeply disturbing) sonnets.

Most writers today agree that the first of these were written to Southampton. There are a number of excellent reasons for thinking so. Firstly, the initial seventeen sonnets were written to try to persuade a very handsome young man to marry—and we know that at this time, the marriage of Southampton and Lady Elizabeth de Vere was planned. Secondly, the biographical details which emerged in these sonnets all applied to the young Henry Wriothesley. Sonnet III, for example, mentioned a beautiful mother, still living:

> Thou art thy mother's glass, and she in thee
> Calls back the lovely April of her prime.

Sonnet XIII mentioned a deceased father; "You had a father, let your son say so," and this also applied to Southampton whose father had died in 1581.

It may be that Shakespeare had been commissioned to write these sonnets, but after the first seventeen, the subject changed to the poet's own growing passion for the young man, who, in the Hilliard miniature painted in 1594, was revealed to be very attractive in a rather feminine way: "A woman's face with nature's own hand painted" (Sonnet XX). If the sonnets did chronicle a real relationship, then they shed some light on the dedications, and they gave a time frame for this same relationship. The earliest sonnets seem to have been written perhaps as early as 1590 or 1591, when Burghley was engineering the marriage of his granddaughter. A much later sonnet, CVIII, often called the "mortal moon" sonnet, seems to have been written after the death of Elizabeth in 1603, when Southampton was released from the Tower.

It seems that the relationship between the poet and the young man to whom he wrote his sonnets lasted about thirteen years, although obviously, not at the same level as was apparent in the earlier sonnets and in the dedications of 1593 and 1594. In the later sonnets and with the introduction of the "dark lady" and the "rival poet", it was obvious that all was not well in this rather uncomfortable quadrangular relationship, but there is no evidence that the relationship with Southampton (if it was indeed he to whom the sonnets were written) was terminated. For the purposes of this book, since I shall argue that Southampton may have been responsible for the Italian influence in Shakespeare's work, these dates are significant.

In Southampton's background and life there was a strong Italian influence. The Southampton country seat was Titchfield House, between Portsmouth and Southampton. The house was, as can be seen from the drawing made in 1732, strongly influenced by Italian ideas. Ian Wilson wrote that the design "would have been intentionally very much along the lines of Florentine and northern Italian palaces. These were likewise mostly built around a square with the principal rooms on the first floor, or *piano nobile*, approached by an ornate staircase".[1]

We do not have specific information on Southampton's library, at least not as it was at this time. One recorded incident, however, suggests that his library was extensive. Some days after Southampton had organised to have *Love's Labour's Lost* staged at Southampton House for King James and Queen Anne in January 1605, it was recorded that his home was searched by London authorities, who discovered a large collection of incriminating Catholic literature. The event was reported in a letter from a trusted steward of the household, who wrote on 26 January 1605:

> eight or ten days since, there were above 200 pounds worth of
> Popish books taken about Southampton House and burned
> in Poules Churchyard.[2]

Although it is not my intention to rely on speculation to prove any part of my argument, Mrs Stopes' imaginative recreation of Southampton's library is interesting, evocative and not at all improbable:

In the first place, his grandfather, Thomas, founder of his title and fortune, had nearly a free hand in going through the freshly surrendered abbeys and priories at the Dissolution. He had no special literary tastes, but whatever books the houses owned would probably be left for him in Titchfield, Beaulieu, Quarr Abbey, and the branches of Hyde Abbey. Again, in 1596, Southampton had eagerly desired to go as a volunteer with his adored friend the Earl of Essex to the taking of Cadiz, and was forbidden to do so at the last by the Queen's mandate. At the subsequent sacking of the city Essex had chosen for his share the contents of the library. Judging from the characters of the two men, what would be more likely than that on his return the Earl of Essex should console his friend for his disappointment by giving him a share in the spoil? Thirdly, he had travelled in at least three countries, Ireland, France, and the Netherlands, and he might have picked up many a prize, for he was known to be a patron of letters and rarities would be offered him. There were several notices of recusant books having been found in and confiscated from Southampton House, but now that he had himself given up the old ritual, and yet remained appreciative of the beauty and value of the old books, the Earl might wish to secure some of his prizes from future spoliation by enclosing them in the walls of St John's.[3]

This last sentence probably referred to the very substantial gift Southampton's wife had made to the library at St John's College after the death of her husband and in the knowledge that this had been his intention. About 1615 Southampton had bought a large collection for the library from William Crashaw, who was in financial trouble. The library was unable to accommodate these books at that time, but when new premises were built for the purpose, the books were sent there. Among the collection were some "3,000 volumes and 500 manuscripts, some very ancient, some very rare, and some never printed".[4] All of this, of course, was far too late to be of any use to Shakespeare, but clearly Southampton had an interest in books and may well have owned some of the Italian texts which Shakespeare used. Again, however, this is only speculation.

In the same social circle and close acquaintances of Southampton, were the two brothers, Sir Charles and Sir Henry Danvers. Their mother, Lady Elizabeth Danvers, was noted for her great beauty and also her Italian birth. This latter fact would probably account for her son's importation of the Italian books mentioned below and would also suggest that the brothers may have been Italian speaking. Sir Charles was about five years older than Southampton. Akrigg tells us:

> He was an experienced courtier ... and a man of educated taste. A list of some 200 books that he imported in 1593 includes a copy of Petrarch's poems, along with a commentary, Montemayor's *Diana,* and a treatise on Dante's *Inferno,* though the vast majority of the books are military, historical and geographical.[5]

It was probably this "treatise on Dante's *Inferno*" which was presented to the Bodleian Library in 1602 by Sir Henry Danvers and which was described in the catalogue of 1602–3 as "Dante con Espos di Bern. Daniello di Luca". By then Sir Charles was dead, having been executed for his part in the Essex rebellion in 1601.

In October 1594 there had been an incident in which both brothers were involved in a murder. There had been a long-standing feud between the Danvers and Long families. At an inn, the Danvers brothers had encountered the Long brothers, one of whom drew his sword on Sir Charles. To save his brother, Sir Henry Danvers shot Henry Long. The Danvers brothers fled to Whitley Lodge, owned by Southampton, and close to Titchfield. By organising a series of fake hunting parties, Southampton managed to get the two fugitives closer to the coast and eventually to the port of Southampton. A boat was chartered for them and, after several close shaves and a quite violent incident in which Florio was involved, they escaped to France and the court of Henry IV. The relationship between the Danvers brothers and Southampton continued. Both of them accompanied Southampton on his campaign in Ireland in 1599. When Sir Charles Danvers was condemned to death for his part in the Essex plot in 1601, Southampton was also condemned, but eventually this sentence was commuted to life imprisonment in the Tower, from which he was released in 1603. Danvers was not so fortunate.

Here again we have an Italian connection. The Danvers family was in possession of a copy of Dante from 1593 (when Sir Charles imported a copy) to 1602 (when Sir Henry donated this copy to the Bodleian Library). In this period Shakespeare is supposed to have written some of his plays. Given Southampton's knowledge of the language and interest in things Italian, it is not unlikely that he would have seen this copy and discussed it with the owners. He may also have discussed it with Shakespeare, who presumably spent some time in his company in the period of the earlier sonnets and who must have had access to some library well furnished with Italian books in the same period and earlier.

To this point, however, I have not accounted for Shakespeare's knowledge of the Italian language. In the social circle in which Southampton moved, was John Florio. He had been born in England in 1553 but his parents had fled with him in 1554 to Europe. It is not recorded when he returned to England, but his first book, *Firste Fruites*, was published in England in 1578 and in the dedication, Florio writes, "Di Londra a di 10 Agosto, 1578." The book, a language teaching manual, was dedicated to Robert Dudley, Earl of Leicester, and in it, Florio mentions his father's services to the Dudley family.

Firste Fruites was a series of dialogues, graduated in difficulty, and printed in columns with the Italian on the left and the English on the right. The dialogues treated a number of situations—dining, going to an inn, wandering the streets of London—and while at the time they may have been useful to the newcomer to England or the traveller, today they give some interesting insights on life at the time. In one of the dialogues, "Discourses upon Musicke and Love," Florio wrote:

> We neede not speake so much of love, al books are ful of love, with so many authours, that it were labour lost to speake of Love.

Robert Giroux comments:

> These humourless lines not only gave Shakespeare a comical title for his play, but a light suddenly breaks when we find Florio in his next dialogue, a "Discourse upon Lust," proving pedantically and anticlimactically that "Lust was the cause that Troy was ruinated ... Sodom and Gomorrah were destroyed, and ... Holofernes fell in love with Judith." The name Shakespeare chose for his pedant in *Love's Labour's Lost* is Holofernes.[6]

There is certainly a similarity[7] between Florio's remark and the title *Love's Labour's Lost* and indeed in a number of studies of this play, Florio is seen in several of the characters. Shakespeare's apparent familiarity with Florio's comment, suggests that he had read Florio's book, and since it is a language text-book, we could assume that Shakespeare read it to learn Italian, or because he knew the author, or both.

By 1580 Florio was in Oxford, where he matriculated at Magdalen in 1581, and was also tutoring Emmanuel Barnes,[8] as we see in the dedication of his translation from the Italian of Ramusio's work.[9] He wrote that he was making this translation "at the requests and earneste solicitations of divers my very good friendes heere at Oxford".[10]

From 1583 he was at the French Embassy in London, where Giordano Bruno also resided from 1583 to 1585. Florio was employed here for two years as tutor to the daughter of the French Ambassador, as an interpreter and in other capacities. One of these other capacities seems to have been to deliver letters to dignitaries such as Walsingham and Sir Walter Raleigh. Even after the Ambassador departed with Bruno in October 1585, it seems that Florio continued to work at the Embassy. Frances Yates[11] mentions a letter calendared 1606, addressed to "Signor Giovanni Florio, at his room at the house of the French Ambassador"—though she believed that the date may have been the error of an official. The French embassy seems to have been a hotbed of spies, since it was through this office that the imprisoned Mary Queen of Scots communicated with her friends abroad. Florio may well have been spying for Walsingham, as, it seems, was Bruno.

In 1591, the year that he was appointed as Southampton's tutor, Florio's *Second Frutes* appeared. It was structured in the same way as the first book and in one of the dialogues there was a conversation between "young Henry" and "Master John". Clara Longworth de Chambrun[12] believed that this may have been a conversation between the young Henry Wriothesley and Florio himself, given that the topics of discussion included tennis and the theatre, both interests of the young Southampton. However, this is only speculation, and it is not until October 1594 that we have definite evidence of Florio being in Southampton's employ. This evidence is in documentation concerning the episode with the Danvers brothers, mentioned earlier in this chapter. It was recorded that:

> one Florio, an Italian, and one Humphrey Drewell the saide Earle of Southampton's servants, beinge in the saide passage Boate, threatned to cast him the saide Grose over board, and saide they woulde teache him to meddle with his fellowes, with many other threatninge words.[13]

At about this time Florio and Shakespeare must have crossed paths. In 1594 Shakespeare's dedication of *The Rape of Lucrece* to Southampton made it clear that their relationship still existed. Florio's involvement in the Danvers affair in the same year demonstrated that he must have been seen by Southampton as a trusted collaborator in what was certainly a very shady business. Florio was clearly part of the household to which Shakespeare must have been a frequent and welcome visitor. Already the playwright had written the first of the Italian plays, *Two Gentlemen of Verona,* and *The Taming of the Shrew,* the subplot of which is based on Ariosto's *Suppositi,* or its translation, *Supposes,* by George Gascoigne. He would also have written *A Comedy of Errors* and several of the historical plays. His interest in Italian plots and settings and his acquaintance with Florio's work was already clearly apparent.

In 1598 Florio's dictionary, *A Worlde of Wordes,* appeared. It had been licensed to Edward Blount in 1596, and was dedicated to "the right honorable the Earle of Southampton", in "whose pay and patronage" Florio had been living "for several years". The dedication was shared with the Earl of Rutland, and also the Countess of Bedford, all of whom had been his pupils, and all of whom would have been able to read the Italian words and phrases scattered throughout the dedication. At the end of the dictionary there was a list of the many works (largely Italian) used to compile it, in which Dante was not mentioned.

By 1598 Shakespeare had written (in addition to more history plays) *Romeo and Juliet, A Midsummer Night's Dream, The Merchant of Venice* and *Much Ado About Nothing.* All of these have Italian sources.

In this year Southampton was in France and whether Shakespeare or Florio had access to his library we do not know. Certainly Florio had his own library, but whether it was extensive enough to contain all seventy-two of the books he lists as sources for his 1598 dictionary is unknown, and whether he kept it at Southampton House is also a mystery. In 1599 Southampton was, for part of the year, in Ireland on the ill-fated expedition with Essex. It seems that at this time Florio lived elsewhere and in March, 1600 he wrote a letter *di casa sua in fretta* (from his own house in a hurry) requesting payment for fees from Sir Robert Cotton. However, he still had a number of wealthy patrons. Florio had been asked by his friend Sir Edward Wotton to translate one chapter of Montaigne. He did this in the house of the Countess of Bedford; she approved of it, and encouraged him to continue with a translation of the whole work. Two other ladies to share the dedication of Florio's *Montaigne* were the Countess of Rutland and

Lady Rich. Two others were two ex-pupils of his, Lady Elizabeth Grey and Lady Mary Neville.

In 1604 Florio began his court service. A document dated March 1619 mentions Florio as having been employed for fifteen years as one of Queen Anne's "Grooms of the Privy Chamber". He was also employed as a reader in Italian and private secretary to the queen and tutor in Italian to Prince Henry. Florio had then reached the highest point of his busy career and it is clear that he moved in very elevated circles. His friends and acquaintances, most of whom we know of through the dedications of his works, were prominent figures of the period in literary or political circles, and Clara Longworth de Chambrun found that the majority of these could also be linked, usually directly, with Shakespeare.

There is no doubt that Shakespeare used many of Florio's own works as source material for his plays. I have already mentioned the fact that Shakespeare's title *Love's Labour's Lost* probably comes from Florio's dialogue on "Musicke and Love" in *Firste Fruites* (1578). Clara Longworth de Chambrun found fourteen proverbs listed by Florio in his *Firste Fruites* which Shakespeare also used in his plays. She also investigated the many parallels between passages in Florio's translation of Montaigne's Essays and in Shakespeare, including the famous one in *The Tempest* (II.1.147–56) where Gonzago lists the features of his ideal "commonwealth".

Frances Yates commented on the work done by G. C. Taylor, who found:

> about one hundred close correspondences in thought and language between Shakespeare and Florio's *Montaigne* and about one hundred passages where the affinity is there, though less clearly defined ... He also compiles a glossary of about seven hundred and fifty words used by Florio in the translation and "used by Shakespeare during and after, but not before 1603". About twenty of these had been used for the first time in English by Florio. He does not claim that Shakespeare took all these seven hundred and fifty

words from Florio, but he urges that the coincidence of this expansion in Shakespeare's vocabulary with the appearance of the vast word-treasury of the *Montaigne* is significant.[14]

In fact, the influence of Florio's *Montaigne* is to be seen throughout Shakespeare's work after about 1600—*before* the publication of Florio's work. It was the custom in this period in literary circles to circulate work in manuscript, as were Shakespeare's sonnets, long before publication. In 1600, Cornwallis had written of Florio's *Montaigne,* "Montaigne now speaks good English,"[15] and although he was derogatory about Florio's appearance, he praised his wisdom as "beyond either his fortune or education".

Many actual facts and all the circumstantial evidence lead us to think that Florio and Shakespeare may have worked together. Firstly, there was the link with Southampton. Both Florio and Shakespeare must have had access to his library. Florio was employed as tutor and in this capacity he must have used this facility. Shakespeare, in the closeness of his relationship with Southampton, and given his love of words and constant search for material, must have browsed there. Secondly, Shakespeare's undisputed use of Florio's work showed that he found it valuable and that he therefore might have accepted guidance from Florio on which Italian sources would be of use to him. Thirdly, and most importantly, there was the list of books used by Florio to compile his second dictionary, *Queen Anna's New World of Words* (1611), which included the much smaller list given at the end of the 1598 edition. Included in the longer list are the titles and authors of some two hundred and forty-nine volumes, mostly Italian, which Florio claimed "have been read of Purpose for the collecting of this Dictionarie".[16] There were many plays, collections of letters and of poetry, novels, histories, travel books, religious treatises, natural histories, dictionaries and copies of the classics.

In the last chapter, forty definite or possible Italian sources for Shakespeare's plays were named. Of those sources, nineteen were to be found in Florio's lists.[17] These include:

Aminta	Torquato Tassso
Arcadia	Sanazzaro
Decamerone	Boccaccio
Dialoghi Piacevoli	Guazzo
Hecatommithi	Geraldi Cinthio
Il Canzoniere	Petrarch
Il Cortegiano	Castiglioni
Il Sacrificio (induction to *Gl'Ingannati*)	no author given
Il Viluppo	Parabosco
Inganni	no author given
La Divina Commedia	Dante, Commentato da Velitelli
La Divina Commedia	Dante, Comentato da Danielo
La Divina Commedia	Dante, Commentato da Boccaccio
La Divina Commedia	Dante, Commentato Dal Landini
Le opere burlesche del Berni e d'Altri	
Le opere di Petrarca	
Le quatro comedie del Arentino	
Novelle	Bandello
Ore de Recreazione	Giucciardini
Orlando Furioso	Ariosto
Pastor Fido	Guarini
Tutte le opere di Machiavelli	

The different commentaries on Dante have been counted as just one source. Added to these the following books were also on Florio's list:

Cornelio Tacito	tradotto da Bernardo Davanzati
Epistole di Cicero in volgare	
Herbario Inglese	Giovanni Gerardi[18]
Historia naturale	C. Plinio secondo[19]
Il Terentio	commentato in lingua Toscana
Metamorphosi d'Ovidio	tradorto [*sic*] dall Anguillara
Tito Livio	tradotto del Narni
Vite de Plutarce	

All of these texts we know Shakespeare to have used, though he may well have had access to them elsewhere. Also on Florio's list were an Italian-English and an Italian-French dictionary, both of which would have been very useful for Shakespeare.

From the similarity between the sources used by Florio and those used by Shakespeare we could probably conclude that they were working from the same library, possibly Southampton's, but which may have included many of Florio's own books. Clara Longworth de Chambrun wrote (in English this time) in 1938 about her discoveries concerning Florio's influence on Shakespeare:

> It was Giovanni Florio who gave Shakespeare the rudiments of French and Italian, just as it was his large library of books which furnished easy access to the Peninsular authors of whom the English poet made use ... I began to wonder why partisans of the traditional doctrine neglected such an important factor in the poet's culture since there need be no mystery in Shakespeare's knowledge of Italy, with Florio, so to speak, at his elbow.
>
> With naive enthusiasm I wrote to a noted scholar of that day asking why he never made use of Florio's writings to explain the facilities which the poet, without leaving England, possessed for learning the small amount of French and Italian necessary for the purpose. Professor Furness replied that he and other American scholars were unable to consult Florio's original and pre-Shakespearean publications. Apart from a set of stock quotations repeated at second hand from the nineteenth century critics, Hunter and Malone, and often incorrectly quoted at that, the works of Florio—with the exception of his celebrated English version of Montaigne's Essays—were buried in oblivion.[20]

She went on to recount that she had managed to acquire a copy of Florio's extremely rare *Firste Fruites*, of which there was only one other (mutilated) copy possessed by the British Museum:

> I soon found that Florio's conversation manuals contained as much and even more than Shakespeare required and that the list of the grammarian's books shows the original sources of his Italian plots. "In Venice we say on the Rialto, just as Londoners employ the term on the Exchange," quoth Florio, and printed it too in his *Worlde of Wordes*.
>
> As I proceeded in the study of his *Second Frutes*, I gained enlightening glimpses of my pet subject, and observed thirty proverbs which Shakespeare had borrowed and a quantity of allusions and parallels throughout the whole dramatic production, which attest the strength and durability of this Italian influence. Of course the passage from Montaigne which Shakespeare borrowed in *The Tempest*, was recognised long ago by an early commentator, but I discovered scores of new ones and felt certain that I had enough to prove that the old tradition which says that the pedant Holofernes in *Love's Labour's Lost*, was an intentional caricature of Giovanni Florio was correct.[21]

But she found that no-one was interested. Eventually, the vice president of an Anglo-American house explained to her that "unless such a discovery as mine was exploited by a well-known critic or distinguished professor, no scholarly publishing house of any repute would think of accepting it."

But even if she is correct in her belief that Florio was Shakespeare's Italian source, it is the relationship between Florio and Shakespeare which does not sit well with my argument. It is often claimed that the character Holofernes in *Love's Labour's Lost* may be, at least in part, a representation of Florio. Clara Longworth de Chambrun pointed out that the name Holofernes was an anagram of Florio's name (I Holofernes—Iohnes

Floreo), and anagrams were very fashionable in this period. She claimed that this portrait of Florio was not cruel:

> Le pauvre Pédant est representé, il est vrai, comme un autolâtre un peu vantard, comme un philologue précieux, qui cite l'italien à tout propos, mais le fond du personnage est un homme plutôt aimable et bien intentionné.[22]

> [The poor Pedant is represented, it is true, as a rather boastful "autolâtre"[23] as a rather precious philologue, who quotes Italian at all opportunities, but fundamentally, he is a rather aimiable and well-intentioned man.]

This may be an indication of how Shakespeare saw Florio, but how did Florio see the playwright?

Florio's dedications revealed much about their writer, and in his dedication of the *Worlde of Wordes*, 1598, Florio, having lavished compliments on Southampton, Rutland and the Countess of Bedford, continued angrily with his address to the Reader. Much of this was really directed to a much hated enemy, H.S., who must have been highly critical of his *Second Frutes*. Clara Longworth de Chambrun argued that this H. S. was in fact Shakespeare, claiming that to have used the initials W. S. would, in Elizabeth's reign, have prevented the publication of any criticism of a person with powerful friends. Frances Yates, however, identified this H.S. as Henry Sanford, who had been tutor to William Herbert, Earl of Pembroke, and who had edited the 1593 *Arcadia*.

But Florio's attack was not directed exclusively at H. S. He also remarked:

> Let Aristophanes and his comedians make plaies, and scoure their mouthes on Socrates; those very mouthes they make to vilifie, shall be the means to amplifie his virtue.[24]

This was probably a reference to Shakespeare and his plays, while the reference to Socrates was no doubt to Florio himself, the teacher.

In either case, if Shakespeare was among Florio's critics, it is unlikely that there was a happy relationship between them. Shakespeare's contact with Florio, at least on an intellectual level, may have been through a third person, the most obvious candidate being Southampton. Shakespeare was certainly acquainted with Florio's work and made good use of it, the language manuals, the dictionaries, and the translation of Montaigne. It would seem, too, that he also made good use of Florio's reading list. In the words of the Clara Longworth de Chambrun:

> Il ne faut laisser à Florio que ce qui lui appartient: il fut bon linguiste et excellent traducteur. Mais il eut un mérite, et un rôle gros de conséquences; il contribua à faire connaître, dans un milieu anglais des plus intellectuels, la renaissance italienne et la belle prose francaise du XVI siècle. Par ses écrits et ses conversations, il ouvrit aux yeux ardents de Shakespeare des horizons nouveaux. Le dramaturge se servit de lui comme d'un dictionnaire vivant, d'une source féconde de renseignements, jusqu'au jour où, s'affranchissant de ses premiers modèles, il donna libre essor à son génie.[25]

> [One must leave to Florio only that which belongs to him: he was a good linguist and an excellent translator. But he had one merit, and a role filled with consequences; he contributed to making known, in an English circle of the most intellectual, the Italian renaissance and the beautiful French prose of the sixteenth century. Through his writing and his conversations, he opened the ardent eyes of Shakespeare to new horizons. The dramatist used him as a living dictionary, a fertile source of information up until the day when, liberating himself from his first models, he gave full scope to his genius.]

The facts, then, are as follows. John Florio had an excellent knowledge of both English and Italian. In his list of the Italian books he used for his dictionaries, appeared, amongst others, nineteen or more titles which have also been suggested as possible sources for Shakespeare's plays. At least one of these (Cinthio's *Hecatommithi*) was not translated into English. He also listed as sources for his second dictionary of 1611, Dante's *Divina Commedia* and four different commentaries.

Today, as in Shakespeare's time, it would be virtually impossible to read Dante's *Divina Commedia* without the use of a commentary. So numerous are the allusions—biblical, liturgical, literary, mythological, classical, historical, geographical, political, philosophical, scientific, astronomical, linguistic, even personal—that a native speaker of Italian would have difficulty comprehending the full meaning of Dante's intricately woven and multilayered text without some explanation. In modern copies, as in those of the fifteenth and sixteenth centuries, there is often more space on the page devoted to the commentary than to the text. Without these explanations, the *Divina Commedia* loses much of its depth, as indeed it does in translation.

The question of Renaissance libraries is an interesting one. The most comprehensive and impressive collections of manuscripts and printed books were once the property of the monasteries. After the Dissolution of these institutions and at the end of the sixteenth century and the beginning of the seventeenth, many of their books gradually found their way into the College and University libraries. Many private citizens also profited greatly from this movement. It was becoming fashionable to read and collect books as part of the code of gentility among the nobility—a custom borrowed from Italy. The clergy, too, acquired libraries for perhaps more scholarly motives. At a slightly lower level of society, the other groups of people who owned books were physicians and University scholars. Sears Jayne believed:

> [O]utside the Universities very few people before 1590 owned
> as many as 15 different books; even at Cambridge the typical
> personal library included only a dozen books or so in the

first decade of the century ... By 1580 the average scholar at Cambridge owned about seventy books ... but laymen owned very few books indeed.[26]

Citing the experience of a researcher of the 1950s who transcribed more than a hundred detailed inventories of personal belongings of ordinary London householders (excluding the nobility), Jayne noted that not a single list of as many as fifteen separate titles of books in the period 1500–1640 was discovered.[27] In the five volume survey of private libraries in Renaissance England edited by R. J. Fehrenbach and published in 1992,[28] there is no copy of Dante's work listed. If we are to trace the source of Shakespeare's access to copies of Dante's work, it will not be found among the libraries of the theatrical people of his daily life.

In 1602, Thomas James, who was appointed by Sir Thomas Bodley to look after the library which the latter had recently presented to the University of Oxford, compiled the first of the catalogues of that library. Two of these, dated respectively 1602–3 and 1613, were preserved in manuscript and the other two were printed and published in 1605 and 1620. From his first catalogue it appears that, so far as Dante's works are concerned, the Bodleian started with one edition of the *De Monarchia* and two of the *Divina Commedia*, which in the catalogue of 1620 had increased to five.[29] This apparently rising popularity of Dante's work in England may have followed on from a rebirth of interest in the poem from the 1540s to the 1570s in Italy. Richardson in his article, "Editing Dante's *Commedia*", tells us that "the history of the reception of the *Commedia* up to modern times shows that there was particular interest in the poem at moments of religious and political crisis and renewal ... The poem must have spoken even more directly to Italians in the mid-sixteenth century, after the emperor Charles V had driven the French from Italy, firmly establishing imperial power in the peninsula."[30]

When the Bodleian Library had opened in November 1602, in its catalogue for 1602–3 were listed:

Dantis de Monarchia

Dante con Espos. di M. Bern. Daniello di Luca.

Dante dell inferno et purgatorio, Ven. 1515

The copy with the commentary by Daniello, as we noted earlier, had been the gift in 1602 of Sir Henry Danvers. The provenance of the copy printed in Venice in 1515 is not known. In the first ever printed catalogue of the Bodleian library—the first printed catalogue in any large library in England—in 1605 were listed:

Dante con la espositione di Aless. Velutello, Ven. 1544

Dante con com di Christ. Landino, Ven. 1512

Dante con com di Landino, Ven. 1484

Dante con l'espos di M. Bern. Daniello, Ven. 1568

The copy with the commentary by Landino, published in 1512, had been purchased in 1600 with a sum of 100 pounds given to the library by Sir Thomas Sackville, Chancellor of the University. The copy printed in 1484 had been given by Sir Michael Dormer in 1603. The copy printed in Venice in 1515 was no longer listed. In the catalogue of 1613 there were still only these same four copies, but in the catalogue of 1620, the copy listed in the 1602–3 catalogue as printed in Venice in 1515, reappeared.

In his list of sources for his *Queen Anna's New World of Words*, published in London in 1611, John Florio listed, among a large number of Italian texts:

Dante. Commentato da Alessandro Velitelli [*sic*]

Dante. Comentato [*sic*] da Bernardo Danielo [*sic*]

Dante. Commentato da Giovanni Boccaccio

Dante. Commentato da Landini [*sic*]

These may have been recent acquisitions to his own large library, as they were not listed among the sources of his 1598 dictionary, the *Worlde of Words*—although words from Dante were mentioned in the original dictionary itself. Frances Yates pointed out that Florio must have read Dante's work carefully, since he included in his revised dictionary some Dantean archaisms peculiar to this writer, and gave English equivalents.[31] He had also commented on Dante's use of words as far back as 1578 in his *Firste Fruites,* written while he was in Oxford and showing a detailed knowledge of Dante's work.

But Florio, although he had seen Dante's work some twenty years earlier, may have used the copies in the Bodleian Library for the compilation of his dictionary since three of the commentaries are the same and they had been in the library since the catalogue of 1605. Unfortunately Florio did not give the date or place of publication of the copies he used, or it may have been possible to identify them more precisely with those in the Bodleian Library. He may have also had access to the library of an Italian-minded aristocrat, of which there were several in his circle. If Southampton had possessed these copies of Dante, it would seem likely that Florio would have used them in the compilation of his earlier dictionary in 1598. The important fact, however, is that the books were accessible to and used by Florio, who was in the immediate social environment of Shakespeare.

There is, if we assume these are the copies of Dante used by Shakespeare, no problem with dates. The earliest passage which we have claimed as a "borrowing" is from *Richard II,* generally believed to have been written in 1595. At that time Sir Charles Danvers was still the owner of the copy with the commentary by Daniello. He had, in 1594, with Southampton's (and Florio's) assistance, fled to France with his brother. Might he have allowed Southampton or Florio access to his library while he was in exile? Florio listed Dante among his sources in 1611, but he must have used the books earlier, perhaps from immediately after the publication in 1598 of his first dictionary, or even earlier, without acknowledgement of Dante as a source. He had certainly seen Dante's work as early as 1578. It may also have been that he preferred not to mention his interest in these copies when Elizabeth was on the throne. Florio—a protestant himself—would have had enough understanding of Dante's work to see that the *Divina Commedia* was not supportive of the protestant movement, and could certainly be classified as "popish".

Two copies then, of the *Divina Commedia,* both with a commentary by Landino, were owned by the Bodleian Library in 1602–3, but unlisted in the catalogue for those years. One (Landino 1512) was missing from 1600 to late 1603 and possibly till 1605. The other (Landino, 1484) was missing from presumably late 1603 to whenever the catalogue was revised in 1605. Equally puzzling is the fact that the copy (the second Aldine edition—without commentary) printed in Venice in 1515 and listed in the 1602–3 catalogue, disappeared from the 1605 and 1613 catalogues, and then reappeared mysteriously in 1620. This copy was at least very portable. The first edition in 1502 was without commentary and was therefore pocket sized. When it was republished in 1515 it had new diagrams. But Florio did not acknowledge it as one of his sources. Did someone else perhaps borrow it for all those years? Shakespeare died in 1616—and the Aldine copy reappeared in the next catalogue of the Bodleian Library in 1620.

It could be that from 1593 to 1602, Shakespeare, through his connection with Southampton, had access to the copy of the *Divina Commedia* owned by Sir Charles Danvers, although from the end of 1594 to 1598 Danvers was in exile in France and in 1599 he was in Ireland. Perhaps Shakespeare would have had access to the library at Drury House while the Danvers brothers were not in residence. From 1600 to 1605, two other copies (Landino 1512 and Landino 1484) were, for all or part of this time, in the possession of the Bodleian library, but not catalogued. Also at large from 1605 to 1620 was the copy known as the second Aldine edition, which had no commentary and was therefore portable. Could Shakespeare, or Florio, have been the phantom borrower? Peter Levi believed that in the years of Shakespeare's mature tragedies, he spent some time in Oxford, attracted by the Bodleian Library. "Entry cost a shilling and scholars from all over the world were very soon visiting and using it. But its books were accumulating for years before it formally opened, and even before that Oxford was full of books; as a society, it was the kind that books always create. That is why it is impossible to rule out Shakespeare's access to sources that might seem beyond his personal scholarly attainment".[32]

It may be possible to establish which copy Shakespeare used. Sometimes in the commentaries, the explanation of a word of phrase can vary significantly from one commentator to another. If we found evidence of an interpretation given exclusively by one commentator in one of the Shakespearean passages which we believe to be a "borrowing" from Dante, we could perhaps determine which commentator Shakespeare was using.

One "borrowing" considered earlier where we see a slightly different interpretation among the commentators, is the passage where Dante's ancestor predicts Dante's experience of exile. The parallel passage is the "bitter bread" comment from *Richard II* which we considered in Chapter 1. Dante's lines were as follows:

> Tu proverai come si sa di sale
> lo pane altrui, e come è duro calle
> lo scendere a 'l salir per altrui scale.
>
> *Paradiso* XVII.58–60

> [You shall come to know how salt is the taste of another's bread, and how hard the path to descend and mount by another man's stairs.]

Shakespeare's similar passage also concerns exile, where Bolingbroke describes how he has:

> ... sigh'd my English breath in foreign clouds,
> Eating the bitter bread of banishment.
>
> *Richard II* III.1.20–1

The key phrase in the passage from Dante is *sa di sale*. Literally, it means "tastes of salt" and indeed that is how Singleton has translated it. If Shakespeare worked with a commentary from one of the copies of the

Divina Commedia which was catalogued in the Bodleian Library in 1602–3 and 1605, or one of the copies listed by Florio, which look to be the same, there are some interesting interpretations of this phrase.

The commentary by Vellutello (Venice, 1544)[33] on the two lines concerning exile is lengthy:

> Ma quello che prima più t'affligera, sarà che tu lascerai ogni tua diletta cosa, che tu più ami, ciò è, la patria, parenti, amici, case, possessioni, e questo è lo strale, che l'arco de l'esilio saetta prima, ciò è. E questo è il dolore con l'esilio tormenta prima il cuore. Seguita poi, in dire, quanto gli abbia ad esser dura cosa l'haver a viver a la mercè d'altri, e l'habitar de l'altrui case.[34]

> [But that which first will afflict you, will be that you will leave behind all of your favourite things, that you love most, that is your country, relatives, friends, houses, possessions and this is the wound that the bow of exile makes first with its arrow. And this pain of exile torments first the heart. It follows then to say how hard it is to have to live on the charity of others and to live in other people's houses.]

There is no mention of bread here, bitter, salty or otherwise, since the writer probably believed that the unpalatable bread was merely an image for the unpleasantness of living off charity. Shakespeare's "bitter bread" has not been suggested by anything here.

The commentary by Bernardino Daniello, of which there is a reprint,[35] made no mention at all of the reference to bread in *Paradiso* XVII.58. He must have assumed that the meaning was self-evident. It was not possible to access copies of the other two commentaries (Landino, Venice, 1512 and Landino, Venice 1484) listed in the Bodleian catalogues of 1602–3 and 1605. However, a later edition in 1564 combined the comments of Landino with those of Vellutello (who died in 1566 or 1559), as did an even later one in 1596. These combined commentaries gave a short section of text in the centre of the page and then the comments of Vellutello and Landino on opposite sides of the page. The comments of Vellutello have not changed since the 1544 edition. The relevant comment of Landino in the 1564 edition read as follows and was the same in the 1596 edition. Landino died in 1504 or 1508, so his comment would certainly not have changed since the 1512 edition, which was in the Bodleian Library:

> ma nondimeno tu, nel tuo esilio sarai percosso dal la prima saetta, che trahe l'esilio: e quello è, che li converà lasciar le cose a te più care, cioè, la patria, i parenti, gli amici, le case, le possessioni, & simili & proverai, come sa di sale, cioè quanto pare amaro.[36]

> [But nevertheless you, in your exile, will be struck by the first arrow, which exile shoots: and that is, that you will have to leave all the things which are most dear to you, that is, the country, relatives, friends, houses, possessions and similar things, and you will feel, how it tastes of salt, that is, how bitter it seems.]

The comments by Vellutello and Landino on the lines concerning exile were remarkably similar. The image of the pain of exile as a bow and arrow attack was in the lines immediately preceding those we have quoted, the list of the things to be missed was almost identical, but the Landino comment introduced the word *amaro*, or "bitter". The wording was a little ambiguous in that we did not know if the word "bitter" was meant to translate literally *sa di sale* or whether it was a metaphor for the distastefulness of being obliged to accept charity. But it was the word that Shakespeare also used in his "bitter bread of exile".

Of course the alliteration of the phrase "bitter bread" has its own attraction, but it is interesting that Shakespeare, like Dante, should have chosen two essentials of life—Dante had food and lodging, Shakespeare, breathing and food—to symbolise the pains of exile. Both writers could have used the generic "food" or they could have chosen something equally basic, "meat" or "water" for example. It seems that the coincidence of "bread"—added to the same adjective, "bitter"—was unlikely, when both poets were describing exile in very similar circumstances. And it looks very much as though Shakespeare was using one of Landino's commentaries. Since the "bitter bread" phrase is from 1595, perhaps the copy Shakespeare was using was *not* the Danvers copy, since Daniello did not mention the word "bitter" in his commentary on *Paradiso* VII, 58–60. But Florio had seen Dante's work much earlier than this—perhaps with a Landino commentary, and he may have discussed this with Shakespeare.

Landino's commentary, according to Toynbee:

> which was the classical commentary of the Renaissance, and has been reprinted more often probably than any other, was first published in 1481, in the famous first Florentine edition of the *Divina Commedia*, with the designs of Sandro Botticelli. Landino made considerable use of the *Comento* of Boccaccio, whom he describes as *huomo, et per dottrina, et per costumi, et per essere proprinquo a tempi di Dante, degno di fede* (a man, for doctrine, for customs, and for being near to the times of Dante, worthy of faith).[37]

It seems likely that Landino's commentary would have been the most common one in existence, and even if Shakespeare were working from the library of another aristocrat, this was the copy he seems to have used.

Florio too, listed four different commentaries which he used and which he identified as those of Vellutello, Daniello, Boccaccio and Landino. The Bodleian Library listed three of these, and they were probably the same copies, excluding Boccaccio. In fact, the commentary by Boccaccio was of little use. Boccaccio had been appointed by the Signoria of Florence in 1373 to write a commentary on the *Divina Commedia*. He began the work but had completed only sixteen cantos and seventeen lines of Canto XVII of *Inferno* when he died on 21 December 1375. In Shakespeare's time this commentary was not printed. In any case, Shakespeare must have read more than seventeen cantos of *Inferno,* since the "borrowings" are widely spread throughout the whole work.

I have established, then, that Shakespeare had some considerable knowledge of Italian, since he used, as sources for his own work, several untranslated Italian plays. He also used a number of lines of authentic Italian dialogue. I have also established that there were a number of copies of Dante's work which were accessible to John Florio and no doubt to others in his circle. One other copy was in the possession of Sir Charles Danvers from 1593 until his death in 1601, and then presented by his brother to the Bodleian Library in 1602. All three of these men were within the circle of Shakespeare's acquaintance through his relationship with Southampton. Since Shakespeare certainly used many Italian books, copies of which were in the libraries of Florio and probably Southampton, it would seem unlikely that he would have made an exception of Dante's works, if they were also there. However, his knowledge of Dante was evident as early as 1595 in *Richard II,* so at some period prior to this he must have had time to study and consider ideas from the *Divina Commedia*—perhaps from about 1591, when probably he first encountered Southampton and Florio.

The copies used by Florio may have been Southampton's, they may have belonged to another aristocratic library,[38] they may have been Florio's own, or they may have been from the Bodleian Library at Oxford, in which town Florio had worked in 1580. In the 1605 Catalogue were listed copies of Dante's work with commentaries by Velutello, Landino (2), and Daniello. This last commentary had from 1593 to 1602, been in the possession of the Danvers family, close friends of Southampton. In this period it may well have been accessible to both Florio and Shakespeare. Florio's list of sources included these same three commentaries and also a commentary by Boccaccio, which was not in the Bodleian library catalogue of 1605. It was not printed till 1724, but Toynbee[39] believed that Florio might have known of it from Gelli's *Letture* (the first of which was published in 1553) in which Boccaccio's *Comento* is frequently quoted.

Certainly, from 1593 (perhaps even 1591) to at least 1605, Shakespeare and Florio mixed in the same circles and shared a number of common acquaintances. Shakespeare knew and used Florio's work, sometimes even before it was published. The strong Italian influence in Shakespeare's plays began at the same time as his acquaintance with Southampton, whose tutor was at this time, Florio. Southampton's knowledge of Italian was, according to Florio, good enough for the tutor to "be not now of any further use to your self sufficiencie being at home so instructed for Italian as teaching or learning could supplie". Through Florio, Dante was accessible certainly to Southampton, and through him to Shakespeare.

CHAPTER 6

The Verdict

But the images of men's wits and knowledges remain in books, exempted from the wrong of time and capable of perpetual renovation. Neither are they fitly to be called images, because they generate still, and cast their seeds in the minds of others, provoking and causing infinite actions and opinions in succeeding ages.

Of the Advancement of Learning,[1] Francis Bacon

The number of close parallels between passages in the works of Shakespeare and Dante is too great to attribute them all to chance or coincidence. Many of these parallels demonstrate a remarkable similarity of idea, of phrasing (in spite of the fact that they were written in different languages), and, most convincingly, a striking similarity of context. It is as though the English playwright, pondering on a character, a philosophical view or a setting, recalled a similar concept in Dante and turned to the Italian poet for ideas. Shakespeare may have easily recalled the image or idea he wished to use, but it seems more likely that he was also able to consult a copy of the *Divina Commedia* and examine the relevant passage closely, adapting it as required.

In English literary circles in the nineteenth and twentieth centuries there was strong resistance to such a notion, perhaps inspired by national or religious loyalties. Many refused to entertain the idea on the quite rational grounds that Dante's work had not been translated into English in Shakespeare's time. However, there is today considerable supporting evidence for the belief that Shakespeare had sufficient knowledge of the Italian language to use other untranslated Italian sources for his plays, probably with the assistance of an Italian-speaking acquaintance and often with an English translation to facilitate the exercise.

The most often stated objection was that if Shakespeare had known Dante's work he would have used it extensively and so we would be left in no doubt as to his familiarity with this resource. I believe that these preceding chapters present enough evidence of his knowledge of Dante for us to be no longer left in doubt. The fact is that the playwright adapted and used these "borrowings" so successfully and seamlessly in his work that they became part of the fabric of his plays—and this ability is surely yet another of the skills that constitute his genius.

There is at least one passage where his knowledge of Dante's work is, I believe, indisputable. In *Measure for Measure,* in the passage where Shakespeare describes Isabella as "enskied and sainted", the close parallel with Dante's account of Saint Clare and her follower Piccarda Donati, the exactly similar neologisms created by both writers, and the striking parallel of context cannot all be explained as coincidence.

If we accept that any of the close parallels here considered are indeed evidence of Shakespeare's knowledge of Dante, and that his knowledge of the Italian language was sufficient to allow this, it remains only to demonstrate that there was at least one copy of the *Divina Commedia* available for Shakespeare's use, constantly and over the period in which he was writing his plays. In Chapter 5 it was established that there were a number of copies of the *Divina Commedia* owned or used by people in the social circles in which Shakespeare must have mixed and in the period in which he was writing his plays. He must have had contact with Sir Charles and Sir Henry Danvers, close friends of Southampton, and the Danvers brothers owned a copy of the *Divina Commedia* which was probably kept at their London mansion, Drury House, from 1593 to 1602. Shakespeare must also have had contact with John Florio, tutor to Southampton from about 1591 onwards, and who, we know, used four copies of the *Divina*

Commedia with four different commentaries in the compilation of his 1611 dictionary, *Queen Anna's New World of Wordes.*

From the fact that so many of the Italian texts believed to have been used by Shakespeare appear in the comprehensive list of Italian books which Florio acknowledged as source material for his 1611 dictionary and published with it, we could perhaps conclude that Shakespeare was using the same library. If this were so, it would seem unlikely that the playwright would ignore Dante's masterpiece while he consulted so many other Italian volumes listed there. This collection of more than two hundred and fifty books may have belonged to Florio—certainly when he died he left a total of "Three hundred and Fortie" books to William, Earl of Pembroke.[2] This legacy included Italian, French and Spanish books in addition to the books he had written himself, some printed and some unprinted. But Florio died in poverty, and if his own library had been as well-stocked as the one he used to write his dictionary, one might imagine he could have sold some of these volumes to alleviate his financial problems.

It is more likely that many of the books Florio used were owned by the Earl of Southampton, and in this case, Shakespeare, too, would almost certainly have had access to them from the time he met Southampton, c.1591, when the first sonnets were written until, perhaps, the completion of his last play. The copies of the *Divina Commedia* used by Florio were published with the same commentators as those copies listed in the catalogue of the Bodleian Library from 1602 onwards. Florio had worked in Oxford, and may well have had connections there which allowed him to work with these books, or even to borrow them. They were weighty tomes, but this would not present an insurmountable problem. Some of these volumes seemed to appear and disappear from the catalogue from time to time and we can only conclude that the cataloguer was rather careless or that someone was finding them very useful.

There would have been of course, other copies owned by other members of aristocratic society, and of which we have no record. But Florio had several aristocratic patrons, and Shakespeare too, given his link with Southampton, would probably have had access to libraries belonging to some of the other literary minded and italophile aristocrats, such as the Earl of Rutland, the Earl of Oxford, and the Earl of Derby. Mary Sidney Herbert, Countess of Pembroke, had a library which contained a large number of Italian books.[3] Her son, William, to whom Florio left his books, had been tutored by Samuel Daniel, who was Florio's brother-in-law. Florio may well have had access to this library.

John Dee, the learned philosopher and seance-organiser "was reputed to have the best library in the country".[4] Dee had been tutor to Sir Philip Sidney, who in 1583 was in charge of a trip to Oxford in the queen's barge up and down the river. Giordano Bruno was also invited and befriended John Florio, with whom he later shared accommodation at the home of Michel de Castelnau. On the return trip to London they called in to visit Dee, and no doubt his library. Through this connection, too, then, Florio may also have had access to Dee's library. The Earl of Essex also owned a very substantial library, to which Shakespeare may have had access through Southampton. On the disastrous occasion of his ill-conceived "rebellion" on Sunday, February 8, 1601, history records that the doors of Essex House had been barricaded and its windows had been closed with piles of books.[5] Peter Levi believed it likely that Shakespeare knew Stow, the antiquary, historian of London and editor of Chaucer, and used his vast collection of books and manuscripts. "I cannot otherwise explain" Levi wrote, "how Shakespeare had access at this time to all the books and the unprinted manuscripts he is known to have used."[6]

The *Divina Commedia* is virtually impossible to understand without a commentary, even for a native speaker of Italian. From the variations in how Dante's lines are interpreted, it is perhaps possible to determine which of these commentaries Shakespeare may have used. There is not a great deal of evidence, but as I have argued in Chapter 5, it seems likely that he was using the commentary by Landino, which was, in fact, the most published and the most popular at the time.

The primary conclusion of my argument—that Shakespeare had read the *Divina Commedia* in the original Italian and used images and ideas from it in his plays—rests on a number of facts established in the preceding chapters. The similarities to be found in the two works are enough to justify the claim that Shakespeare used Dante as a source. He had some knowledge of the Italian language, and the possibility of access to a copy of the *Divina Commedia*. He was accustomed to "borrowing" material for his plays. There is no reason why he would not have made use of this material if it was available to him, and the evidence presented here attests that he did so.

But there are a number of secondary conclusions which can also be drawn from this investigation. One could assume that Shakespeare would not have read all of the *Divina Commedia* with equal interest and equal comprehension. Many readers of Dante find some parts tedious or too difficult to understand—and remember perhaps only the parts that are most dramatic or most relevant to their own lives. The passages from Dante considered as possible sources for Shakespeare in the preceding chapters are to be found in all three books of the *Divina Commedia,* as illustrated in the next table where the cantos apparently used are marked "#".

It seems from this table that *Inferno* was the most popular with Shakespeare—as it is with many readers. One reason for this is that the language is simpler than that used in *Purgatorio* and very much simpler than that used in *Paradiso*. Another reason is that the characters and action in *Inferno* are considerably more colourful and dramatic, and perhaps for these reasons more suitable as material for the stage. In *Inferno*, the characters are humanly flawed and spectacularly damned. The settings are vividly and terrifyingly the stuff of our worst nightmares—and all of this is excellent material for the theatre. If Shakespeare were searching for images or details to flesh out his own characters or ideas to lure an audience into the world of his play, *Inferno* would certainly be an ideal place to find them.

He also found parts of *Purgatorio* useful, but not the opening cantos, and nothing at all after Canto XXIII, when Dante (the Pilgrim) leaves his old friend Forese Donati and Dante (the Poet) moves into philosophical discussions on poetic style, the nature of the generative principle and the need for chastity. The Earthly Paradise does not seem to provide any material for him. In *Paradiso,* the material Shakespeare uses is only that provided by the Heaven of the Moon, the Eagle, and the idea of exile.

Apparent "borrowings" from the *Commedia*

Inferno		*Purgatorio*		*Paradiso*	
I	#	I		I	
II	#	II		II	#
III	#	III		III	#
IV		IV		IV	
V	#	V	#	V	
VI		VI	#	VI	#
VII	#	VII		VII	
VIII		VIII		VIII	
IX	#	IX	#	IX	
X		X		X	
XI		XI		XI	
XII	#	XII		XII	
XIII	#	XIII		XIII	
XIV	#	XIV	#	XIV	
XV		XV	#	XV	
XVI		XVI	#	XVI	#
XVII		XVII	#	XVII	#
XVIII		XVIII		XVIII	
XIX		XIX		XIX	
XX		XX	#	XX	
XXI		XXI		XXI	
XXII		XXII		XXII	
XXIII		XXIII	#	XXIII	
XXIV		XXIV		XXIV	
XXV		XXV		XXV	
XXVI	#	XXVI		XXVI	
XXVII	#	XXVII		XXVII	
XXVIII	#	XXVIII		XXVIII	
XXIX	#	XXIX		XXIX	
XXX		XXX		XXX	
XXXI		XXXI		XXXI	
XXXII	#	XXXII		XXXII	
XXXIII	#	XXXIII		XXXIII	
XXXIV	#	–		–	

Often (as the table demonstrates) Shakespeare's interest seems to focus on blocks of Dante's work—groups of sequential cantos. He is interested in the opening Cantos I, II and III of *Inferno*, where Dante (the Pilgrim) finds himself in the wood of error, decides, after some hesitation, to journey through Hell with Virgil, and meets the opportunists. After that, Shakespeare's interest focuses on the carnal and the avaricious. (Cantos V and VII). He glances perhaps at the Erinyes[7] in Canto IX, then moves on to the fate of the violent, tyrants and suicides (Cantos XII, XIII and XIV) and the river of blood. Passing rapidly over ten cantos, he seems to regain interest with some of the worst offenders in *Inferno*: the thieves, the evil counsellors, and the sowers of discord (Cantos XXV, XXVI, XXVII and XXVIII). Most of all, he is interested in the traitors (Cantos XXXII, XXXIII and XXIV).

He does not find anything he can use in the fate of the virtuous pagans, the wrathful (though he is interested in their expiation in *Purgatorio*), the heretics, or Virgil's lengthy and detailed explanation of the structure of the lower part of Hell (Cantos X and XI). Nor does he use any material from the account of the sodomites, the usurers, the monster Geryon, or the occupants of Malebolgia: panderers, seducers and flatterers, simoniacs, fortune-tellers, grafters, and hypocrites (Cantos XV–XXIV). His interest does not seem to be caught by long philosophical treatises (except perhaps for the discussion on the cause of social disorder, the "universal wolf" of avarice) or religious diatribes.

In *Purgatorio* Shakespeare finds material in the account of the late-repentant, at least those who died violently (Cantos V and VI). He then moves on to the consideration of the nature of repentance and the eagle dream in Canto IX, the latter of which seems to interest him particularly in the use of the Eagle as a symbol of the god Jove, of the Roman Empire and of Divine Justice. Shakespeare also shows interest in the cantos on the envious, the wrathful, and the consequent discussion on free will (Cantos XIV, XV and XVI). After that, he focuses on the hoarders and wasters, and the gluttons (Cantos XX and XXIII). He is not interested in the arrival of the penitent on the shore of Purgatory, the ritual of purification, the late-repentant who did not die violently, the proud, the slothful, the lustful, nor any cantos on the Earthly Paradise.

In *Paradiso,* his interest seems to be rather diminished. This last *cantica* is often said to be he most medieval part of the *Divina Commedia* and Shakespeare's attention seems to be confined to the circle of the Moon (Cantos II and III), the Roman Eagle (Canto VI) and Dante's meeting with his ancestor Cacciaguida (Cantos XVI and XVII). After that, Shakespeare seems to have found nothing he could use, and indeed, Dante's language becomes increasingly difficult as he tries to express ideas which are mystical and virtually inexpressible. Perhaps Dante's ascent to the higher spheres, and his meeting with the saints and eventually God, is a little overwhelming, and in any case, outside the very human world in which Shakespeare's plays are set.

But disregarding the parts where Dante is inclined to sermonize—and he does so quite often—his writing is highly dramatic, so that characters, action and settings are eminently suited to the stage. Dorothy Sayers points out:

> Had he lived at a time when drama was the dominant form, the plays of Dante might be holding the stage to this day. His work has all the marks: the solid planting and setting of a dramatic action; the brisk economy of the dialogue; the instinctive avoidance of scenic incongruities; the sure recognition of the "scène-a-faire"; the knack of relieving a situation with a touch of high comedy; the ability to establish a character in a line or two; the rejection of ramblings and embroideries: the knowledge of when to stop. It is this compact and sinewy quality in his narrative which holds the reader's attention.[8]

Shakespeare would have noted these qualities immediately—and imitated them to considerable effect.

There are a number of conclusions about Shakespeare himself which can perhaps be implied from his selection of passages from the *Divina*

Commedia. He is certainly interested in Dante's view of Hell. The pictures he presents of it himself in *Richard III, Measure for Measure* and *Macbeth* seem strongly influenced by Dante's vision, though some ideas here may certainly be traced to *The Aeneid,* Dante's own primary source. Associated with this is his interest in some of the "sins" with which Dante deals, avarice, the cause of all corruption (symbolized by the wolf) and considered in *Troilus and Cressida,* and the nature of betrayal or treachery, considered in *King Lear* and *Macbeth* particularly. Repentance too, interests him, genuine repentance as seen in *Cymbeline* or hypocritical repentance where the sinner fears the torments of the afterlife, but does not wish to give up what the "sin" has won for him, as seen in *Hamlet.* The reason for the existence of evil and the question of free will also concern him, as we see particularly in *King Lear.*

For those who wish to speculate, it may be possible to relate these preoccupations to incidents in Shakespeare's own life—if we can consider the sonnets as autobiographical—but that is not the subject of this book. It is also possible to relate these interests to historical incidents of the period, particularly to the trial and execution of Essex and his co-conspirators. On 7 February 1601, the evening before the abortive rebellion of Essex, the conspirators had requested that *Richard II* be performed, though the representative for the Lord Chamberlain's Men protested that the actors were reluctant to perform the play and had only done so for the "forty shillings more than their ordinary" which they were paid.[9] On 24 February, the Queen requested a performance by the Lord Chamberlain's men, which is believed to have been *Richard II.*[10] On 25 February, Essex was executed. If Shakespeare were mixing with Southampton and his associates, he could not have been exempt from the swirling currents of loyalty and betrayal in the society in which he moved at this time.

Shakespeare is also fascinated by some of the images Dante uses which so clearly delineate character. Dante's initial fear when he is lost in the *selva oscura,* his hesitation at the prospect of entering Inferno, Francesca's eternal and moving torment for surrendering to an over-riding passion,

Forese's sadly diminished state, Piccarda's forced broken vow of chastity, and Dante's own sad experience of exile, all appear in Shakespeare in a slightly different form. Even Dante's language, experimental as it often is, intrigued him, so that he, also an experimenter, "invented" exactly the same word in English (enskied) as Dante had invented (*inciela*) in Italian.

Shakespeare was clearly interested in the story of the eagle which carried off the beautiful Ganymede and which had its origins in Ovid (*Metamorphoses* X.155–61) and Virgil (*Aeneid*, V.252–5). Dante uses this image to describe the dream of the eagle which carried him to the gates of Paradise. Shakespeare uses the eagle dream in *Cymbeline* and also uses the Roman Eagle to describe the power of ancient Rome. As discussed in Chapter 2, VII, there is an interesting link between the Derby family whose emblem was an eagle carrying off a child, and various elements of Shakespeare's life and his plays.

Equally interesting is the following table in which can be traced the time at which Shakespeare's interest in Dante began, the period in which he seems to have most frequently used Dante's text, and the times at which his interest waned.

Title[11]	Date	Borrowing
Edward III	1590	doubtful authorship
1ˢᵗ Part of the Contention (2H6)	1591	? doubtful authorship
Richard Duke of York (3H6)	1591	? doubtful authorship
1 Henry 6	1592	doubtful authorship
The Comedy of Errors	1592	
Two Gentlemen of Verona	1593	
Richard III	1593	? ?
Titus Andronicus	1594	
The Taming of the Shrew	1594	?
Romeo & Juliet	1595	
Love's Labour's Lost	1595	
A Midsummer Night's Dream	1595	? ? ?
Richard II	1595	X X ?

Title	Date	Borrowing
Sir Thomas More?	1595	3 other writers
Henry V	1595	
King John	1596	
The Merchant of Venice	1596	
1 Henry IV	1597	?
II Henry IV	1597	
Much Ado About Nothing	1598	
Love's Labour's Won	1598	lost
As You Like It	1599	
Julius Caesar	1599	
The Merry Wives of Windsor	1600	
Twelfth Night	1600	
Hamlet	1601	X ?
Troilus & Cressida	1602	?
All's Well That Ends Well	1602	D's *Convivio?*
Measure for Measure	1604	X X X ? ? ?
Othello	1604	? ? ?
King Lear	1605	X ? ?
Macbeth	1606	X X ? ?
Antony & Cleopatra	1607	?
Timon of Athens	1607	
Pericles	1608	
Coriolanus	1608	
Cymbeline	1609	X
The Winter's Tale	1610	
The Tempest	1611	X combination factors
Cardenio	1613	lost? with Fletcher?
All Is True (Henry VIII)	1613	with Fletcher?
Two Noble Kinsmen	1613	

In this table I have included all parallels considered in this book, on the basis that if *any* of them is a genuine "borrowing"—then all of them *could* be. Those marked "X" are those which fulfil the criteria established in the Introduction. Those which have been considered, but do not fulfil these criteria, are marked "?" I have not marked the plays in which Shakespeare seems to write with some knowledge of the *Divina Commedia,* but where there is no actual passage which clearly demonstrates this.

Some trends emerge. Shakespeare may have used ideas from Dante in the earliest of his plays, but certainly he "borrowed" more in the plays written after 1600. One of the first plays which seems to show some real knowledge of the *Divina Commedia* is *Henry VI,* Part III, in which occurs the image of Richard "lost in a thorny wood", very similar to the first and perhaps most famous image of *Inferno.* Another is a brief reference in *Richard III* to "the melancholy flood/ With that grim ferryman that poets write of". That this was a reference to Dante was claimed by Clara Longworth de Chambrun in 1921 and supported by Frank Kermode in 2000. In each of these cases, the knowledge Shakespeare demonstrates is from early cantos of *Inferno*—Cantos I and V.

The parallel passages I have noted before *Richard III* could all be explained as biblical allusions (2, *Henry VI*) or coincidence (3, *Henry VI*). *Richard III* was written c.1593. In that year, Sir Charles Danvers had imported his copy of the *Divina Commedia.* It may be that the mention of "that grim ferryman" was an indication that Shakespeare had recently been reading or had been told about Dante's *Inferno.*

After *Richard III,* the next evidence of Shakespeare's use of Dante is in *Richard II,* allegedly written in 1595. For the first time passages from *Paradiso* appear as a source for Shakespeare in both the *Dream* and *Richard II.* If he began to read *Inferno* in 1593, it may have taken him two years to arrive at *Paradiso.* Near the end of 1594, Sir Charles Danvers and his brother had escaped to France to avoid a murder charge, and there they remained in exile until they were pardoned by Elizabeth in 1598. If Shakespeare were using the copy of Dante belonging to the Danvers family, he may not have had access to it from the end of 1594 until after their return in 1598—or even after this, as both of the Danvers brothers accompanied Southampton to Ireland in 1599. In 1601 Sir Charles Danvers was arrested for his part in the Essex rebellion, and he was executed in March of that year. Their copy of the *Divina Commedia* was presented to the Bodleian Library in 1602.

None of the parallel passages which fulfil the requirements of a "borrowing" in Shakespeare are from his poems. There are two possible reasons for this. Firstly, the earliest date at which we have any evidence that Shakespeare may have read Dante's work is 1593, if the theory that he saw the copy imported by Sir Charles Danvers in that year is correct. By this date, some of the Sonnets were already written, as was *Venus and Adonis*. *The Rape of Lucrece* was dedicated to Southampton in May 1594, so we can assume that it was written in the year between the publication of *Venus* in April, 1593 and the following May.

In writing these two poems, Shakespeare is working closely from Ovid's *Metamorphoses* and *Fasti*. His tone in *Venus and Adonis* is one of romantic comedy and a light, almost mocking humour distances us from the actual tragedy of the tale. Even if Shakespeare were aware of Dante's work at this time, it would be surprising if he considered something so different in subject, tone and style as the *Divina Commedia* as a source material for this particular work. Shakespeare's tone in *The Rape of Lucrece* is tragic and perhaps here, Dante could have provided some useful images. But no "borrowings" have been noted.

In the case of the Sonnets, there is another factor. They are mostly very personal: written perhaps sometimes spontaneously and in many cases to consider some aspect of the poet's own immediate and private experience. Some of them seem almost like emotionally charged letters, written because the love, or suffering, or bewilderment experienced *must* be expressed. Writing in these circumstances, I doubt that many poets would pause to consult other writers for useful images or ideas. It may be, of course, that an image already heard or read may have come to mind, but none of these seem to be from Dante. Some of the sonnets were written when Dantean ideas were appearing in the plays, but even in the "mortal moon" sonnet, believed to be the latest and written after Southampton was released from the Tower in 1603 after the death of Elizabeth, I can find no evidence of Shakespeare's knowledge of Dante.

In the plays, by 1601 and from *Hamlet* onwards in the great tragedies, Shakespeare is concerned with philosophical and moral problems—the afterlife, the causes of corruption, the problem of justice, Divine or human, the reasons for evil, the existence of free will, the precise meaning of betrayal and treachery, the impermanence of loyalty and the nature of repentance—all of which are subjects treated at length by Dante in the *Divina Commedia*.

Florio did not acknowledge the use of Dante in the compilation of his 1598 dictionary, the *Worlde of Words*, although he mentioned the name of the Italian poet and commented that his work was difficult to understand. In his 1611 revised work, *Queen Anna's New World of Words*, he claimed to have used four different copies of the *Divina Commedia* with commentaries by Velitello (*sic*), Danielo (*sic*), Boccaccio and Landini (*sic*). Perhaps we can assume that he began work on this second version immediately after the first was published—in 1598 or 1599—and that in this period he had access to the four copies of the *Divina Commedia*. We do not know from where he acquired these, but he must have consulted them for about ten years. In this same period, Shakespeare too, seems to have been using a copy of Dante. Shakespeare's latest use of Dante seems to have been in 1611 in *The Tempest* and this is the same year that Florio published his revised dictionary. Did Florio then return the copies of Dante to wherever they came from? Three more plays are attributed to Shakespeare after this date. *Cardenio* is often said to be lost, though recently an edition of a play claimed to be this one, has been published. *Henry VIII* has two possible parallels with Dante but may be in part the work of a collaborator, and in *Two Noble Kinsmen*, no parallels have been noted.

A comparison of the above table with a similar table compiled by Ann Thompson and listing chronologically Shakespeare's references to Chaucer,[12] leads to some interesting conclusions. Firstly, in the earliest works by Shakespeare (*Henry VI*, Parts I, II, and III, *Richard III*, and *Venus and Adonis*), Thompson finds no evidence of Chaucer's ideas. The first Shakespearean work to demonstrate his influence is *The Rape of Lucrece* (1593–4). Perhaps in these early years, Shakespeare had not yet gained access to the library in which so many of his later ideas were mined. Or perhaps he had not yet learned to use the ideas of other writers in an effective and profitable way. Neither does she find any of Chaucer's ideas in the sonnets—perhaps for the very reasons I have suggested above to account for the absence of "borrowing" from Dante in these poems. Beyond that there is no correlation between the two tables, but it is interesting to speculate that perhaps Shakespeare's interest in Dante *was* a response to his reading about him in Chaucer. The earliest Shakespearean reference to Chaucer was in *The Rape of Lucrece* (1593–4). The earliest sign of his knowledge of Dante was in *Richard III* (1593).

Whitaker observed in the last chapter of his study of Shakespeare's use of learning that:

> No characteristic of Shakespeare's thinking is more significant than this slow germination of concepts after he encountered them. He probably knew the Homilies even before he came to London, and traces of their teaching on the kingship appear in his earliest plays. But their full impact upon his mind took almost five years to develop and reached ultimate expression in *Richard II*. Similarly, if we assume that he read Hooker shortly after *Of the Laws of Ecclesiastical Polity* appeared in 1594, he mulled over it for three or four years before showing its influence in his plays, and the elaborate exposition of its ideas in *Troilus and Cressida* came after six or seven years. This lag agrees remarkably well with the interval between his major sources and the plays based on them.[13]

If we assume this to be so, we can perhaps apply this time-lag rule of several years to Shakespeare's use of Dante. Shakespeare's earliest access to the *Divina Commedia* could have been to the copy imported by the Danvers family in 1593. The earliest "borrowing" we believe was in *Richard III* in 1593. The time of most frequent "borrowing" was from about 1604 onwards, and it would mean that Shakespeare may have studied Dante several years earlier. If he was working from the same library as Florio, and Florio acknowledged his use of Dante for the 1611 dictionary but not the 1598 edition—then perhaps Shakespeare was reading Dante from 1598 onwards, as was, presumably, Florio. Shakespeare was not at first using the *Divina Commedia* for deeply intellectual ideas. His use of Dante seems to be limited mainly to images in *Richard II*, though he touched on more complex ideas later in the "borrowed" images of *Troilus and Cressida*, *Macbeth* and *King Lear*.

Another conclusion to be drawn from this study is the vast variety of sources from which Shakespeare has drawn his material. It is hardly possible to find one idea used by him which has one source only. In his plays are, variously combined, ideas from classical writers, from contemporary writers in several languages, biblical tales, church doctrine, accounts of recent exploration, medieval scientific theories, medieval notions of witchcraft and the occult, theatrical advice, proverbial wisdom, words and phrases from other languages, legal procedures, political theories, and an extensive variety of images from almost every aspect of life. This is a quality that Shakespeare and Dante have in common, an almost infinite data bank from which to draw and recycle ideas in a new way. Perhaps this quality is one of those which make a truly great writer.

Kenneth Muir, commenting on Shakespeare's use of Florio's translation of Montaigne in *King Lear*, wrote:

> This account of the sources of the play may serve to throw light on Shakespeare's method of creating a unity from heterogeneous material. When he amplified and complicated his original fable, his *donnée*, he pressed into service incidents, ideas, phrases and even words from books and plays; and the remarkable richness of texture apparent in *King Lear* may be explained, at least in part, by Shakespeare's use of such a method.[14]

This comment could be applied to all Shakespeare's plays, and illustrates precisely the method we have just outlined.

It is difficult to understand why so many English writers have rejected even the possibility that Shakespeare may have been familiar with Dante's work. It is also difficult to explain the total absence of any discussion of Dante's influence on English writers (even Chaucer) in Lewis Einstein's work *The Italian Renaissance in England: Studies.*

Dante's works were to be found in the Bodleian Library from 1602 onwards and presumably also in some private collections even earlier. If a considerable number of people had some knowledge of the Italian language, it would be amazing if no-one read the *Divina Commedia* and no-one was in any way influenced by it. In the fourteenth century Chaucer had certainly read it, evidence for which claim is clear in his writing. Two hundred years later John Florio read it—and carefully. Edmund Spenser and Sir Philip Sidney had certainly read it and used some of the ideas in their own work. Ben Jonson seems to have known about it, and perhaps used some ideas from it. John Marston, half Italian, seems also to have known something about it. Toynbee tells us that Greene, Whetstone, Harington, Drayton, Meres, and Donne knew something of Dante and mentioned him. Shakespeare had read or seen the works of all those named above. Is it conceivable that he would not have known something of Dante?

If Shakespeare knew and used ideas from Dante, then the result was the enrichment of his own work. If Dante's ideas are there in the plays, then there is more for us to understand. We have only to think how an English expression such as "a pound of flesh" or "the sticking-place" or "one fell swoop" is enriched for the person who knows the Shakespearean origin of such phrases and, hearing the phrase, recalls the circumstances in which it was earlier used, feeling again the emotions which were felt in that earlier context. Such references are allusive, though we may not always be conscious of this. In his essay "Dante and the Art of Citation", Christopher Kleinhenz considers how Dante's writings were influenced by his extensive reading and his constant citations from other texts. He claims that:

> We have come to an increased understanding of how Dante incorporates the textual citation for his own purposes and

how he is able to enhance the meaning of his text by evoking/invoking other texts and their context.[15]

Dante's most frequent citations are from the Bible and when in *Purgatory* XXX.19, the crowd hails Beatrice with the cry "Benedictus qui venis!", the reader must remember the cry in Matthew 21:9 when the Jews hailed Christ's arrival in Jerusalem on Palm Sunday with "Benedictus qui venit in nomine Domini".[16] Shakespeare's most frequent citations are also from the Bible and he uses exactly the same device in *King Lear* IV.4, when Cordelia says, "O dear father!/ It is thy business that I go about". We cannot miss the echo of Luke 2:49: "Knew yee not that I must go about my father's businesse?"[17] In each case the analogy to be made between Beatrice and Christ, and Cordelia and Christ is unmistakable to those familiar with the Bible. This extremely effective device of course, could have been arrived at quite independently by Shakespeare, but it may have been learned from Dante who used it constantly.

Similarly, Shakespeare's references to Dante enhance the meaning of his own text and bring with them (for the reader of Dante) all the connotations they had in the original. Thus, when we imagine Isabella, "enskied and sainted", we must also think of Saint Clare, *inciela* (enheavened), and particularly of her follower, Piccarda Donati, who, snatched from the *dolce chiostro* by men *a mal più ch'a bene usi*, manages to convey her fate as a result of men's rapacity, though her words are veiled in shame. The emotions we feel for her, we understand, must also be felt for Isabella—faced with the same fate. And when we think of Bolingbroke, eating "the bitter bread of banishment" we must also think of Dante, grieving for his beloved but forbidden Florence and for the rest of his life, ascending and descending *per l'altrui scale*. Similarly, Shakespeare's mention of the "universal wolf" brings with it all Dante's loathing for avarice, *la lupa*, and his conviction that the insatiability of this beast was the cause of all human misery. And as Saner pointed out in his "Gemless Rings", Dante's shock at seeing his friend Forese so terribly altered is recalled by Edgar's shock at seeing his father blinded, and "so the parallel is not merely verbal—striking as is the literal similarity—but emotional."[18] Jonathon Bate captures this effect precisely in his *Shakespeare and Ovid* where he argues that Shakespeare's imitation is an allusion, that "the source text is *brought into play* (from Latin *al-ludo*, to play with); its presence does significant aesthetic work of a sort which cannot be performed by a submerged source".[19]

Bate explains, and although his argument is concerned with Shakespeare's use of Ovid, it applies equally to his use of Dante:

> That good imitation involves difference as well as similarity is a cardinal principle of Renaissance poetics. Again and again, sixteenth-century theorists make the point which was first made by Petrarch in his letter to Boccaccio written from Pavia on 28 October 1366. The "proper imitator should take care that what he writes resembles the original without reproducing it"; the resemblance should be that "of a son to his father", not that of a portrait to the sitter; individual features will diverge, but the whole will, through some mysterious power, have the feel of the original. Petrarch continues, "Thus we writers must look to it that with a basis of similarity there should be many dissimilarities. And the similarity should be planted so deep that it can only be extricated by quiet meditation. The quality is to be felt rather than defined. Thus we may use another man's conceptions and the colour of his style but not his words. In the first case the resemblance is hidden deep; in the second it is glaring. The first procedure makes poets, the second makes apes. This is the substance of Seneca's counsel, and Horace's before him, that we should write as the bees make sweetness, not storing up the flowers but turning them into honey, thus making one thing of many various ones, but different and better."[20]

Shakespeare's work, then, is immeasurably rich not just intrinsically but also for what it evokes in our memory. All of our perceptions and emotions are linked to some earlier experience and the more experiences we have had, the more we can feel about what we see or read. For the reader of the Bible, Shakespeare evokes all kinds of moral and religious emotions and associated ideas. For the reader of the *Divina Commedia,* Shakespeare can recreate elements of Dante's tale, recalling the intensity of human passions which the Italian poet so vividly described and with which, I believe, the English playwright so empathised.

To attribute to Shakespeare a knowledge of Dante is hardly surprising. The evidence is persuasive. The possibility is a probability. As the most derisive critics of this theory have repeatedly said, "If Shakespeare had known Dante he'd have used him, and so often as to leave no doubt on the point." They are right. It is my contention that Shakespeare *did* know Dante, and used his work often enough to leave me in no doubt on the point. If I am correct, something more has been added to the picture we have of our great literary icon. We can see him as a man aware of and interested in the very best of Italian literature and with insights into medieval religious, philosophical and political thought. We can see him as a man reaching out beyond the confines of his own culture and prepared to consider ideas not always in accordance with current English tradition and policy. Mary Augusta Scott claimed, "It is a truism that the noblest English poetry bears the mark of high Italian descent."[21] There can be no nobler English poetry than that of Shakespeare—and I believe it bears the mark of the very highest Italian descent, a direct line from Dante's *Divina Commedia.*

Epilogue

The material in the chapters you have read is taken from my doctoral thesis, submitted in 2002. It was passed but there was an unpleasant complication. One of the three examiners wrote:

> The candidate has set herself an impossible task, but that said, it is clear that she has worked very hard, and presented a thesis that is of an acceptable level in everything but its central argument. It is clearly and correctly expressed, wide ranging in its reading, and accurate in its citations. In some ways I wish I could recommend its acceptance, but I am afraid I cannot do so, nor can I suggest a way in which this hard work can be rescued, unless the candidate is prepared to abandon her claim to have proved her case, and that, in spite of her diligent search, the evidence is simply not there.

Fortunately for me a University committee agreed that the discrepancy between this assessment (the lowest possible mark, 5), and those given by the other two examiners (1 and 2), was unjustified and unacceptable. A fourth examiner was employed and awarded me the highest possible mark, 1.

This was my first experience of the unshakeable conviction of the stalwart "Stratfordians", as they have become known in the angry world of the Authorship Question. Their vision of Shakespeare is set in stone. Shakespeare did not know Dante's work—and woe betide anyone who might claim differently.

Their argument was always the same. Shakespeare could not have read *La Divina Commedia* as it was not translated at that time. But there is any amount of proof (see Chapter 4) that he did use material from other untranslated Italian sources and this is acknowledged widely.

Having read Brenda James' astonishing revelations in *The Truth Will Out*, I also read some of the responses to this on the internet and realised that the Flat Earth Society is still alive and well.

The Authorship Question has fascinated people for more than three hundred years. Many readers and writers have marvelled at the vast fields of knowledge accumulated by the actor from Stratford. How did he manage to acquire such an enormous store of detailed history, accurate knowledge of Italy and the Italian language, familiarity with the conversation of Kings and courtiers, a firm grasp of politics, the law, modern scientific and medical theories and most of all—a profound understanding of human nature?

Shakespeare may have spent a few years at Stratford Grammar School (although there is no record of this) but this would hardly account for his achievements in the afore-mentioned areas of learning. He was not a University Man. He had not travelled outside England. He was not an aristocrat with a vast library. He had not taught his wife and children to read or write. He did not own a single book at the time of his death. No one has ever found any letters he had written, or autograph manuscripts of his poetry and plays.

Many a candidate has been suggested as the real writer of this body of work—usually he is a highly educated aristocrat who had travelled, mixed with the upper classes, read widely and could write well—but for one reason or another, the shoe never did quite fit.

Several writers in the last few decades have challenged the traditional biography of Shakespeare. Richard Roe in *The Shakespeare Guide to Italy*, using only the text from Shakespeare's plays, has investigated Italian towns, street names, churches, travel routes and local geography to test the accuracy of Shakespeare's settings. His conclusions are beyond question. Shakespeare had been in Italy.

Brenda James had noticed, as have many others, that the Dedication of the Sonnets was decidedly strange—for its setting out on the printed page, for its awkward syntax and for the identity of Mr W. H. It was not even clear who had written it. She recognised that it was a code and she was able to break it. Almost immediately she found a name, Sir Henry Neville. She began to research it and found a man who had all the qualities we might have expected in the author of the most wonderful literature in the English language. She did not disclose her method of decoding in her first book (with W. D. Rubenstein) *The Truth Will Out*, but it is explained in detail in her next two books, *Henry Neville and the Shakespeare Code*, and *Understanding the Invisible Shakespeare*. At this point she has published three books on the subject and is working on more.

Also intrigued by the first of this series, two Australians, Professor James Goding and Bruce Leyland set about decoding the Dedication by their own method. Astonishingly, although this was slightly different from that used by James, the same name appeared—Sir Henry Neville—and they extended their investigation into the sonnets as well as the dedication. Their book, *Who Will Believe My Verse?*, reveals some of the hidden meanings in the tantalizingly mysterious and enigmatic sonnets.

James establishes the real author as Sir Henry Neville, a wealthy aristocrat (untitled), from a family which could be traced back to William the Conqueror. He was educated at Merton College, Oxford and very widely read. While still a student he embarked on a four year tour (1578–82) of Europe with a small group lead by Sir Henry Savile, spending much of this time in Northern Italy and France. Savile was collecting manuscripts and books for the Merton College Library at Oxford.

Neville married Anne Killigrew, daughter of a wealthy Cornish landowner in 1584 and they had eleven children. They lived mostly at Billingbear in Berkshire but also occasionally in London. Neville's father-in-law served as a diplomat and was fluent in French and Italian.

At 22 Neville had became a Member of Parliament and held a position as Ambassador to France for two years (1599–1601). He became involved in the failed Essex Rebellion in 1601. He was arrested, tried and betrayed by his two friends, Essex and Southampton (a lifelong friend), who named him as being at the first meeting to plan this coup. He was sent to the Tower. Essex and a number of others were executed. Neville and Southampton were condemned to the Tower indefinitely and not released until after the death of Elizabeth in 1603. At this time they must have developed a close relationship and indeed it seems that some of the sonnets were written in this period.

After his release Neville pursued a life in politics and later in business, investing in the London Virginia Company along with Southampton, whom he had forgiven. James believes that the "WELL-WISHING ADVENTURER" of the Dedication refers to an investor in this company which received its charter on 23 May 1609. The Sonnets were published on 20 May, 1609. The Dedication is simply one "ADVENTURER" (Neville) wishing another (Southampton) "ALL HAPPINESSE".

Many people have noted the change in the mood of Shakespeare's work from 1600 onward. The plays from this period, often called the "problem plays", were much more serious than his earlier work and perhaps the events in the writer's own life were responsible for this. One of the most interesting aspects of James' research is the way in which she manages to relate the plays to events in the writer's own life. The early history plays tend to focus on characters from the Neville family, the later light-hearted comedies, often set in Italy are cheerful, romantic—reflecting perhaps on his travel experiences. The "problem plays" look at the notions of loyalty, betrayal, justice, and punishment—all ideas which would have preoccupied him during and after the Essex affair. It is difficult to make such a comparison with the life of the actor from Stratford.

Neville chose to publish his work under the name of William Shakespeare for a number of reasons. Firstly it was not acceptable for aristocrats to write for the theatre, or at least for the public theatre. Secondly he held views not always consistent with those of Elizabeth and others holding political power, and these are sometimes evident in his plays. Rather than draw attention to this fact, he chose to protect himself and his family by writing under the pseudonym of William Shakespeare, an actor from Stratford and very distantly related to Neville himself.

He died in 1615, one year before the actor from Stratford.

James' revelation was for me one of the most exciting discoveries in my lifetime. No more do we need to hear talk of "native intelligence" or "genius", which somehow enabled the actor from Stratford to recreate cities he had never seen, to capture so exactly the language of a class to which he did not belong, and above all to create characters so psychologically convincing that we can talk about them as though they are real. No more do we have to pack a world of knowledge into the syllabus of Stratford Grammar, or try to imagine Shakespeare learning Italian from Italian sailors at the Mermaid Inn, or endlessly scratching away in his wobbly handwriting with a quill and ink behind the scenery at the Globe.

I recommend Brenda James' books to all those who have, as I have, wondered how these plays and poems were ever created. But regardless of who was the real author, the evidence presented here of "Shakespeare's" knowledge of Dante's great work, still stands. In Chapter 1, I wrote that I used the name "Shakespeare" to describe the author of the plays and poems which we understand to be the work of this great playwright and poet, whoever he may have been. The parallels are still there and must be explained.

On the other hand, the information I provide on Shakespeare's knowledge of Italian, is hardly necessary when we realise that Sir Henry Neville travelled for quite a long period in Italy and was certainly familiar with the cities he describes in his plays. He was also familiar with contemporary Italian literature, from which he borrowed many of his plots, and which were not all translated. Neither is it necessary to ponder on where he may have seen a copy of *La Divina Commedia*.

Florio, in the writing of his dictionary in 1611 acknowledged his use of three different copies of the work. The same three copies were in the catalogue for the Bodleian Library from 1605. Florio would have had access to these as he had lived and worked in Oxford where he matriculated from Magdalene College in 1581. Sir Henry Neville, a graduate from Merton

College would also have had access to these books. Sir Charles Danvers, also a close friend of Southampton and Neville, possessed a copy of the book. Neville may well have had a copy in his own large library.

Florio, I note on re-reading my thesis, may have exposed the true identity of Shakespeare when he commented:

> Let Aristophanes and his comedians make plaies, and scoure
> their mouths on Socrates; those very mouthes they make to
> vilify, shall be the means to amplifie his virtue.[1]

The reference to Socrates was clearly to himself, as a teacher, philosopher and intellectual. It is generally believed that the reference to Aristophanes was to Shakespeare. If the Greek names have been chosen for their similarity to the real object of his criticism, it is interesting to note that Aristophanes was born into a wealthy family. He had an excellent education and was well versed in literature, especially the poetry of Homer and other great Athenian writers. His writings suggest a strong knowledge of the latest philosophical theories.

Is this the man from Stratford? I believe it describes "Shakespeare"— Sir Henry Neville. And Florio knew very well his real identity.

In the world of literature Shakespeare ranks in stature perhaps only with Dante, who also read widely and used the material he found in such a way that we can only wonder at his encyclopaedic knowledge of the learning and literature of his time. "Dante and Shakespeare divide the world between them," claimed T.S. Eliot, "there is no third".[2] Few who have read both writers would dispute this claim, and if "Shakespeare" used ideas from Dante, as he did from so many other writers, then this is one of the multitudinous factors which give his work its universal and timeless appeal.

Acknowledgements

Whilst I have been absorbed in researching and writing my thesis and then transforming it into this book, I have been aware of and very grateful for the enormous support I have received from friends, family and those whose expertise in either Shakespeare or Dante (or both) has been invaluable to me.

I have already thanked Dr Richard Madelaine (dec.) from the University of New South Wales for his interest in my subject and his informed suggestions on courses of thinking I might pursue. With characteristic good humour and reassuring rational thought, he steered me through a subject which is neither fashionable nor popular today but which, combining as it does my interest in English literature and Italian culture, has fascinated me for many years. His willingness to consider my theories and his objectivity in assessing them have kept me from the many hazards to which my longstanding passion for this subject may have exposed me – and all without ever dampening my enthusiasm.

I also thank Dr Mary Dwyer, from the University of New England for introducing me many years ago to Dante and *Divina Commedia*, and thereby starting me on this long trail. I thank her too for her continuing interest in my progress and her assistance whenever I have asked for it.

Especially I thank Professor James Goding whose assistance and encouragement have been invaluable. His experience and advice on the practical problems encountered along the way were indispensable.

And, of course, I thank Nick Walker, Anastasia Buryak and Wayne Saunders at Australian Scholarly Publishing, all of whom have worked with skill and patience to make this the book that I hoped it would be.

My friends and family have listened to me over the years with patience and humour. My husband especially has patiently suffered gruelling hours of television while I was absorbed in writing. I suspect that their interest in my subject was not always undivided, but I know that their support for me was unstinting.

But without the smiling man from the Indian Pacific, Don Heussler, this book would never have been written. It was he who recounted to me the astonishing revelations of Brenda James in her book *The Truth Will Out* and who has followed with interest the creation of my book.

I wrote to Brenda James to tell her how her discovery had impacted on my thesis and how it had provided the answers which had eluded me, to so many questions. She replied offering to help in any way she could and encouraging me to write this book.

For me, the research and writing of my thesis and this book have been an illuminating and exciting adventure and I thank again all those who have shared even parts of this with me.

Notes

Introduction: The Saints of Poetry

1   Thomas Carlyle, *Lectures on Heroes,* Chapman and Hall, London, 1840, p. 248.

2   Alexander Pope, *The Dunciad* (IV), ed. Valerie Rumbold, Longman, New York, 1999, pp. 288–9.

3   Selma Guttman, *The Foreign Sources of Shakespeare' Works,* Kings Crown Press, New York, 1947, p. xiv.

4   Geoffrey Chaucer, "The Monk's Tale", D. Lang Purves, ed., *The Canterbury Tales, and The Faerie Queene,* William P. Nimmo, Edinburgh, 1870.

5   John Ciardi, *The Divine Commedia. The Inferno,* Translated by John Ciardi, a Mentor Book, New York, 1954, p. 28.

6   C. H. Grandgent, *La Divina Commedia,* edited and annotated by C. H. Grandgent, revised by Charles S. Singleton, Harvard University Press, Cambridge, Mass., 1972, p. 626.

7   This essay was entitled "Dante's Moral Philosophy in Shakespeare's *Macbeth*" and was awarded the Frederick May Memorial Prize for 1995 by the Italian Department of Sydney University.

Chapter 1 – The Question: Had Shakespeare read Dante?

1   H.F. Cary, *The Vision,* Frederick Warne & Co. London, 1814.

2   James Russell Lowell, "Shakespeare Once More", in *Among My Books,* J.M. Dent, London, 1925. The essay had been first printed in 1868.

3   Wilhelm König, "Shakespeare und Dante" in *Jahrbuch der Deutschen Dante-Gesellschaft* VII (1872), Kraus Reprint, Vaduz, 1963, p. 206. Translation from German by Maxie Shreiner.

4   Erato Hills, "Dante and Shakespeare", in *Notes and Queries,* 5th Series, Vol. 10 (1878), p. 166.

5   F. J. Furnivall, "Dante and Shakespeare", in *Notes and Queries,* 5th Series, Vol. 10 (1878), p. 396.

6   Lorenzo Mascetta-Caracci, "Dante in Shakespeare", in *Giornale Dantesco,* 1 della Nuova Serie, Leo S. Olschki, Firenze-Venezia, 1897.

7   Mascetta-Caracci, p. 114. Translations from Italian by the present writer unless otherwise acknowledged.

8   Lewis Einstein, *The Italian Renaissance in England,* The Columbia University Press, Macmillan (Agents), New York, 1902.

9   Einstein, p. 317.

10 Ibid., p. 371.

11 Ibid., p. 321.

12 Quoted from E. Moore, *Dante and his Early Biographers,* London, 1890, p. 65, in Einstein, p. 317.

13 Paget Toynbee, *Dante in English Literature—from Chaucer to Cary, 1380–1844.* Methuen, London, 1909, p. 30.

14 Cary points out in his brief "Life of Dante" which precedes his famous translation, *The Vision,* that "One copy only of the version and commentary is known to be preserved, and that is in the Vatican. I would suggest the probability of others existing in this country". Cary, *The Vision,* 1883, p. xii.

15 Toynbee, *Dante in English Literature,* p. 30.

16 Ibid.

17 Einstein, p. 11.

18 Brian Richardson, "Editing Dante's Commedia" in Theodore J. Cachey, Jr, ed., *Dante Now,* University of Notre Dame Press, Notre Dame, 1995, p. 249.

19 I have omitted the examples he gives here as they are all discussed later in this book.

20 Toynbee, *Dante in English Literature,* Introduction, p. xxiv.

21 Michele Renzulli, *Dante Nella Letteratura Inglese,* Societa Editrice "La Via", Firenze, 1925, p. 44.

22 From this point onwards, I refer to this author as "Clara Longworth de Chambrun" in the text, as her full title and name are rather cumbersome and this shortened version is the name she used beneath her Preface to *Shakespeare Rediscovered.*

23 Clara (Longworth), Comtesse de Chambrun, *Giovanni Florio,* Payot, Paris, 1921, p. 131. Translation from the French by the present writer unless acknowledged otherwise.

24 Ernesto Grillo, *Shakespeare and Italy,* Robert Maclehose and Co. Limited, The University Press, Glasgow, 1949, p. 31.

25 Reginald A. Saner, "'Gemless Rings' in *Purgatorio* XXIII and *Lear*", in *Romance Notes,* 10 (1968), 163–7, 164–6.

26 Ibid., p. 166.

27 Ibid. I have not been able to accommodate the "sea-captains" or the "quiet room in the Mermaid" in the argument presented in this book.

28 Joseph Satin, "Macbeth and the Inferno of Dante", *Forum* (Houston), IX, 2 (1971), pp. 19–23.

29 Eric Vincent, entry under "Shakespeare, William", *Enciclopedia Dantesca,* Istituto Dell'Enciclopedia Italiana, Roma, 1976, p. 209.

30 Francis Fergusson, *Trope and Allegory: Themes Common to Dante and Shakespeare,* The University of Georgia Press, Athens, 1977, p. 1.

31 Ibid., p. 2.

32 Robin Kirkpatrick, *English and Italian Literature from Dante to Shakespeare*, Longman, New York, 1995, p. 279.

33 Stuart Gillespie, *Shakespeare's Books—A Dictionary of Shakespeare's Sources,* The Athlone Press, London, 2001, p. 132.

34 David Wallace, "Dante in English", in Rachel Jacoff, ed., *The Cambridge Companion to Dante,* Cambridge University Press, Cambridge, 1993, p. 245.

35 See Chapter IV.

36 Leonard Barkan, "What did Shakespeare read?" in Margreta De Grazia, ed., *The Cambridge Companion to Shakespeare,* Cambridge University Press, Cambridge, 2001, pp. 41–2.

37 Lowell, *Among My Books,* p. 164.

38 Grillo, p. 132.

39 Jonathan Keates, *Italian Journeys,* Picador, London, 1991, pp. 143–4.

40 *Love's Labour's Lost,* ed. Richard David, The Arden Shakespeare (2), Methuen, London, 1994 (London, 1951), Introduction, p. xxviii.

41 T. W. Baldwin, *William Shakespeare's Small Latin & Lesse Greeke,* University of Illinois Press, Urbana, 1944. Baldwin examines the Grammar School curriculum at the time that Shakespeare is assumed to have attended Stratford Grammar School. His argument depends on the fact that this assumption is correct—but even if it is not, the fact is that Shakespeare's works show an extensive knowledge of many of the Latin and Greek texts used in the schools throughout Elizabethan England.

42 Selma Guttman, *The Foreign Sources of Shakespeare's Works,* Kings Crown Press, New York, 1947. Ms Guttman begins her study in 1904, "the date of H. R. D. Anders' *Shakespeare's Books,* and extends it up to 1940. It deals with English, French, and German commentary concerning Shakespearean sources originally written in foreign languages", p. xiv. She concedes that "some of the source suggestions herein recorded are implausible and far-fetched", p. xiv. In the study she lists a total of 40 Latin sources, 24 Greek sources, 17 French sources, 28 Italian sources, 9 Spanish sources and 7 sources from various other languages.

43 Mario Praz, "Emblems and Devices in Literature" in *Studies in Seventeenth Century Imagery,* Edizioni Di Storia e Letteratura, Roma, 1964, pp. 205–321.

44 Timothy Murray, *Theatrical Legitimation: Allegories of Genius in Seventeenth Century England and France,* New York & Oxford: Oxford University Press, 1987, p. 70.

45 Jeffrey Masten, *Textual Intercourse,* Cambridge University Press, Cambridge, 1997, p. 74.

46 Jonathon Bate, *Shakespeare and Ovid,* Clarendon Press, Oxford, 1993, p. 5.

47 Robert S. Miola, *Shakespeare's Reading,* Oxford University Press, 2000, pp. 152 ff.

48 Grillo, p. 89.

49 Furnivall, p. 396.

50 Roland Barthes, "From Work to Text" in *Image—Music—Text,* translated by Stephen Heath, Hill and Wang, New York, 1977, p. 160.

51   Gillespie, pp. 2–3. The quotations from Robert S. Miola are from "Shakespeare and his Sources: Observations on the Critical History of *Julius Caesar*", *Shakespeare Survey* 40 (1987), 69–76 (p. 71).

52   cf. Ann Thompson, *Shakespeare's Chaucer,* Liverpool University Press, 1978.

53   Saner, pp. 164–5.

54   Ibid.

55   J. M. Robertson, *The Baconian Heresy,* Herbert Jenkins, London, 1913, p. 435. The date of the passages considered here disallows any possibility of a third alternative—that Shakespeare may have read Bacon.

56   H. F. Cary, *The Vision or Hell, Purgatory, and Paradise,* a new edn., corrected, George Bell And Sons, London, 1883.

57   James Lowell, "Shakespeare Once More" in *Among My Books,* 1925.

58   Wilhelm König, "Shakespeare und Dante", in *Jahrbuch der Deutschen Dante-Gesellschaft* VII (1872), translation by Maxie Schreiner.

59   Erato Hills, author of a brief note on parallels in *Notes and Queries,* 1878.

60   Lorenzo Mascetta-Caracci, author of "Dante in Shakespeare", in *Giornale Dantesco,* 1897.

61   Paget Toynbee, author of *Dante in English Literature,* 1909.

62   Clara (Longworth) Comtesse de Chambrun, author of *Giovanni Florio,* 1921.

63   Kenneth Muir, "*Macbeth* and Dante", in *Notes and Queries,* 16th Series, Vol. 194 (1949), p. 333.

64   Reginald A. Saner, author of "Gemless Rings".

65   Eric Vincent, author of the entry on Shakespeare in *Enciclopedia Dantesca,* 1976.

66   Joseph Satin, author of "Macbeth and the Inferno of Dante", in *Forum* ix 2 (1971).

67   Richmond Noble, *Shakespeare's Biblical Knowledge,* Society for Promoting Christian Knowledge, London, 1935, p. 76.

Chapter 2 – The Evidence

1   *Macbeth,* ed. Kenneth Muir, The Arden Shakespeare (2), Methuen, London, 1951, p. 60.

2   Muir, "*Macbeth* and Dante", p. 333.

3   Satin, pp. 19–23.

4   Ibid., p. 20.

5   Dante, *Inferno,* a cura di Natalino Sapegna, "La Nuova Italia" Editrice, Firenze, 1963, p. 104

6   *Macbeth,* Arden (2), p. 49. The footnote refers us to another footnote on p. 84 on "black Hecate" which tells us "As Shakespeare was aware Hecate is properly another name for Diana and Luna, so that "black" might seem to be an inappropriate epithet." All this is rather confusing: however, the footnote in the Arden (2) *A Midsummer Night's Dream,* p. 124, explains that "She was Hecate (or Proserpina) in Hades, Diana (and occasionally Lucina) on earth; and Luna (or Phoebe or Cynthia) in the heavens."

7 A. C. Bradley, *Shakespearean Tragedy*, Macmillan, London, 1956 (London,1904), p. 244.

8 Bradley, p. 247.

9 While I do not necessarily accept Bradley's view on the subject of staging, the fact remains that he is constantly reminded of Dante's *Inferno* by the atmosphere and setting of Shakespeare's play.

10 Bradley, p. 261, quoting from *Inferno* X. 36.

11 Wilhelm König, "Shakespeare und Dante", p. 211.

12 G. Wilson Knight, "*The Lear* Universe" in *The Wheel of Fire*, Methuen, London, 1972 (London, 1949), p. 179.

13 Reginald A. Saner, "'Gemless Rings' in *Purgatorio* XXIII and Lear", pp. 164–5.

14 Ibid., p. 166.

15 Ibid.

16 John Ciardi, *La Divina Commedia, The Paradiso.* Translated by John Ciardi. A Mentor Book, New York, 1954, p. 235.

17 *King Lear,* ed. Kenneth Muir, The Arden Shakespeare (2), Methuen, London, 1973 (London, 1952), p. 198.

18 Caroline Spurgeon, *Shakespeare's Imagery and What It Tells Us,* Beacon Press, Boston, 1960 (Cambridge, 1935), p. 242.

19 John Ciardi, *The Purgatorio,* A Mentor Book, New York, 1961, pp. 69–70.

20 Eric Vincent, entry under "Shakespeare, William", *Enciclopedia Dantesca,* p. 209 (my translation).

21 *Measure for Measure.* Ed. J. W. Lever, The Arden Shakespeare (2). Methuen, London, 1986 (London, 1958), p. lviii of introduction.

22 Lever, introduction to *Measure for Measure,* p. xliv.

23 Shakespeare, *Measure for Measure,* Arden (2), p. 24.

24 *Paradiso,* Translated, with a commentary, by Charles S. Singleton, 1: Italian Text and Translation, Bollingen Series LXXX, Princeton University Press, Princeton, 1975.

25 Dante Alighieri, *Paradiso,* a cura di Umberto Bosco e Giovanni Reggio, Dodicesima ristampa, Le Monnier, Firenze, 1995, p. 57.

26 My Translation of the above footnote.

27 Shakespeare, *Measure for Measure,* Arden (2), p. 58.

28 H. F. Cary, *The Vision, or Hell, Purgatory and Paradise,* p. 370.

29 Dante Alighieri, *The Divine Comedy of Dante Alighieri,* translated by Henry Wadsworth Longfellow, George Routledge & Sons, London, 1903, p. 502.

30 Dante Alighieri, *The Paradiso,* translated by John Ciardi (A Mentor Book, New York, 1970), p. 49.

31 There is some divided opinion about the meaning of "these black masks". The Arden (2) edition (p. 58) comments that the phrase is "taken by Tyrwhitt, Steevens, and others as a direct allusion to the "masks" worn by the ladies in the audience. But "these" might merely indicate something in vogue, as in our

vulgarism "these here". Shakespeare would not wish to distract attention from the stage at this critical point. "Masks" here are probably veils: cf Gent., IV, iv. 160 "her sun expelling mask. N.C.S. (101–2) sees a covert reference to the forthcoming performance of Jonson's *Masque of Blackness* on 5 January 1605. But, as noted in the 1950 edition, masks were not worn by participants on that occasion." The "Clarisse", according to the footnote (22) in the Arden (2) edition, wore white habits. However, the effigy of Saint Clare (until the earthquake of 1997) on display at the church of Santa Chiara in Assisi wore a brown habit and a black veil. The illustration from Bell's (1774) edition of Shakespeare and used on the cover of the Arden (2) edn. shows Isabella in a white habit and a black veil. As a novice, she would certainly have worn a white habit. Even today, the nuns of Santa Chiara in Assisi are a closed order and if, on request, they appear in the church to speak to a visitor, the black veil is still worn over the face. These veils could certainly be described as "black masks". They are also very flattering, since they hide any minor blemishes but reveal good bone structure and well formed features. However, Shakespeare's company may not have known this and need not necessarily have adhered to this tradition.

32 Edward A. Armstrong, *Shakespeare's Imagination,* University of Nebraska Press, Lincoln, 1963 (Lincoln, 1946), p. 20.

33 Ibid., p. 54.

34 Shakespeare, *Measure for Measure,* Arden (2). The footnote to lines 101–4, 60, comments that these lines are "suggested by Cassandra's words to Andrugio, *1 Prom.,* III. 4: 'I rather chose, /With torments sharpe, my selfe he first should kyll'. 'At the beginning of this quotation Death is a beadle whipping a harlot; Isabella thinks of stripping herself for punishment, but the image takes on a sexual meaning.' Kenneth Muir, *London Magazine,* Dec. 1954, p. 106.

35 Dante Alighieri, *La Divina Commedia—Paradiso,* a cura di N. Sapegno, La Nuova Italia Editrice, Scandicci (F irenze), 1996, p. 41. "si stia di continuo giorno e notte".

36 Marina Warner, *Alone of All Her Sex,* Picador, London, 1990, pp. 128–9.

37 Ciardi, The Purgatory, XXII, 70–2.

38 This is a device used by Dante to enable him to place in Hell people who were still alive at the fictive date of his journey, 1300—but who were dead by the time that he wrote his masterpiece.

39 Mascetta-Caracci, p. 114.

40 Virgil K Whitaker, *Shakespeare's Use of Learning.* The Huntingdon Library, San Marino, California, 1964 (San Marino, 1953), pp. 197–8.

41 Ibid., p. 199.

42 Cesare Ripa, *Baroque and Rococo Pictorial Imagery,* Introduction, translations and 200 commentaries by Edward A. Maser. Dover Publications, New York, 1971, p. 115.

43 Cesare Ripa, *Iconologia,* Reprint of 1611 ed. published by P. P. Tozzi, Padua, modern reprint by Garland, New York, 1976, p. 36.

44 Raymond Southall, *"Troilus and Cressida* and the Spirit of Capitalism" in Arnold Kettle, ed., *Shakespeare in a Changing World,* pp. 225–6, quoted in Vivian

Thomas, *The Moral Universe of Shakespeare's Problem Plays,* Croom Helm, London, 1987, p. 131.

45 It is in this same cornice that reference is made to the avaricious Marcus Licinius Crassus, Roman Triumvir with Julius Caesar and Pompey. He was captured in battle by the Parthians and his head was brought to King Hyrodes who ordered that molten gold be poured into his mouth to satisfy his hunger for gold. Dante's reference is in the "rein" of avarice, where the sinners recite examples of those who were entrapped by this sin, one of whom is Crassus. They cry, "Crasso, / dilci, che 'l sai: di che sapore è l'oro?" (Crassus, tell us, since you know, how does gold taste?) (*Purg.* XX, 116–17). The same story occurs in *Antony and Cleopatra,* when Cleopatra, terrified of what news the messenger might bring of Antony, threatens him with, "The gold I give thee will I melt and pour/ Down thy ill-uttering throat." (II. 5. 33–35). Baldwin, in *William Shakespeare's Small Latine and Less Greeke,* Vol. II, p. 576, is puzzled by Shakespeare's source for this story. He comments, "while Plutarch emphasises the avarice of Crassus, I do not find this item of pouring the gold down his dead throat mentioned there ... The riches of Crassus were proverbial, 'Crasso ditior,' but Erasmus does not attach our item to this adage ... This particular item of having the gold poured down the throat of Crassus, Shakespeare is likely to have had eventually from Florus, for Dio Cassius seems to be the only other authority for this particular story, and Shakespeare and his contemporaries were not so likely to come across it there as in Florus. But whether Shakespeare had the story directly from Florus (at that time untranslated) is of course, a different question." Might Shakespeare's source have been Dante?

46 Dante, *Inferno,* Sapegno, pp. 5–6.

47 Dante, *Inferno,* annotata e commentata da Tommaso Di Salvo, Zanichelli, Bologna, 1998 (Bologna, 1993), p. 144.

48 Dante, *Inferno,* di Salvo, p. 144.

49 *King Lear,* Arden (2), "Humanity must perforce prey on itself, / Like monsters in the deep" (IV.2.48–9), p. 146.

50 Dante, *Inferno,* Sapegno, p. 11.

51 Ibid.

52 Whitaker, p. 186.

53 J.E. Hankins, *Backgrounds of Shakespeare's Thought,* The Harvester Press, Sussex, England, 1978, p. 186.

54 Endnote for Hankins, *Backgrounds,* p. 269: "I cite the Prose Edda from Mallett's *Northern Antiquities,* London: Bohn Library, 1859, pp. 451–5."

55 Hankins, *Backgrounds,* endnote p. 269.

56 Vivian Thomas, *Shakespeare's Chaucer,* Liverpool University Press, Liverpool, 1978, p. 25.

57 König, p. 207.

58 Lowell, *Among My Books,* p. 166.

59 Ibid., p. 167.

60 Ciardi, *The Inferno,* 1954, p. 36.

61 *Hamlet,* ed. Harold Jenkins, The Arden Shakespeare (2), Methuen, London, 1982, p. 94.

62 Ibid., p. 492.

63 Ibid.

64 Stephen Greenblatt, *Hamlet in Purgatory,* Princeton University Press, Princeton, 2001, pp. 236–7.

65 Mascetta-Caracci, p. 117.

66 *The Taming of the Shrew,* ed. Brian Morris, The Arden Shakespeare (2). Methuen, London, 1988 (London, 1981), p. 203.

67 Michele Renzulli, *Dante Nella Letteratura Inglese,* Societa Editrice, "la Via", Firenze, 1925, p. 44.

68 These are the lines used by T. S. Eliot as his epigraph for "The Love Song of J. Alfred Prufrock". Here too the speaker confesses because he believes that his story will go no further.

69 Dante, *Inferno,* Sapegno, p. 34.

70 *Antony and Cleopatra,* ed. M. R. Ridley, The Arden Shakespeare (2), Methuen, London, 1962 (London, 1954), p. 37. While the *OED* gives this meaning (Vol. V, p. 989), it does not give any example of Shakespeare's use of the word in this sense. It also gives a number of examples of Shakespeare's use of the word "flag" in the sense of ensign or banner—but it does not mention this example from *Antony and Cleopatra* at all.

71 *Shakespeare—Lexicon,* Alexander Schmidt, 3rd edn., Revised and Enlarged by Gregor Sarrazin, Vol. I, Printed and Published by Georg Reimer, Berlin, 1902, p. 424.

72 *Antony and Cleopatra,* A Facsimile of the First Folio Text, Introduction by J. Dover Wilson, Faber and Gwyer, London (no date given), p. 343.

73 There is some variation in the punctuation of this passage in different editions. The Arden (2) places commas after "body', "stream", "to", "back", and "tide". The Cambridge Edition (*Antony and Cleopatra,* ed. Richard Madelaine, Cambridge, 1998, p. 165) places commas after "body", "stream", and "back", omitting them after "to", and "tide". Editors amend the punctuation to clarify the sense—and it may be that someone (perhaps an early compositor) had omitted a comma after "flag"—thus accidentally changing the sense for posterity. Dover Wilson in his Introduction to the Facsimile edition of this play comments, "The most irritating effect is the unintelligent punctuation, obviously supplied for the most part by the compositors, which accounts for 88 of the 321 "corrections" on the list."

74 Grandgent, *La Divina Commedia,* p. 27.

75 The central plot of the wager seems to have come from Boccaccio's *Decameron,* although this was not translated till 1620. There was, however, a tale in English called *Frederyke of Jennen,* which was printed in Antwerp in 1518 and reprinted in London in 1520 and 1560. This seems to have evolved through various translations from several languages, but its source was an Italian tale.

76 *Cymbeline,* ed. J.M. Nosworthy, The Arden Shakespeare (2), Methuen, London, 1960 (London, 1955), p. 162.

77 Dante, *Purgatorio,* a cura di Natalino Sapegno, "La Nuova Italia" Editrice, Scandicci, Firenze, 1995, p. 100.

78 Peter Levi finds this the funniest stage direction in Shakespeare. Peter Levi, *The Life and Times of William Shakespeare,* Macmillan, London, 1988, p. 304.

79 Andrew Gurr, *The Shakespearean Stage 1574–1642,* Cambridge University Press, 1980, p. 174.

80 Ovid's *Metamorphoses* (translation by Mary M. Innes), Penguin Books, London, 1955, p. 225; Macmillan, London, 1988, p. 304.

81 Peggy Munoz Simonds, *Myth, Emblem, and Music in Shakespeare's Cymbeline,* University of Delaware Press, Newark, 1992, p. 227.

82 Ibid.

83 The message is DILIGITE IUSTITIAM QUI IUDICATIS TERRAM: Love righteousness ye that are judges of the earth.

84 Erich Auerbach, "Aquila volans ad escam", in *Lettura Critica della Divina Commedia,* Vol II, Tommaso Di Salvo, La Nuova Italia Editrice, Scandicci, Firenze, 1995, p. 118. Job, 9, 26 "They are passed away as the swift ships, as the eagle that hasteth to the prey." Job, 39, 27 "Doth the eagle mount up at thy command, and make her nest on high?" Isaiah, 40, 31 "But they that wait upon the Lord shall renew their strength: they shall mount up with wings as eagles; they shall run and not be weary; and they shall walk and not faint." Exodus, 19, 4 "Ye have seen what I did unto the Egyptians, and how I bore you on eagles' wings, and brought you unto myself." (English translations from the Authorised Bible.)

85 *Cymbeline,* Arden (2), Introduction, pp. xxxvii—xxxviii.

86 Harold Bloom, *Shakespeare: The Invention of the Human,* Riverhead Books, New York, 1998, p. 633.

87 Ibid.

88 Ibid., p. 634.

89 Ian Wilson, *Shakespeare: The Evidence,* Headline Book Publishing, London, 1993, p. 338.

90 George Peele, *Polyhymnia,* from D. H. Horne, ed., *Life and Minor Works of George Peele,* Newhaven, 1952, p. 233. Quoted in Ian Wilson, p. 109.

91 Levi, p. 372.

92 Quoted in Ian Wilson, p. 17, from a letter written in 1599 by a Catholic secret agent and discovered by James Greenstreet in London's Public Record Office.

93 Hills, p. 165.

94 Dante, *Inferno,* Sapegno, p. 150.

95 The footnote in the Arden (1) ed. Morton Luce explains "'key'—suggested by the 'keys of office'; then by rapid association, a key for tuning musical instruments; still more rapid is the transition from a 'tuning-key' to 'ivy' etc".

96 F. J. Furnivall had founded the New Shakspere Society in 1873. F. E. Halliday, in *The Cult of Shakespeare,* mentions his "jaunty self-confidence" and "the eccentricity of his spelling", p. 164.

97 Ibid., p. 396.

98 The image of the vine on a tree was common in the emblem books, but its significance as described in these does not seem relevant here. Alciati used the image to signify "Amicitia" (friendship). As in Shakespeare's image, the tree has been deprived of life, but Alciati explains, "the vine tells us to seek friends of such a sort that not even our final day will uncouple them from the bond of friendship". Andrea Alciati, *Emblemata, Lyons 1550,* Scolar Press, Aldershot, 1996, p. 173. Cesare Ripa also used the tree, again an elm, in the background of his emblem for "Amicitia". A grapevine grows on it, which indicates that "true friendship is based on mutual support and interdependence". He notes "that the elm tree is sometimes shown as being dead, and the image would then mean that one true friend does not abandon another in distress". Cesare Ripa, *Baroque and Rococo Pictorial Imagery,* p. 52. Shakespeare used the image of the vine and the tree in this sense elsewhere—"Thou art an elm, my husband, I the vine." *Comedy of Erorrs* II.2.175. The different way in which the image is used here in *The Tempest* seems to emphasise the betrayal involved in this relationship—what should have been an image of mutual support and friendship becomes an image of parasitic destruction.

99 König, p. 208.

100 Virgil, *The Aeneid* (Translation by W. F. Jackson Knight), Penguin, London, 1956, pp. 75, 76, 81.

101 Boccaccio, *Il Decamerone,* V, 8, Editoriale Lucchi, Milano, 1972, pp. 382 ff.

102 *The Third Part of King Henry VI,* ed. Andrew S. Cairncross, The Arden Shakespeare (2), Methuen, London, 1964, Introduction, p. xv. "It is now generally agreed that Q is a reported or bad version of the text later printed in F, and not an early play or version of a play afterwards revised by Shakespeare. There was probably a slight element of revision between the two texts, and of adaptation required by a reduction in the cast or by the censor. The main differences, however, are best explained by reporting ... But the main cuts seem to have fallen on rhetorical, poetical, and allusive passages, which could easily be spared without affecting the progress of the action. Such are ... much of Gloucester's soliloquy (III.2)."

103 Chambrun, *Giovanni Florio,* p. 132.

104 The editors of *Sir Thomas More* (Vittorio Gabrieli and Giorgio Melchiori) in the Revels Plays series, Manchester University Press, Manchester, 1990, note another possible Dantean echo in another dream—though this play is only in part attributed to Shakespeare. More's wife dreams that she and her husband, on a small boat in the Thames, are carried away by the tide from the rest of the group and find themselves opposite the Tower. There the boat "turned / And turned about, as when a whirlpool sucks /The circled waters." (IV.2.23–5). In her dream, they both died. In a footnote we are told that this is "a possible echo from Ulysses' narrative in *Inferno* XXVI/139–41—"Tre volte il fe' girar con tutte l'acque: /alla quarta levar la poppa in suso/e la prora ire in giù,". Since the passage is not considered to be Shakespeare's work then the claim is not relevant to this book—except that it means that perhaps one of Shakespeare's collaborators on this play, *may have known* Dante—which increases the

likelihood that Shakespeare may also have known it. The parallel is not close—but it *did* recall Dante to the present writer, even before reading the footnote.

105 Dante, *Inferno*, Sapegno.

106 Ciardi, *Inferno*.

107 *King Richard III,* ed. Antony Hammond, The Arden Shakespeare (2), Methuen, London, 1981, p. 173. The footnote to the word "poets" says, "Most notably Vergil and Dante, but also Sackville, in his Induction to 'Buckingham' in the *Mirror*. See Introduction, pp. 86–87." There is no mention of Dante on these pages but the aforementioned footnote seems to suggest that Shakespeare could have known something of the content of Dante's work.

108 Frank Kermode, *Shakespeare's Language,* Allen Lane, The Penguin Press, London, 2000, p. 31.

109 Ibid., p. 32.

110 Ibid.

111 "sa di sale" is explained as "di amaro" (bitter) and "sarà amaro" (it will be bitter) in both the Sapegno and the Bosco & Reggio editions of *Paradiso*, even though the phrase means literally, "tastes of salt". Cary translates the phrase as a single adjective, "salt", Longfellow also uses "salt", as does Singleton. Ciardi translates the phrase as "bitter as salt". Landino's commentary (*Dante, con l'espositione di Cristofero Landino, e di Alessandro Velutello,* In Venezia, Appresso Giovambattista, Marchio Sesta, e fratelli, 1564, pp. 58 ff.), which Shakespeare may have seen (see Chapter IV) notes "come sa di sale, cioè quanto pare amaro" (how it tastes of salt, that is, how it seems bitter). It is interesting that of these, the native speakers of Italian incorporate the idea of "bitter" (amaro) which perhaps has a slightly different meaning in Italian from in English. Normally English would not describe the taste of salt as "bitter." The *OED* (*The Oxford English Dictionary*, Second Edition, Vol. II, Prepared by J.A. Simpson and E.S.C. Weiner, Clarendon, Oxford, 1989, p. 232) describes the taste of "bitter" as "having the characteristic taste of wormwood, gentian, quinine, bitter aloes, soot; the opposite of sweet". It does not include salt as an example.

112 Noble, p. 153.

113 Noble tells us that the text of this quotation is "as in the 1585 folio edition of the Bishops' Bible, as are also the chapter and verse numberings". Noble, p. vii.

114 *OED*, Vol. II, p. 232.

115 The same phrase was later borrowed by Fletcher in *The Lover's Progress* (V.1.82–4) "Shall I decline/Eating the bitter bread of banishment, /The course of justice to draw out a life?" Quoted in M.C. Bradbrook, *Themes and Conventions of Elizabethan Tragedy,* Cambridge University Press, London, 1966, p. 94.

116 Dante Gabriel Rossetti, *Poems & Translations,* Oxford University Press, London, 1926, p. 48. Rossetti in his poem "Dante at Verona" uses the Dantean image as his epigraph. The translation is probably his own, and reads, "Yea, thou shall learn how salt his food who fares /Upon another's bread—how steep his path/ Who treadeth up and down another's stairs". While he does not use the word "bitter" here, he uses it in the poem itself, "Some glimpses reach us—somewhat still /Of the steep stairs and bitter bread ..." It is interesting that although he has

not translated using the phrase "bitter bread", he has used it nevertheless as an equivalent—or was he simply borrowing from Shakespeare? The alliteration (in English) is appealing, and perhaps this explains his choice.

117 Mascetta-Caracci, p. 117.

118 It is unfortunate that Singleton has reversed the order of the last two phrases in his translation. This seems to weaken the parallel apparent between the idea in *Richard II* and in *Inferno V,* where both expressions of the idea end on a sad note.

119 Quoted in Mary Augusta Scott, *Elizabethan Translations from the Italian,* Houghton Mifflin Company, New York, 1916, p. 183.

120 Quoted in Scott, p. 183.

121 Cary, *The Vision,* 1883, p. 28.

122 It is in this canto that the names "Montecchi e Cappelletti" are mentioned as examples of serious conflict. They are not two rival families in Verona—but rather two Ghibelline political factions, one based in Verona and the other in Cremona. These names, which became part of the legend of Romeo and Juliet, were borrowed by Shakespeare from Bandello, who took them from Luigi da Porto, who took them from Masuccio da Salerno—who probably took them from Dante.

123 *King Richard II,* Arden (2), p. xlii. The Introduction explains that this book was entered in the Stationers' Register on 11 October 1594, and published as *The First Fowre Bookes of the civile warres between the two houses of Lancaster and Yorke.*

124 *King Richard II,* Arden (2), p. 203.

125 *A Midsummer Night's Dream,* ed. Harold F. Brooks, The Arden Shakespeare (2), Methuen, London, 1979, Introduction, p. lviii.

126 *A Midsummer Night's Dream.* Arden (2) Introduction, p. lviii. A long list of sources however, is given, including Chaucer, Lyly, North's *Plutarch,* Golding's version of Ovid's *Metamorphoses, Huon of Burdeux, The Golden Ass* by Apuleius, *The discoverie of witchcraft* by Reginald Scot, Montemayor's *Diana,* Spenser's *Shephearde's Calender,* Seneca, Mouffet's *Of Silkwormes, and their flies*—and many more.

127 *ysteron-proteron*—a rhetorical figure in which one anticipates an action which in reality must follow.

Here the succession of real acts is inverted, as if one could see, reconstructing mentally, the course of the arrow from the end to the beginning.

128 *A New Variorum Edition of Shakespeare—A Midsummer Night's Dream,* ed. Horace Howard Furness, Dover Publications, New York, 1963 (London, 1895), p. 226.

129 The Cambridge Edition of *A Midsummer Night's Dream* has a footnote, p. 80, on the "bush of thorns". "No-one knows the origin of the ancient and widespread legend that the moon is inhabited by a man with a bundle of sticks on his back. The association of the man in the moon with thorns seems to have two sources, one the identification of the man in the moon with Cain, the other a legend of a man who stole a bundle of thorns and was banished to the moon; both are found in medieval literature, the latter, for instance, in Robert

Henryson's *Testament of Creseid*, 260–4. See Oliver F. Emerson, *"Legends of Cain,* especially in Old and Middle English", PMLA 21 (1906), 840–5. The man in the moon was also often said to have a dog."

130 See Chapter II, Evidence III, in which there is other very persuasive evidence that Shakespeare had used ideas from this same canto in *Measure for Measure.*

131 Spurgeon, p. 260.

132 Ibid.

133 *Shakespeare—Lexicon*, p. 737—Images in Shakespeare where the moon represents change and inconstancy: *Measure for Measure* (III. 1. 25), *Love's Labour's Lost* (V. 2. 212), *Romeo and Juliet* (II. 2. 109), *King Lear* (V. 3. 19), *Othello* (III.3. 178), *Antony & Cleopatra* (V. 2. 240).

134 Demetrius is described by Lysander as "this spotted and inconstant man". It is interesting that the two adjectives which Dante associates with the moon are here paired and applied to a character—as though Shakespeare has remembered the association of ideas in Dante.

135 *Love's Labour's Lost,* Arden (2), p. 99.

136 Ciardi, *Paradiso,* p. 46

137 Bloom, p. 169.

138 *A Midsummer Night's Dream,* Arden (2), p. 104. However, Bloom interprets this line as an anticipation of the fact that Antony will find "Helen's beauty in Cleopatra". Bloom, p. 169.

139 This speech has attracted considerable comment because of the mislineations. The speech in its complete form is printed above, but John Dover Wilson (see The New Cambridge edition of M.N.D., 1984, p. 137) showed that if the irregular lines were removed, the text would still make excellent sense. The "irregular lines" are the those we have printed with this footnote. Dover Wilson believed he could detect a much later layer of composition and formed a theory that the play originated in 1592 and was revised in 1594 and 1598. Since the idea of the "poet" was (if this theory is correct) in a later addition it may be that Shakespeare was reflecting on his own skills—or he may be commenting on Dante since the additional lines describe precisely what Dante has done in *Paradiso* II and III.

140 *A Midsummer Night's Dream,* Arden (2), p. 104.

Chapter 3 – Eliminating the Impossible

1 Toynbee, *Dante in English Literature,* Introduction, p. xvi.

2 Paget Toynbee, *Dante Studies,* Clarendon Press, Oxford, 1921, pp. 175–6.

3 Toynbee, *Dante in English Literature,* p. 6.

4 Cary, *The Vision,* 1883, p. 221.

5 Quoted in Toynbee, *Dante in English Literature,* pp. 6–7.

6 Gurr, Andrew. *The Shakespearean Stage, 1574–1642,* Cambridge University Press 1980, p. 174.

7 Ann Thompson, *Shakespeare's Chaucer,* Liverpool University Press, London, 1978, p. 14.

8   Geoffrey Chaucer, "The Monk's Tale", in D. Laing Purves, ed., *The Canterbury Tales* and *The Faerie Queene*, William P. Nimmo, Edinburgh, 1870.

9   Toynbee, *Dante in English Literature*, p. 82.

10 This image (*Purg.* v, 14–15*)* is one of those noted by Mascetta-Caracci as being adapted slightly and used in *The Taming of the Shrew*, II, 1.

11 Toynbee, *Dante in English Literature*, p. 49.

12 Jonson, *Volpone and Other Plays*, p. 131.

13 Ian Wilson, p. 393.

14 In a copy of *Volpone* now in the British Library is an inscription in Jonson's hand, "To his loving Father & worthy Freind [*sic*] / Mr John Florio: / The ayde of his Muses / Ben Jonson seales his testemony / of Freindship, & Love".

15 Chambrun, *Giovanni Florio*, p. 200.

16 Smith, J.C. and De Selincourt, E., eds, *Spenser: Poetical Works*, Oxford University Press, Oxford, 1970, Introduction, p. vii.

17 In *Volpone* there is, I suspect, a passing reference to a character in *Inferno*—and the similarity of context convinces me that I am probably correct! In the play (I. 3. 29–30), Volpone is acting out his own death. "I feel I am going—uh! uh! uh!— /I am sailing to my port—uh! uh! uh!— /And I am glad I am so near my haven." The image of approaching death as a coming into port, is a familiar one to readers of Dante. In *Inferno* XXVII, when Guido da Montefeltro is recounting to Dante (the Pilgrim) a decision he made in later life, he presents it thus, "Quando mi vidi giunto in quella parte /di mia etade ove ciascun dovrebbe /calar le vele e raccoglier le sarte" (XXVII, 79–81) (When I saw before me all the signs /of the time of life that cautions every man / to lower his sail and gather in his lines). The wording of these lines is such that one sees in him still the calculating strategist that he always was, not a man genuinely preparing for death. In fact, earlier in the canto, he has reported how when he was alive, "l'opere mie /non furon leonine, ma di volpe" (XXVII, 74–5) (my deeds were not of the lion, but of the fox). He was renowned as a strategist, and his decisions were not always honest or just. It may be that Jonson had discussed his character Volpone with Florio, who probably helped with the Italian detail of this play, and Florio recalled the similar character in Dante. However, it it not an image that Shakespeare also borrowed, though he does seem to have taken an interest in this character.

18 Kenneth Muir, *The Sources of Shakespeare's Plays*, Methuen, London, 1977, p. 255.

19 Ludovico Ariosto, *Orlando Furioso*, Vol. II, Arnaldo Mondadori Editore, Milano, 1976, p. 884.

20 Translation by the present writer.

21 Rudolph Gottfried, ed., *Ariosto's Orlando Furioso*, Selections from the Translation of Sir John Harington, Indiana University Press, Bloomington, 1971, p. 277.

Chapter 4 – The Last Remaining Option

1   Mario Praz, "Shakespeare's Italy", in *Shakespeare Survey 7*, ed. Allardyce Nicoll, University Press, Cambridge, 1954, p. 104.

2   John Florio, *His Firste Fruites*, London, 1578, Reprint by Da Capo Press,

Theatrum Orbis Terrarum Ltd, Amsterdam, 1968, New York, p. 50.

3　Giordano Bruno, *La Cena de la Ceneri*, 1584, dialogue III, quoted in Frances Yates, "Renaissance and Reform", *Collected Essays*, Vol. II, Routledge and Kegan Paul, London 1983, p. 165.

4　Florio, *His First Fruites*, London 1578, p. 51.

5　Scott, p. 1.

6　*Cal. State Pap, Ven.*, VII, 524 *et seq.* quoted in Einstein, p. 99.

7　Chambrun, *Giovanni Florio*, p. 201, quoting from the dedication of John Florio, *A Worlde of Wordes* (1598).

8　Guttman, Introduction, p. xiv.

9　Ibid., pp. 111–12.

10　Murray J. Levith, *Shakespeare's Italian Settings and Plays*. St Martin's Press, New York, 1989, p. 3.

11　Gillespie, Index, pp. 521–8.

12　William Theobald, *The Classical Element in the Shakespeare Plays*, ed. R. M. Theobald, London, 1909, p. 388, quoted in Guttman, p. 102.

13　Naseeb Shaheen, "Shakespeare's Knowledge of Italian", in *Shakespeare Survey* 47, ed. Stanley Wells, Cambridge University Press, Cambridge, 1994, p. 164.

14　Kenneth Muir, footnote in *Othello*, The Arden Shakespeare (2), Methuen, London, 1986, p. 42.

15　Muir, *The Sources of Shakespeare's Plays*, p. 182.

16　Praz, "Shakespeare's Italy," 1954, p. 103.

17　Translation by Mario Praz.

18　R. H. Moore, "Shakespeare's Deviations from *Romeus and Juliet*", PMLA, 52 (1937): 68–74, quoted in Guttman, pp. 121–2.

19　Grillo, p. 125.

20　Ibid.

21　Ibid., p. 127.

22　*Twelfth Night*, ed. Morton Luce, The Arden Shakespeare (1), Methuen, London, 1906 (revised 1937).

23　See list of Levith's suggested sources above.

24　*Twelfth Night*, Arden (1), Introduction, p. x.

25　Ibid., Introduction, p. xii.

26　Ibid., p. 181.

27　*The Two Gentlemen of Verona*, ed. R. Warwick Bond, The Arden Shakespeare (1), Methuen, London, 1906.

28　J. L. Klein, *Geschicte des Drama's*,1866, bd. iv. 785–791, in *The Two Gentlemen of Verona*, Arden (1), Introduction, p. xx.

29　Carlo Segre, "Le Fonti Italiani Dell'*Othello*", in *Relazioni Letterarie Fra Italia e Inghilterra*, Successori Le Monnier, Firenze, 1911, pp. 14–15.

30　Giovanni Battista Nenna, *A Treatise on Nobility*, Israel Universities Press,

Jerusalem, 1967, Introduction, p. x.

31 Chambrun, *Giovanni Florio,* pp. 134–5.

32 Ibid., p. 135.

33 Ibid.

34 Grillo, p. 132.

35 The dates of these plays present some problems here, since *The Taming of the Shrew* was written before *Romeo and Juliet,* according to Harbage and Schoenbaum, *Annals of English Drama.* All dates however are conjectural and this publication gives a range for the *Shrew* of 1594–98 and for *Romeo and Juliet* of 1591–1597, pp. 58–60.

36 Grillo, pp. 132–3.

37 Ibid., p. 136.

38 John Michell, *Who Wrote Shakespeare?* Thames and Hudson, London, 1996, p. 215.

39 Levi, p. 345.

40 Praz, "Shakespeare's Italy", p. 100.

41 Ibid., p. 104.

42 Ibid., p. 105.

Chapter 5 – The Antique Book

1 Ian Wilson, p. 142.

2 H. Hutschmann and K. Wentersdorf, *Shakespeare and Catholicism,* Sheed and Ward, New York, 1922, p. 112.

3 Charlotte Carmichael Stopes, *The Life of Henry, Third Earl of Southampton, Shakespeare's Patron,* Cambridge, 1922, pp. 374–5.

4 Stopes, *The Life of Henry, Third Earl of Southampton, Shakespeare's Patron,* p. 371.

5 G. V. P. Akrigg, *Shakespeare and the Earl of Southampton,* Hamish Hamilton, London, 1968, p. 41.

6 Robert Giroux, *The Book Known as Q–A Consideration of Shakespeare's Sonnets,* Weidenfeld and Nicolson, London, 1986, p. 144.

7 Tilley claims the origin of this title is the proverb "You lose your Labor". Morris Palmer Tilley, *A Dictionary of The Proverbs of England in the Sixteenth and Seventeenth Centuries,* Ann Arbor. University of Michigan Press, 1950, p. 365. The parallel with Florio seems closer since his comment includes all three words of Shakespeare's title.

8 Giroux, p. 107.

9 A. Lytton Sells, *The Italian Influence in English Poetry,* George Allen & Unwin Ltd, London, 1955, p. 94.

10 Frances Yates, *John Florio,* Cambridge University Press, 1934, p. 56.

11 Yates, *John Florio,* p. 76.

12 Chambrun, *Giovanni Florio,* p. 23.

13 Yates, *John Florio,* p. 125.

14 Ibid., p. 245.

15 Ibid., p. 168.

16 Chambrun, *Giovanni Florio*, pp. 210–16.

17 Ibid. The spelling is Florio's.

18 We are often referred to this text in footnotes to Shakespeare editions. For example, in a reference to "ginger" in *Twelfth Night*, Arden (1), "'Gerarde (Herball, p. 62) classes ginger 'candid, greene, or condited,' among the aphrodisiacs,' Furness", p. 61. Also, in *Othello*, Arden (2), in a reference to "locusts", the footnote tells us, "This clearly means something that was sweet and a delicacy. Of the many passages to attempt to define it more precisely, and adjudicate between carob and honeysuckle, the most significant is that from Gerarde's *Herball* (1597) 'The carob groweth in Apulia . . . and other countries eastward, where the cods are so full of sweet juice that it is used to preserve ginger. Moreover both young and old feed thereon with pleasure. This is of some called St John's bread, and thought to be that which is translated *locusts*.'" p. 42.

19 *Twelfth Night*, Arden (1), footnote in Introduction, p. xxv, "... as reflected in the mass of literature to which he had access—Pliny's *Natural History*, for instance".

20 Clara Longworth, Comtesse de Chambrun, *Shakespeare Rediscovered*, Charles Scribner's Sons, New York, 1938, p. 5.

21 Chambrun, *Shakespeare Rediscovered*, 1938, p. 6.

22 Chambrun, *Giovanni Florio*, p. 169.

23 I have not been able to find a translation for this word—but by analogy ("'idolâtre' = idolater) take it to mean one who worships himself.

24 Chambrun, *Giovanni Florio*, pp. 205–6.

25 Ibid., p. 179.

26 Sears Jayne, *Library Catalogues of the English Renaissance*, University of California Press, Berkeley, 1956, p. 14.

27 Jayne, p. 14.

28 R. J. Fehrenbach, ed., *Private Libraries in Renaissance England*, Medieval and Renaissance Texts and Studies, New York, 1992.

29 Toynbee, *Dante in English Literature*, p. 103.

30 Brian Richardson, "Editing Dante's *Commedia*, 1472–1629", Theodore J. Cachey, Jr., ed., *Dante Now*, University of Notre Dame Press, Notre Dame, 1995, p. 249.

31 Yates, *John Florio*, pp. 266–7.

32 Levi, p. 293. Levi's evidence for Shakespeare's frequent presence in Oxford is Aubrey's anecdote about Davenant's claim that Shakespeare was his father.

33 This publication is in the Fisher library at Sydney University.

34 Alessandro Vellutello, *La Comedia di Dante Aligieri con La Nova Espositione di Alessandro Vellutello*, comment on *Paradiso* XVII.58 ff.

35 Daniello, Bernardino, *L'Espositione di Bernardino Da Lucca Sopra La Comedia di Dante*, ed. Robert Hollander and Jeffrey Schnapp with Kevin Brownlee and Nancy Vickers. Published for Dartmouth College by University of New England, Hanover and London, 1989.

36 *Dante, con l'espositione di Christofero Landino, e di Alessandro Vellutello,* In Venezia, Appresso Giovambattista, Marchio Sesta, e fratelli, 1564. Comment on *Paradiso* XVII, pp. 58 ff.

37 Toynbee, *Dante Studies,* p. 66.

38 Lawrence claims in his *Notes on the Authorship of The Shakespeare Plays and Poems,* p. 164, that "Florio ... was on intimate terms with Bacon and ... was one of his literary assistants at Gorhambury ..." In this case, he would have had access to his library, and Bacon may have possessed a copy of Dante's work.

39 Toynbee, *Dante in English Literature,* p. 85.

Chapter 6 – The Verdict

1 Francis Bacon, *Of the Advancement of Learning,* ed. W.A. Wright, Oxford, 1926, p. 72, quoted opposite the title page in John Leon Lievsay, *Stefano Guazzo and the English Renaissance,* Chapel Hill, The University of North Carolina Press, Durham, 1962.

2 Ian Wilson, p. 392.

3 Scott, Introduction, p. xlix.

4 John Bossy, *Giordan Bruno and the Embassy Affair,* Vintage, London, 1963, p. 23.

5 Peter Quennell, *Shakespeare,* Weidenfeld and Nicholson, London, 1963, p. 240.

6 Levi, p. 68.

7 Shakespeare could also have read of the Erinyes in the *Aeneid.*

8 Sayers, p. 27.

9 Ian Wilson, p. 278.

10 R. B. Sharpe, *The Real War of the Theatres,* D.C. Heath & Oxford University Press, London, 1935, p. 183, "Elizabeth was perfectly capable of both bravado to conceal her real feelings and a very grim sort of humour. It may be that as a gesture of contempt, triumph and warning, she called Shakespeare and his fellows before her that evening ... and commanded them to perform the play in which she believed they had pointed out her weakness and foretold her deposition by Essex, the play of which they had given a special performance by request of the Essex conspirators on the eve of the rebellion—*Richard II.*" (Quoted in Ian Wilson, pp. 279–80)

11 The titles and dates listed here are from Alfred Harbage, revised by S. Schoenbaum, *Annals of English Drama, 975–1700,* Methuen, London, 1964, pp. 231–92.

12 Thompson, Appendix, pp. 220–221. Thompson uses dates taken from J. G. McManaway, "Recent studies in Shakespeare's chronology", *Shakespeare Survey,* 3 (1950), pp. 22–3.

13 Whitaker, p. 326.

14 *King Lear,* Arden (2) Introduction, p. xxxix.

15 Christopher Kleinhenz, "Dante and the Art of Citation", in Cachey, ed., *Dante Now,* p. 45.

16 *Purgatorio,* Sapegno, p. 335. Footnote to "Benedictus"—"Son le parole con cui gli Ebrei salutarono la venuta di Cristo a Gerusalemme: 'Benedictus qui venit in nimine Domini' (*Matteo,* xxi, 9 : *Marco,* xi, 10: Luca, xix, 38; e cfr. *Salmi,* cxvii, 26).

17 *King Lear,* Arden (2), p. 155 gives a footnote to "father!" ... about] Bethell, *Shakespeare and the Popular Dramatic Tradition,* 1946, p. 60, compares Luke, ii, 49: "Knew yee not that I must goe about my father's businesse?"

18 Saner, pp. 164–5.

19 Jonathon Bate, *Shakespeare and Ovid,* Clarendon Press, Oxford, 1993, p. 10. Roland Barthes may not subscribe to this view, thus imposing a limit on the extent to which the reader or audience can appreciate much of Shakespeare's work.

20 *Le familiari,* xxiii. 19, in *Letters from Petrarch,* selected and trans. Morris Bishop, Bloomington, Ind., 198–9, quoted in Bate, *Shakespeare and Ovid,* pp. 87–8.

21 Scott, Introduction, p. xlix.

Epilogue

1 Chambrun, *Giovanni Florio,* pp. 205–6.

2 T.S Eliot, *Dante,* Faber & Faber Limited, London, 1965, p. 46.

Bibliography

Primary Sources

Alciato, Andrea, *Emblemata*, Lyons 1550, Scolar Press, Aldershot, 1996.

Ariosto, Ludovico, *Orlando Furioso,* Vol. II, Arnaldo Mondadori Editore, Milano, 1976.

Aristotle, *The Nicomachean Ethics,* English translation H. Rackam, William Heinemann, London, MCMXXVI.

Boccaccio, Giovanni, *Il Decamerone,* Editoriale Lucchi, Milano, 1972.

Bruno, Giordano, *La Cena de la Ceneri,* 1584, dialogue III, quoted in Francis Yates, "Renaissance and Reform", *Collected Essays, Vol. II,* Routledge and Kegan Paul, London, 1980.

Chaucer, Geoffrey, *The House of Fame,* eds., Nicholas R. Havely, Durham Medieval Texts, Durham, 1994.

––– "The Monk's Tale", in D. Laing Purves ed., *The Canterbury Tales* and *The Faerie Queene,* William P. Nimmo, Edinburgh, 1870.

Dante Alighieri

Dante, con l'espositione di Christoforo Landino, e di Alessandro Vellutello in Venezia, Appresso Giovambattista, Marchiò Sesta, e fratelli, 1564.

Dante, con l'espositione di Christoforo Landino, e d'Alessandro Vellutello in Venetia, Appresso Gio. Battista, e Gio. Bernardo Seffa, fratelli, 1596.

La Commedia di Dante Alighieri con La Nova Espositione di Alessandro Vellutello, Impresa in Vinegia per Francesco Marcolini instantie di Alessandro Vellutello del mese di giugno MDXLIII (1544).

La Divina Commedia. Edited and Annotated by C. H. Grandgent. Revised by Charles S. Singleton, Harvard University Press, Cambridge, Massechusetts, 1972.

La Divina Commedia: Inferno. a cura di Natalino Sapegno, "La Nuova Italia" Editrice, Firenze, 1963; *Purgatorio.* a cura di Natalino Sapegno, "La Nuova Italia" Editrice, Scandicci, Firenze, 1995; *Paradiso.* a cura di Natalino Sapegno, "La Nuova Italia" Editrice, Scandicci, Firenze, 1996.

La Divina Commedia: Inferno. annotata e commentata da Tommaso Di

Salvo, Zanichelli editore S.p.A., Bologna, 1993.

La Divina Commedia: Paradiso. a cura di Umberto Bosco e Giovanni Reggio, Le Monnier, Firenze, 1995.

L'Espositione Di Bernadino Daniello Da Lucca Sopra La Comedia Di Dante, eds. Robert Hollander & Jeffrey Schnapp with Kevin Brownlee and Nancy Vickers, Darmouth College, University Press of New England, Hanover and London. 1989.

The Divine Comedy: Inferno. Translated, with a Commentary, by Charles S. Singleton, 1: Italian text and Translation, Bollingen Series LXXX, Princeton University Press, Princeton, 1970; *Purgatorio.* Translated, with a Commentary, by Charles S. Singleton, 1: Italian Text and Translation, Bollingen Series LXXX, Princeton University Press, Princeton, 1973; *Paradiso.* Translated, with a Commentary, by Charles S. Singleton, 1: Italian Text and Translation, Bollingen Series LXXX, Princeton University Press, Princeton, 1975.

The Divine Comedy: The Inferno. Translated by John Ciardi, A Mentor Book, New York, 1954; *The Purgatorio.* Translated by John Ciardi, A Mentor Book, New York, 1961; *The Paradiso.* Translated by John Ciardi. A Mentor Book, New York, 1970.

The Divine Comedy. Translated by Henry Wadsworth Longfellow, George Routledge & Sons, Limited, Ludgate Hill, MDCCCCIII.

The Divine Comedy: *Purgatory.* Translated by Dorothy L. Sayers, Penguin Books, Edinburgh, 1955.

The Vision: Or Hell, Purgatory, and Paradise. Translated by the Rev. Henry Francis Cary, a new edn., corrected, George Bell and Sons, Covent Garden, 1883.

Florio, John, *A Worlde of Wordes (1598)*, Reprint by Georg Olms Verlag, Hildesheim, New York, 1972.

——— *His Firste Fruites,* London, 1578. Reprint by Da Capo Press, Theatrum Orbis Terrarum Ltd, Amsterdam, New York, 1968.

———*Queen Anna's New World of Words.* Blount and Barrett, London, 1611.

———*Second Frutes. (1591)* Scholars' Facsimiles and Reprints, Delmar, New York, 1977.

Jonson, Ben, *Volpone and Other Plays*, Penguin Books, London, 1998.

Munday, Anthony et al., *Sir Thomas More,* Revised by Henry Chettle, Thomas Dekker, Thomas Heywood & William Shakespeare, Manchester University Press, Manchester, 1990.

Nenna, Giovanni Battista, *A Treatise on Nobility*, translated by William Jones, 1597, reprinted by Israel Universities Press, Jerusalem, 1967.

Ovid, *Metamorphoses,* Translated by Mary M. Innes, Penguin, London, 1955.

Petrarca, Francesco, *Canzoniere,* Garzanti Editore, Milano, 1987.

Ripa, Cesare, *Baroque and Rococo Pictorial Imagery,* Introduction, translations and 200 commentaries by Edward A. Maser, Dover Publications, New York, 1971.

———*Iconologia,* Reprint of 1611. ed. Published by P.P. Tozzi, Padua, modern reprint by Garland, New York, 1976.

Shakespeare, William

A New Variorum Edition of Shakespeare, A Midsummer Night's Dream, ed. Horace Howard Furness, Dover Publications, New York, 1963.

A New Variorum Edition of Shakespeare, Antony and Cleopatra, ed. Martin Spevack, Modern Language Association of America, New York, 1990.

A New Variorum Edition of Shakespeare, Measure for Measure, ed., Mark Eccles, Modern Language Association of America, New York, 1980.

A Midsummer Night's Dream, Arden edn., ed. Harold F. Brooks, Methuen, London, 1979.

A Midsummer Night's Dream, ed. R. A. Foakes, University Press, Cambridge, 1984.

Antony and Cleopatra, Arden edn., M. R. Ridley, Methuen, London, 1962.

Antony and Cleopatra, A facsimile of of the first folio text. Introduction by J. Dover Wilson. Faber and Gwyer, London, n.d.

Antony and Cleopatra, ed. Richard Madelaine, Cambridge University Press, Cambridge, 1988.

Coriolanus, Arden edn., Philip Brockbank, Methuen, London, 1976.

Cymbeline, Arden edn., ed. J. M. Nosworthy, Methuen, London, 1955.

Hamlet, Arden edn., ed. Edward Dowden, Methuen, London, 1919.

Hamlet, Arden edn., ed. Harold Jenkins, Methuen, London, 1982.

King Henry IV, Part One, Arden edn., ed. A. R. Humphreys, Methuen, London, 1961.

King Henry VIII, Arden edn., ed. R. A. Foakes, Methuen, London, 1957.

King Lear, Arden edn., ed. Kenneth Muir, Methuen, London, 1973.

King Richard II, Arden edn., ed. Peter Ure, Methuen, London, 1959

King Richard III, Arden edn., ed. Antony Hammond, Methuen, London, 1981.

Love's Labour's Lost, Arden edn., ed. Richard David, Methuen, London, 1994.

Macbeth, Arden edn., ed. Kenneth Muir, Methuen, London, 1951.

Macbeth, Arden edn., ed. Kenneth Muir, Methuen, London, 1977.

Measure for Measure, Arden edn., ed. J.W. Lever, Methuen, London, 1971.

Othello, Arden edn, ed. M. R. Ridley, Methuen, London, 1958.

Romeo and Juliet, Arden edn., ed. Edward Dowden, Methuen, London, 1940.

Shakespeare's Poems, Arden edn., ed. C. Knox Pooler, Methuen, London, 1911.

Sonnets, Arden edn., ed. C. Knox Pooler, Methuen, London, 1918.

The Complete Works of William Shakespeare, Spring Books, London.

The Famous History of the Life of King Henry VIII, Arden edn., ed. C. Knox, Pooler, Methuen, London, 1936.

The First Part of King Henry the Sixth, Arden edn., ed. Andrew S. Cairncross, Methuen, London, 1962.

The Second Part of King Henry the Sixth, Arden edn., ed. H. C. Hart, Methuen, London, 1931.

The Third Part of King Henry the Sixth, Arden edn., ed. Andrew S. Cairncross, Methuen, London, 1964.

The Taming of the Shrew, Arden edn., ed. Brian Morris, Methuen, London, 1988.

The Tempest, Arden edn., ed. Morton Luce, Methuen, London, 1938.

The Tempest, Arden edn., ed. Frank Kermode, Methuen, London, 1954.

The Two Gentleman of Verona, Arden edn., ed. R. Warwick Bond, Methuen, London, 1906.

The Two Noble Kinsmen, with Fletcher, John, ed. N. W. Bawcutt, Penguin Books, Middlesex, England, 1977.

The Winter's Tale, A New Variorum edn., ed. Horace Howard, Furness, Dover Publications, New York, 1964.

Timon of Athens, Arden edn., ed. H. J. Oliver, Methuen, London, 1959.

Troilus and Cressida, Arden edn., ed. K Deighton, Methuen, London, 1932.

Twelfth Night, Arden edn., ed. Morton Luce, Methuen, London, 1906.

Virgil, *The Aeneid,* translation by W. F. Jackson Knight, Penguin, London, 1956.

Secondary Sources

Akrigg, G.P.V., *Shakespeare and the Earl of Southampton,* Hamish Hamilton, London, 1968.

Anders, H.R.D., *Shakespeare's Books,* Georg Reimer, Berlin, 1904.

Armstrong, Edward A., *Shakespeare's Imagination,* University of Nebraska Press, Lincoln, 1963.

Baldwin, W., *William Shakespeare's Small Latine and Less Greek.* University of Illinois Press, Urbana, 1944.

Barkan, Leonard, "What did Shakespeare read?" in Margarita de Grazia edn., *The Cambridge Companion to Shakespeare,* Cambridge University

Press, Cambridge, 2001.

Baron, Dennis, *De Vere is Shakespeare,* The Oleander Press, Cambridge, 1997.

Barthes, Roland, "From Work to Text", in *Image—Music—Text,* translated by Stephen Heath, Hill and Wang. New York, 1977.

Bate, Jonathon, *Shakespeare and Ovid,* Clarendon Press, Oxford, 1993.

Bloom, Harold, *Shakespeare: The Invention of the Huma,* Riverhead Books, a member of Penguin Putnam Inc., New York, 1998.

Boitani, Piero, *Chaucer and the Italian Trecento,* Cambridge University Press, Cambridge, 1983.

Bossy, John, *Giordano Bruno and the Embassy Affair,* Vintage, London, 1991.

Bowden, Henry Sebastian, *The Religion of Shakespeare,* Burns & Oates Ltd, London, 1899.

Boyde, Patrick, *Dante: Philomythes and Philosopher,* Cambridge University Press, 1981.

Bradbrook, M. C., *Shakespeare: The poet in his world,* Weidenfeld and Nicolson, London, 1978.

Bradley, A. C., *Shakespearean Tragedy,* Macmillan & Co Ltd, London, 1956.

Cachey, Theodore J. ed., *Dante Now.* University of Notre Dame Press, Notre Dame and London, 1995.

Carlyle, Thomas. *Lectures on Heroes.* Chapman & Hall, London, 1840.

Churchill, R. C., *Shakespeare and his Betters,* Max Reinhardt, London, 1958.

Clemens, Wolfgang H., *The Development of Shakespeare's Imagery,* Methuen & Co. Ltd., London, 1959.

de Sousa, Geraldo U., *Shakespeare's Cross-Cultural Encounters,* Macmillan Press Ltd, London, 1999.

Di Salvo, Tommaso, *Lettura Critica della Divina Commedia,* Volume II, Purgatorio, La Nuova Italia Editrice, Scandicci, Firenze, 1995.

Douglas, Lieutenant Colonel Montagu, *The Earl of Oxford as "Shakespeare",* Cecil Palmer, Oxford, 1931.

Eagleton, Terry, *Literary Theory: An Introduction,* Blackwell, Oxford UK and Cambridge USA, 1983.

Einstein, Lewis, *The Italian Renaissance in England,* The Columbia University Press, Macmillan Agents, New York, 1902.

Eliot, T. S., *Dante,* Faber & Faber, London, MCMLXV.

Fehrenbach, R. J., ed., *Private Libraries in Renaissance England, Mediaeval and Renaissance texts and Studies,* New York, 1992.

Fergusson, Francis, *Trope and Allegory: Themes Common to Dante and Shakespeare,* The University of Georgia Press, Athens, 1977.

Freeman, Rosemary, *English Emblem Books,* Chatto & Windus, London, 1948.

Furnivall, F. J., "Dante and Shakespeare" in *Notes and Queries,* 5th Series, Vol. 10, 1878.

Gillespie, Stuart, *Shakespeare's Books: A Dictionary of Shakespeare's Sources,* The Athlone Presss, London, 2001.

Giroux, Robert, *The Book Known as Q – A Consideration of Shakespeare's Sonnets,* Weidenfeld & Nicolson, London, 1982.

Gottfried, Rudolph, ed., *Ariosto's Orlando Furioso: Selections from the Translation of Sir John Harington,* Indiana Universtiy Press, Bloomington, 1971.

Grillo, Ernesto, *Shakespeare and Italy,* Robert Maclehose & Co., Ltd., The University Press, Glasgow, 1949.

Greenblatt, Stephen, *Hamlet in Purgatory,* Princeton University Press, Princeton, 2001.

Guttman, Selma, *The Foreign Sources of Shakespeare's Works,* Kings Crown Press, New York, 1947.

Halliday, F. E., *The Cult of Shakespeare,* Gerald Cuckworth & Co., Ltd, London, 1957.

Hankins, John Erskine, *Backgrounds of Shakespeare's Thought,* The Harvester Press Ltd., Oxford, Maine, USA, 1978.

––– *Shakespeare's Derived Imagery,* University of Kansas Press, Lawrence, 1953.

Harbage, Alfred, revised by Schoenbaum, *Annals of English Drama, 975– 1700,* Methuen & Co. Ltd, London, 1964.

Hills, Errato, "Dante and Shakespeare" in *Notes and Queries,* 5th Series Vol. 10, 1878.

Hoffman, Calvin, *The Murder of the Man Who Was "Shakespeare",* Julian Messner Inc., New York, 1955.

Hotson, Leslie, *I, William Shakespeare,* Jonathon Cape, Thirty Bedford Square, London, 1937.

Hutschmann, H., & Wentersdorf, K., *Shakespeare and Catholicism,* Sheed & Ward, New York, 1952.

Jacoff, Rachel, ed., *The Cambridge Companion to Dante,* Cambridge University Press, Cambridge, 1993.

James, Montague Rhodes, *A Descriptive Catalogue of the Manuscripts in the Library of St John's College, Cambridge,* Cambridge University Press, 1913.

Jayne, Sear, *Library Catalogues of the English Renaissance,* University of California Press, Berkeley, 1956

Keates, Jonathan, *Italian Journeys,* Picador, Pan Books, London, 1991.

Keen, Alan and Lubbock, Roger. *The Annotator.* Putnam, London, MCMLIV.

Kermode, Frank, *Shakespeare's Language,* Allen Lane, The Penguin Group, London, 2000.

Kirkpatrick, Robin, *English and Italian Literature from Dante to Shakespeare,* Longman, New York, 1995.

Kleinenz, Christopher. "Dante and the Art of Citation" in Cachey, ed., *Dante Now,* University of Notre Dame Press, Notre Dame and London, 1995.

Konig, Wilhelm, "Shakespeare und Dante" in *Jahrbuch der Deutschen Dante-Gesellschaft* VII (1872), Kraus Reprint Ltd., Vaduz, 1963 (Translation by Maxie Schreiner, M.A.)

LeFranc, Abel, *Under the Mask of William Shakespeare,* translation by Cecil Cragg, Merlin Books, Braunton, Devon, 1988.

Levi, Peter, *The Life and Times of William Shakespeare,* Macmillan, London, 1988.

Levith, Murray J., *Shakespeare's Italian Settings and Plays,* St Martin's Press, New York, 1989.

Longworth de Chambrun, Clara, *Giovanni Florio,* Payot, Paris, 1921.

—— *Shakespeare Rediscovered,* Charles Scribner's Sons, New York, 1938.

—— *The Sonnets of William Shakespeare: New Light on Old Evidence,* G. P. Putnam's Sons, NewYork & London, The Knickerbocker Press, 1913.

Lowell, James Russell, *Among My Books,* J. M. Dent & Sons, London, 1925

—— *Literary Essays IV,* Macmillan & Co., Ltd., London, 1901.

Lucas, F. L., *Seneca and Elizabethan Tragedy,* Haskell House Publishers Ltd., New York, 1969.

McPherson, David C., *Shakespeare, Jonson, and the Myth of Venice,* Newark: University of Delaware Press, London and Toronto, Associated University Press, 1990.

Marrapodi, Michele, ed., *Shakespeare's Italy,* Manchester University Press, Manchester, 1993.

Mascetta-Caracci, Lorenzo, "Dante in Shakespeare" in *Giornale Dantesco, N.S.1,* Leo S. Olschki, Firenze-Venezia, 1897.

Masten, Jeffrey, *Textual Intercourse: Collaboration, Authorship and Sexualities in Renaissance Drama,* Cambridge University Press, Cambridge, 1997.

Michell, John, *Who Wrote Shakespeare?,* Thames & Hudson, London, 1996.

Miola, Robert S., *Shakespeare's Reading,* Oxford University Press, Oxford, 2000.

Muir, Kenneth, *The Sources of Shakespeare's Plays,* Methuen & Co Ltd., London, MCMLXXVII.

––– and O'Loughlin, Sean, *The Voyage to Illyria,* Barnes & Noble, Inc., and Methuen & Co. Ltd., New York, 1970.

––– "Macbeth and Dante" in *Notes and Queries,* 16th Series, Vol. 194, 1949.

Murray, Timothy, *Theatrical Legitimation: Allegories of Genius in Seventeenth Century England and France,* New York & Oxford: Oxford University Press.

Nicholl, Charles, *The Reckoning,* Jonathon Cape, London, 1992.

Noble, Richmond, *Shakespeare's Biblical Knowledge,* Society for Promoting Christian Knowledge, London, 1935.

Plimpton, George A., *The Education of Shakespeare,* London & New York, Oxford University Press, 1933.

Pope, Alexander, *The Dunciad* IV, ed. Valerie Rumbold, Longman, New York, 1999.

Praz, Mario, "Shakespeare's Italy", in *Shakespeare Survey,* 7th edn., Allardyce Nicoll, University Press, Cambridge, 1954.

––– *Studies in Seventeenth Century Imagery,* Edizione di Storia e Letteratura, 2nd edn., Sussidi Eruditi, 16, Roma, 1964.

Price, Diana, *Shakespeare's Unorthodox Biography,* Greenwood Press, Connecticut, 2000.

Quennell, Peter, *Shakespeare,* The World Publishing Company, Cleveland, Ohio, 1963.

Renzulli, Michele, *Dante Nella Letteratura Inglese,* Societa Editrice "La Via", Firenze, 1925.

Robertson, J. M., *Croce as Shakespearean Critic,* George Routledge & Sons, Carter Lane, E. C., London, 1922.

––– *The Baconian Heresy,* Herbert Jenkins Ltd., London, MCMXIII.

Roe, Richard Paul, *The Shakespeare Guide to Italy,* Harper Perennial, HarperCollins, New York, 2011.

Rossetti, Dante Gabriel, *Poems and Translations,* Oxford University Press, London, 1926.

Rowse, A. L., *Shakespeare's Southampton,* Macmillan, London, 1965.

––– *William Shakespeare,* Macmillan & Co, Ltd, London, 1963.

Sammartino, Peter, *The Man Who Was William Shakespeare,* Cornwall Books, Cranbury, New Jersey, 1990.

Saner, Reginald A., "Gemless Rings" in *Purgatorio* XXII and *King Lear,* in *Romance Notes, 10: 163–7,* Chapel Hill, N. C., 1968.

Satin, Joseph, "Macbeth and the Inferno of Dante", *Forum.* 9 (1):18–23, Houston, Texas, 1971.

Schoenbaum, S., *William Shakespeare: A Documentary Life,* The Clarendon Press, Oxford in association with The Scolar Press, 1975.

——— *Shakespeare's Live,* Clarendon Press, Oxford, 1991.

Scott, Mary Augusta, *Elizabethan Translations from the Italian,* Houghton Mifflin Company, Cambridge, 1916.

Segre, Carlo, *Le Fonti Italiani Dell' "Othello", in Relazioni Letterarie Fra Italia e Inghilterra,* Sucessssori Le Monnier, Firenze, 1911.

Sells, A. Lytton, *The Italian Influence in English Poetry,* Allen & Unwin Ltd., London, 1955.

Shaheen, Naseeb, *Biblical References in Shakespeare's Tragedies,* Newark: University of Delaware Press, 1987.

——— "Shakespeare's Knowledge of Italian", *Shakespeare Survey* 47, Cambridge University Press, Cambridge, 1994.

Simonds, Peggy Munez, *Myth, Emblem, and Music in Shakespeare's "Cymbeline",* University of Delaware Press, Newark, 1992.

Smith, J. C., and de Selincourt E., *Spenser: Poetical Works,* Oxford University Press, Oxford, 1970.

Sobran, Joseph, *Alias Shakespeare: Solving the Greatest Literary Mystery of All Time,* The Free Press, New York, 1997.

Spurgeon, Caroline, *Shakespeare's Imagery and What It Tells Us,* Beacon Press, Boston, 1960.

Stoke, Francis Griffin, *Who's Who in Shakespeare,* Studio Editions, London, 1992.

Stopes, Charlotte Carmichael, *Burbage and Shakespeare's Plays,* Alexander Morning Ltd., The De La Mare Press, 32 George Street, Hanover Square, London, 1913.

——— *The Life of Henry, Third Earl of Southampton, Shakespeare's Patron,* Cambridge University Press, 1922.

——— *Shakespeare's Environment,* G. Bell & Sons, Ltd., London, 1914.

Thomas, Vivian, *The Moral Universe of Shakespeare's Problem Plays,* Croom Helm, 1987.

——— *Shakespeare's Chaucer,* Liverpool University Press, 1978.

Thompson, Ann, *Shakespeare's Chaucer,* Liverpool University Press, 1978.

Toynbee, Paget, *Dante in English Literature: From Chaucer to Cary,* Methuen & Co. Ltd., London, 1909.

——— *Dante Studies,* Clarendon Press, Oxford, MDCCCXXI.

Twain, Mark, *Is Shakespeare Dead?,* Harper & Brothers, New York, MCMIX.

Ure, Peter, *The Problem Plays,* British Council and the National Book League,

Longmans, Green & Co., London, 1961.

Warner, Marina, *Alone of All Her Sex,* Picador, London, 1990.

Whitaker, Virgil K., *Shakespeare's Use of Learning,* The Huntingdon Library, San Marino, California, 1964.

Whalen, Richard F., *Shakespeare: Who Was He?,* Praeger, Westport, 1994.

Wharton, T. F., *Measure for Measure,* Macmillan, London, 1989.

Williamson, Hugh Ross, *Kind Kit,* Michael Joseph Ltd., London, 1972.

Wilson, Frank. P., "A Supplement to Toynbee's *Dante in English Literature*" in *Italian Studies, III,* 1946.

Wilson, Ian, *Shakespeare: The Evidence,* Headline Book Publishing, London, 1994.

Wilson, Knight, G., *The Wheel of Fire,* Methuen & Co. Ltd., London, 1972.

Yates, Frances A., *A Study of Love's Labour's Lost,* Cambridge University Press, 1936.

––– *John Florio,* Cambridge University Press, 1934.

––– *Renaissance and Reform: The Italian Contribution,* Vol II, Routledge & Kegan Paul, London, 1983.

General Works

A New and Complete Concordance in the Dramatic Works of Shakespeare, John Bartlett, A.M., London, Macmillan and Co., 1894.

Enciclopedia Dantesca, Vol. V, Istituto Dell'Enciclopedia Italiana, Roma, 1976.

Shakespeare: Lexicon, Alexander Schmidt, 3rd edn., Revised and Enlarged by Gregor Sarrazin, Vol. I & II, Georg Reimer, Berlin, 1902.

William Shakespeare: A Textual Companion, Stanley Wells & Gary Taylor, eds., Oxford, 1987.

Index

CPSIA information can be obtained
at www.ICGtesting.com
Printed in the USA
BVHW032257180719
553811BV00002B/233/P